Eva Emery Dye

Romance with the West

T0338174

Eva Emery Dye

Romance with the West

Sheri Bartlett Browne

Oregon State University Press
Corvallis

For my children
Elizabeth, Ian, and Samuel

Cover photo courtesy Oregon Historical Society, negative number CN021678

The paper in this book meets the guidelines for permanence and durability of the Committee on Production Guidelines for Book Longevity of the Council on Library Resources and the minimum requirements of the American National Standard for Permanence of Paper for Printed Library Materials Z39.48-1984.

Library of Congress Cataloging-in-Publication Data
Browne, Sheri Bartlett.
  Eva Emery Dye : romance with the West / Sheri Bartlett Browne.– 1st ed.
      p. cm.
Includes bibliographical references and index.
  ISBN 0-87071-008-7 (alk. paper)
  1. Dye, Eva Emery, 1855-1947. 2. Women and literature–United States–History–20th century. 3. Novelists, American–20th century–Biography. 4. Suffragists–United States–Biography. 5. Western stories–Authorship. 6. Oregon–In literature. 7. Oregon–Biography. I. Title.
  PS3507.Y33 Z53 2004
  813'.52–dc22

2003018485

Oregon State University Press
101 Waldo Hall
Corvallis OR 97331-6407
541-737-3166 • fax 541-737-3170
http://oregonstate.edu/dept/press

Contents

vi   Acknowledgements

1   Introduction

6   The Emergence of "Jennie Juniper"
1855-1875

21   "The Gates of Heaven": Oberlin College
1875-1882

37   Wife, Mother, Writer: A Time of Transition
1882-1890

54   The Literary Missionary
1890-1900

72   Envisioning the West: Sacagawea, Lewis and
Clark, and *The Conquest*
1898-1902

100   Sacagawea, the Women's Club Movement,
and Suffrage Activism
1903-1912

126   Romance with Hawaii
1905-1947

152   Epilogue

156   Notes

175   Bibliography

181   Index

Acknowledgements

This book has its roots in a conversation held long ago with Stephen Dow Beckham, professor of history at Lewis and Clark College. He told me then that it would be a difficult challenge to assemble the necessary pieces of Dye's life in order to write her biography. It is my hope that the final product meets his expectations and honors his commitments to teaching and public history. For his constant encouragement and sage advice, and for reading drafts of this work, I offer my deepest thanks.

Gratitude also goes to the family of Eva Emery Dye, who granted access to their extensive family papers and provided cheerful hospitality each time I visited. Without their assistance, this book could never have been written.

Many others gave sound criticism and supported my efforts. Sara M. Evans helped me find my own voice as a historian and biographer and never wavered in her enthusiasm for Eva Emery Dye. Tom Edwards shared his vast knowledge of the Pacific Northwest and gently guided my prose. Michael Bertrand graciously offered to read the final draft of the manuscript, and his astute comments markedly improved several chapters. His insights also initiated a career-changing, ongoing conversation about popular culture, race, and gender. Jeffrey Pilz, Janice Kragness, Jean Ward, and Elaine Maveety read earlier versions, provided helpful advice for the publication process, and convinced me that there was light at the end of the tunnel. Fellow writer Arlene Williams supplied invaluable observations about content and style. George Green, John Howe, Lisa Norling, MJ Maynes, and Mary Dietz, all at the University of Minnesota, shaped my ideas and believed in my abilities. Librarians Sharon Campbell (Washoe County Library) and Tammy Martin (Oberlin College Archives) tracked down obscure sources and references. I also would like to thank the editorial board at OSU Press and the anonymous reviewers for their comments and suggestions as well as Mary Braun for shepherding me through this process. Managing Editor Jo Alexander deserves special praise for her editorial skills and patience.

My parents, Gary and Donna Bartlett, have participated in this project from the very beginning, listening to endless stories, sharing their love of history, and giving me their time and support when I most needed it. Like my parents, my children have also given the most precious gifts–time and love–so that I might realize a dream. This book is dedicated to them.

Introduction

Tenacious, determined, ambitious, enthusiastic, and dedicated are all words that describe Eva Emery Dye. Although Oregonians may know her name, few know much about her life and work. A poet and author of history and romance, a temperance and suffrage activist, a popular speaker and Chautauqua organizer, Dye devoted her life to researching and writing about the West. She lived her life in the public sphere and until recently few documents were available to illuminate the roles she fulfilled as a wife and mother. This biography connects her private life to her public accomplishments and offers a window into her personality and motivations that has been missing from earlier analyses of her contributions and achievements.

Prior to her graduation and marriage in 1882, twenty-seven-year-old Eva L. Emery underwent a phrenological examination at Oberlin College. One can easily dismiss this popular nineteenth-century medical practice as unscientific; but this examination of the shape and dimensions of her head was uncannily accurate in its assessment of her strengths and weaknesses:

> Like father in characteristics. Plenty of grit, firmness, endurance.
> Perception and memory strong. Fact-gatherer rather than
> abstract thinker … believes in self. W[oul]d look forward to
> family. Socially considerate and liberal. Loves the sublime.[1]

What the phrenological inspection does not reveal, however, is the history that preceded and followed it, and the particular circumstances that shaped and influenced Dye's life. Dye was a woman of strong and deeply held convictions that were Jeffersonian in nature and vision. Central among these was her firm belief that pursuing the "life of the mind" would enable her to exercise public virtue, that study and thought and writing would result in positive public service as a wife, mother, and citizen. She found solace, inspiration, and guidance in the classics, in history, and in poetry. Dye founded a life's work on the written word; she read widely and deeply in literature and poetry that inspired her to compose her own poetry, essays, editorials, and historical novels. She taught, lectured, chastised, and encouraged several generations of Americans to enjoy and engage in their own history. The roots of her passion and determination to write historical fiction, the history of her involvement in women's rights, and her lifelong interest in promoting educational opportunities for Oregonians are the subjects of this biography.

Dye was a woman who brought extraordinary enthusiasm, energy, and dedication to her work as a writer and to her years of community service. Born in Illinois in 1855, she left as a young woman for Ohio and later settled with her husband and children in Oregon City, Oregon. She held bachelor's and master's degrees from Oberlin College and was part of the first generation of college-educated women in the United States. Like many women who graduated from college in the 1880s, Dye faced career and family choices of which earlier generations had only dreamed.

Possessing a love of poetry and classical Greek literature, she began her literary endeavors at the age of fifteen when she published her first poem. What followed was a seventy-five-year effort to combine her love of history and literature into works that would inspire her readers in an uncertain and unpredictable modern age. Ultimately she published several historical essays, one grade-school primer, four works of historical fiction, and numerous poems. She also left behind an unpublished book-length manuscript, an array of speeches, and voluminous personal correspondence that is rich with details of middle-class family life in Oregon during the late nineteenth and early twentieth centuries.

Dye was committed to the belief that history should enliven and educate the reader, and she chose as her models the historical fiction of Sir Walter Scott and Washington Irving, and the poetry of Henry Wadsworth Longfellow. Enamored of the British Romantics and the authors of the American Renaissance, Dye adopted a style that lent itself to the heroic and patriotic and reflected an oral tradition of storytelling common in her father's family. Full of dramatic scenes, grand pageantry, romantic interest, adventure, and honor, her books examined subjects that historians and the reading public still find fascinating: the history of the Lewis and Clark Expedition, the Oregon Trail experience, American westward migration and its impact on native peoples, and the biographies of men and women who were important to the development of the Pacific Northwest in the nineteenth century.

Taking the historical accuracy and themes of Irving as her example, Dye pioneered the genre of historical fiction in the Pacific Northwest.[2] During the late nineteenth century, Oregon produced a number of authors, many of them women, who wrote personal reminiscences, fiction and nonfiction dealing with westward migration, and stories about life on the Pacific Northwest frontier. Most notable among these were Abigail Scott Duniway, Ella Higginson, Frances Fuller Victor, and Anne Shannon Monroe.[3] None of these writers, however, matched Dye's ability as a historical researcher. She wanted her characters to come to life in the reader's imagination, but she insisted they do so as accurately as possible. Toward that end she worked tirelessly to collect historical details about her subjects from their friends, acquaintances, and family members.

Dye's research endeavors sometimes had surprising and significant results. She was instrumental in the 1903 discovery of original travel diaries written by William Clark on the Lewis and Clark Expedition. Dye provided Reuben Gold Thwaites with information that led to the previously unknown journals, but unfortunately never received recognition for this. With an eye for detail and an uncanny ability to wrest documents from her informants, Dye also unearthed the diaries of John Colcord and Ranald McDonald. Colcord was one of Honolulu's first American settlers in 1821, and she discovered his journal while researching nineteenth-century American missionaries in Hawaii. McDonald was a world traveler and the son of a chief factor for the Hudson's Bay Company. Research on his life netted the diaries he kept throughout his life, which described his childhood at Fort Colville and eventual travels to Japan during the 1840s. While some of these valuable sources remain in private hands or as part of other manuscript collections, to our benefit she donated most of her research results to the Oregon Historical Society. Her collection contains a vast array of letters, including richly detailed exchanges between Dye and McDonald prior to his death in 1894, valuable correspondence from Clark's grandsons and Meriwether Lewis's nephew, and letters from the son of Hudson's Bay Company chief factor John McLoughlin describing daily life at Fort Vancouver. Although she is best known for the books that arose from this extensive material, particularly *McLoughlin and Old Oregon* (1900) and *McDonald of Oregon* (1906), the results of her historical research are perhaps a more lasting contribution.

Dye's most successful written work was *The Conquest: The True Story of Lewis and Clark* (1902). Beginning with the life of George Rogers Clark and ending with his brother William Clark's tenure as Indian Agent, *The Conquest* covered the period of western expansion from 1774 to the death of William Clark in 1838. It was one of the first works of historical fiction to popularize the Lewis and Clark Expedition and introduced to the general public a new heroine, the Shoshone woman Sacagawea. Dye's portrayal of Sacagawea enhanced the young mother's role and romanticized aspects of the journey, but in the main she adhered to the facts of the expedition. It was not the text itself that turned Sacagawea into an American icon but Dye's subsequent efforts to memorialize her with statues and speeches.

Twentieth-century historians have misunderstood Dye's motivation for writing *The Conquest*, and by taking her work out of context they have perpetuated inaccuracies and oversimplified her efforts. Attributing the portrayal of Sacagawea to Dye's support for woman suffrage, for example, historians have failed to note that Dye's most important work on the vote for women occurred well after publication of *The Conquest*. Without evaluating Dye's other writings or her educational experiences, historians also have perpetuated the myth that *The Conquest* was written solely to feature the life of an Indian woman. Dye set out to write an epic of expansion replete with heroes and heroines, a patriotic tale of westward settlement that boasted of white achievement. When she discovered that one of the "noble" Indians featured in Lewis and Clark's journals was a young woman and a mother, she knew she had the elements of a successful historical novel. Dye did not portray Sacagawea as an independent suffragist-in-waiting, as some have suggested, but as a model of nineteenth-century true womanhood.

From Dye's literary tribute to Sacagawea evolved an organization that became not just the means to memorialize her but also an important training ground for activists in the Oregon suffrage movement during the early twentieth century. A small but vital part of the women's club movement, the Sacajawea Statue Association (1903-1905) provided a bridge between women's cultural activities and direct political action. Dye's work on behalf of the association was the catalyst that brought her into a prominent role in the state suffrage movement as a mediator between conflicting interests and competing leaders. The connections between the women's club movement and suffrage activism have received too little attention from regional historians, and Dye's participation in both endeavors provides an opportunity to understand better the ties that bound women together in a struggle for social change.

Dye's literary pursuits led her down other public service paths. She and her husband Charles formed a committee to save John McLoughlin's home in Oregon City from destruction. After several years of work to raise money and interest civic leaders in the project, they accomplished their goal in 1909. Today McLoughlin's home is a museum in Oregon City and a National Historic Site.

The McLoughlin House was not the only community project on which the Dyes collaborated. One of their greatest achievements was in the arena of cultural education. Both skilled orators and organizers, they put their talents to excellent use when they founded the Willamette Valley Chautauqua Assembly in 1894. Dedicated to providing education and entertainment to the public at low cost, Chautauqua organizers brought thousands to Gladstone, Oregon, for two weeks every summer to hear nationally known speakers and participate in baseball games, musical recitals, and courses in ornithology, American history, and theology, to name just a few of the offerings. The Chautauqua was a logical outgrowth of the Dyes' educational experiences and a reflection of their desire to introduce Oregonians to cultural events they had enjoyed in the Midwest. Their leadership skills and financial commitment kept the Chautauqua alive in Oregon for thirty-four years.

At the age of eighty-two, Dye wrote to her children, "Every little while some young man or woman wants to write the 'story of my life.' I tell them there is nothing to write, or I will write it myself. But all I shall ever write is probably in these letters."[4] She was wrong on two counts. She never did write her autobiography, and the uncharacteristic modesty in her claim that "there is nothing to write" belies the evidence. She was correct that the history of her life would be told through her letters, but until recently none of the documents that bear witness to her personal life were available. Serendipity brought me to the doorstep of her grandson in 1995, and the analysis that follows is based largely on hundreds of family letters and other documents he kindly provided. Much of this evidence of a life richly lived has now joined Dye's collection at the Oregon Historical Society.

The history of women in the Pacific Northwest is still in its infancy. It is hoped that this biography will continue a dialogue about the history of women writers in the region, the meaning of family relationships and educational opportunities in women's lives, and the importance of women's voluntary associations during the late nineteenth and early twentieth centuries.

The Emergence of "Jennie Juniper"
1855-1875

On a spring afternoon in 1923, worshippers of the First Congregational Church in Oregon City gathered together as they had every Sunday for many years. This day—June 3—was a little different than previous Sundays, however. No sanctuary surrounded them, nor were they arriving at the church's entrance on Main Street. Instead, they congregated outside at the corner of Sixth and John Adams streets, the breeze carrying the fragrance of lilacs and freshly turned earth. They had gathered to break ground for their new church and to offer remembrances of the one that was destroyed by fire on February 4, 1923.[1]

This day was exceptional for other reasons. Friends of Eva Emery Dye and her husband Charles would not witness her typical arrival at the church, which normally occurred just before the sermon began. Every Sunday for years Mrs. Dye would advance down the aisle with a quick step, oblivious to the stares from her fellow parishioners. Her sharp brown eyes would light upon her husband in the third row. Hurrying to his side, she would nudge him gently and whisper, "Papa," an endearment she had used ever since their oldest son was born. She would then take her place next to him in the pew. There she would listen attentively but somewhat restlessly to the sermon, rising immediately when it ended, ready to leave.[2]

On this day, however, Mrs. Dye was one of the main speakers. She had recently returned from six months of research and writing in Hawaii and was full of stories about the founders of the Congregational Church and their ties to the islands. Overflowing with enthusiasm, she peppered her audience with dates and tales of the early Congregational Society in Oregon and sprinkled her speech with a dusting of romance and heroism. It was an afternoon filled with hopeful expectations for the new church and for her new book on American missionaries in Hawaii.

Many moments in Dye's life could be used to illustrate her character and motivations, but this church ceremony provides a singular overview of her personality. Civic leader, historian, traveler, researcher, orator, and wife were all roles on display that day, not to mention many traits that defined her: restlessness, enthusiasm, dedication, and energy.

Born on July 17, 1855, in Prophetstown, Illinois, Eva Lucinda Emery was the first child of Cyrus and Caroline Trafton Emery. From her father Eva acquired perseverance, tenacity, avid curiosity, and love of history. Her mother's influence is more elusive, but in many ways more revealing. Caroline Emery did not live to see her daughter reach the age of two. Her absence left Eva with a longing for acceptance and affection not assuaged until her marriage, and with a need to find strong female role models in her life and her work. Caroline's early writings, and her enjoyment of and proficiency in music, also gave her daughter a creative and artistic example that Eva remembered as significant and inspiring in her pursuit of a writing career.

Family letters and Cyrus Emery's reminiscences, which he wrote in 1903 at the age of seventy-two, reveal both the interconnectedness of family networks and the role that antebellum industrialization and urbanization played in disconnecting many New England families from the land of their forebears.[3] The same sources illustrate the importance of strong intergenerational ties in the family and the degree to which early or sudden death shaped family structure and choices. Most importantly, when Eva's parents married, the Emery family, a long line of independent-thinking entrepreneurs, encountered the indomitable spirit and business savvy of Lucinda Clark Trafton, Eva Emery Dye's grandmother. She and Eva's father were omnipresent in shaping her character.

Cyrus Emery was the oldest son of a second marriage for Captain Thomas Salter Emery and his wife Hannah Willard. The Emerys were prolific in Sanford, Maine, and many in the family were prominent landowners and merchants. In 1838, when Cyrus was eight years old, his father died suddenly, and his son learned a valuable lesson about the power of debt to ruin a family. Thomas Emery owned land on which he farmed but when he bought it he had failed to get a clear title. Cyrus remembered in later years,

> my father paid for his land twice. The party from whom he bought first, owned only a tax title. In 1793, when the rightful owners put in their claims, he was obliged to buy of them or forfeit his land. From this misfortune my father never recovered. He was obliged to mortgage and this was never satisfied.[4]

Cyrus Emery also reported that his father "had been obliged to increase his debts by the purchase of a yoke of oxen on credit. Now, on the day of father's funeral, the man, or men, of whom he had bought the oxen, came to our house and threatened to attach my father's dead body for this debt."[5]

The Emerys' financial difficulties occurred against the backdrop of the Panic of 1837, when the combination of widespread land speculation and unstable state banks prevented a sound economic response to a sudden drop in land sales and an astronomical rise in commodity prices. The depression lasted for six years. Many landowners lost their property altogether when the bottom fell out of the market, and others went into crushing debt in order to keep land that they had farmed for generations.

In order to redeem the land after Thomas Emery's death, Salter Emery, Cyrus's half-brother from his father's first marriage, paid the mortgage. The land remained in the Emery family and was never at the disposal of Thomas Emery's unfortunate widow, Hannah Willard Emery, who experienced what countless other women faced in the generation before reforms in married women's property laws. Under common law, she could not inherit her husband's land directly, nor could she prevent her husband's creditors from seizing the land and the oxen to pay his debts. She was at the mercy of the larger Emery family. When Salter Emery paid the debt on the land, she lost all ties to it and its potential economic benefit. Her children might inherit a portion of the farm eventually, but, as Thomas Emery's widow, she could not.

Nor did Hannah find much comfort or assistance in the family of her birth. Her father, Samuel Willard, Jr., "was a very rich man, with hundreds of acres of land, much of it valuable timber land covered with pine, with a saw mill ... not one foot of which did she ever have, or any use from it, except some personal property, one cow and three or six sheep."[6] Hannah's brother Stephen Willard inherited it all, and after her husband's death she was left to eke out an existence on "twenty acres of land about three-fourths of a mile south from home, which she bought with money she earned when a girl working out at fifty cents a week."[7]

This probably means that, perhaps due to the foresight of her father or mother, Hannah Willard Emery had acquired a separate estate. Separate estates were one of the only ways in which women could maintain property they had brought to a marriage; however, they were used not to promote a woman's independence but to keep property in her family and allow for its transmittal from generation to generation. Many women used separate estates to convey property to daughters and granddaughters, especially in the period from 1820 to 1860.[8] Hannah's twenty-acre parcel was used for pasture for both her own livestock and that of Cyrus's grandfather, William Emery. Whether she received remuneration of some kind for the use of her land or was compensated in other ways (with provisions, perhaps) is unknown. What is clear is that the moderate separate estate she held by virtue of her own work as a young woman was not enough land to support a family.

Cyrus Emery shouldered the weighty responsibility of being the oldest child when his father died, despite the poverty he, his mother and two sisters endured. Because of his obligation to support his mother and sisters, his school experiences were limited to three months in the summers.[9] He learned to read at an early age and, judging from the quantity and quality of the storytelling in his reminiscences, Emery found valuable lessons in his family's history and, more generally, in American history. His fondness for literature, history, and rudimentary theology helped him to approach life with an open and inquiring mind and to trust his own observations and experience; these interests and character traits he would share with his daughter Eva.

Cyrus's willingness to question authority was related to the time in which he lived. He grew up in the aftermath of Jacksonian political reform and in an intense period of religious revival and social change in America. He was three months old when Charles Grandison Finney preached his famous sermons in Rochester, New York, touching off the Second Great Awakening. Although Cyrus seems to have been little affected by the most salient characteristics of the revival—the public, fervent style of prayer and conversion and the fostering of communities of zealous evangelicals— he did embody the self-reliant, independent, and empirical thinking of the era.[10] As a boy he once read a story that illustrated the importance of thinking for himself and demonstrated the degree to which religious reform had transformed Puritan New England. The story, which provided frightening examples of Calvinist hell-fire and damnation, taught him,

> first, not to believe stories simply because they [a]re old and second because told by a man with a DD attached to his name. Third, believe nothing no matter from what source it comes, unless it contains the evidence of truth. You must be the judge for yourself of what is the truth, no one else can judge for you.[11]

After his father's death Cyrus hired himself out to neighbors and farmers, usually cutting wood, driving beef cattle to market, hoeing corn, or hauling wood by oxen to ports in Wells Landing and Kennebunkport. In April 1843, at the age of thirteen, he left home in search of more plentiful and permanent work, but returned to Sanford within a year to work as an apprentice tinsmith to his older half-brother William, who was also a deacon in the local Congregational Church. Cyrus worked for "the Deacon" for four years, and in return for "earn[ing] him more money than any apprentice he ever had," William Emery provided his half-brother with room and board, clothing, and the coveted opportunity to go to school four weeks each winter.[12]

Cyrus's apprenticeship to his brother provided the foundation for a successful career as a master craftsman, making and peddling tinware and stoves in small towns and cities all over Maine. He noted that in the 1830s and 1840s, tin peddling "was a lucrative and respectable business." Among the extensive network of Emerys in Maine eleven men including Cyrus participated in family tinning enterprises, and his apprenticeship in Sanford was conducted under the auspices of S. B. Emery & Company, owned by Samuel B., William L., and Caleb S. Emery.[13]

At the age of eighteen, Cyrus's apprenticeship ended, and he struck out on his own. He settled in nearby Biddeford, Maine, and worked for three years as a journeyman tinsmith, eventually going into business with a partner, William Andrews. They founded the firm of Andrews & Emery and became successful making pans, plates, coffee pots, and cookware, and selling stoves.[14] As a craftsman and merchant, Cyrus joined Biddeford's growing middle class and seemed destined to live out his life in Maine, supported not by unyielding soil but by his skills as a tinsmith and salesman.

But Cyrus's life course veered when he began courting the daughter of Colonel John and Lucinda Trafton. The Traftons' youngest child, Caroline Brackett Trafton, was born in Shapleigh, Maine, in June 1833, and attended Maine Wesleyan Seminary and Female College in Kent's Hill as a young woman.[15] She specialized in music, taking courses in organ, voice, and music theory and was known in Shapleigh and Biddeford for her clear alto singing and her talent on the melodeon.

Information on Colonel Trafton is sketchy; however, it is apparent that he had significant land holdings in Biddeford and Shapleigh but suffered severe losses in the Panic of 1837. Once the commander of the York County militia, Trafton owned the waterworks that powered the lumber mill in Shapleigh and "was one of the most extensive manufacturers and dealers in lumber at that time in York County, Maine," according to Cyrus.[16] Lucinda Clark Trafton, his second wife, was a strong-willed, independent woman who was known in the 1850s and 1860s for her varied and extensive business interests. John Trafton's death in the late 1840s had left his wife as trustee to his considerable estate, whose heirs included three children from a previous marriage and three children from his marriage to Lucinda Clark.

Like Hannah Willard Emery, Lucinda Clark Trafton did not inherit her husband's estate outright, but she had the use of the land and the family home in Biddeford during her lifetime and the daunting responsibility of preserving the estate for the benefit of his children and future heirs. Unlike Hannah, Lucinda exercised considerable power, buying and selling portions of the estate in order to increase its value and productivity. Perhaps she was permitted to do so under the conditions of the trusteeship or as a separate provision in her husband's will. Clearly John Trafton had trusted his wife and respected her business abilities. Maintaining buildings, paying taxes, collecting rents for a tenement in Biddeford, and settling her husband's debts became a full-time task for his widow, and the considerable effort was made more difficult in late 1851 when both her stepson Jordan and her oldest son Lewis died of tuberculosis. Once again, as an indicator of her business acumen and her trustworthiness, Lucinda Trafton was named executor of their estates.

Soon the burden of administering three estates became enormous, and she frequently visited the probate judge in Biddeford. That she was more than equal to the management task is apparent in the correspondence with her daughter in 1854 and 1855. She wrote ably of using rents from a tenement in Biddeford to pay the taxes, insurance, and expenses of running it. "Had I not taken the course I have it could have been sold before this for the taxes. I have kept insured, and paid the taxes, and repairs." In 1855 her letters bemoaned the fact that she had been trying without success to collect the debts owed to Jordan Trafton's estate. Above all, she made it clear that none of these activities lined her own pocketbook. "Tell her [daughter Laura Trafton Page] … that I have not gone after the multitude to get rich and am not delaying her portion with a view to benefit myself."[7]

The circumstances that brought Cyrus Emery and Caroline Trafton together are missing from the historical record. It is unclear whether Cyrus had met Caroline's father before his death, and the Traftons' upper-middle-class aspirations and lifestyle seem an unlikely pairing with Cyrus's more modest upbringing and profession. What the evidence does suggest is that Lucinda Trafton had her hands full managing her husband's and sons' estates and that she had a young daughter in her late teens for whose future she was responsible. Emery families had lived in Sanford and Biddeford for generations and were known for their honesty, integrity, and Christian principles. If Cyrus's hammering out tinware clashed with the melodious tones of Caroline's organ playing, the historical evidence does not reveal it. They were married June 5, 1853, just days before Caroline's twentieth birthday.

The newlyweds only spent one year in Maine, and during this time Cyrus extended his sales to include medicinal products made by his mother-in-law's new husband, Dr. Henry Smith. Lucinda Trafton had remarried in early 1854 to Dr. Smith, who was an apothecary. The doctor sold a variety of health elixirs including "beer," which was a health drink the doctor made of roots and herbs, "a warm cordial for children, and a compound for the cure of Lock Jaw." He was also famous in Maine for Smith's Catholican, a painkiller of uncertain origins.[18] With his able wife as broker and bookkeeper, Dr. Smith's small business prospered, and Cyrus Emery traveled the countryside providing the doctor's stock to merchants and collecting the money for items sold in local groceries.

Cyrus was restless, however, and he was adept at recognizing a good opportunity. His wife's older half-sister Laura Trafton Page lived in Garden Plain, Illinois, with her husband Samuel. There they farmed wheat and corn and raised hogs.[19] Like countless others in the 1850s, Cyrus believed there would be greater economic opportunities in the vast expanse of the Midwest than could be found in New England; therefore, in June of 1854, he sold his share in Andrews & Emery to his partner for a thousand dollars. The Emerys headed west. In later years he commented, "I am proud of the country of my birth, but not particularly proud of that location where I was born, for it is a hard, rocky, barren soil … I made my escape as soon as possible and have never regretted the move then made."[20] At the time of the move Cyrus was uncertain in which occupation he would settle, but farming with his wife's brother-in-law seemed to be the logical choice.

The week-long trip via railroad and steamboat to Illinois included a short stay with Cyrus's half-sister Mary Elizabeth and her husband Lyman Crown in Boston. Crown was a book publisher, and Cyrus made arrangements to ship one hundred dollars' worth of books to Rock Island, Illinois, where he planned to sell them. Once in Illinois, Cyrus discovered that he disliked the back-breaking farm labor in the Illinois heat, so he soon borrowed Samuel Page's horse and buggy and peddled books. Bookselling brought him into contact with tradesmen and merchants who suggested that Prophetstown would be an ideal place to begin a tinware business. By October 1854, Cyrus and Caroline were settled in Prophetstown, having purchased "a stock of goods suitable for our business and a set of tinner's tools and machines" in Chicago.[21]

Letters from Lucinda Smith to her family in Illinois are the only extant sources that shed light on this period in the life of Caroline and Cyrus.

The pain of absence from loved ones, the sudden deaths of numerous family members and friends, and her deep spiritual strength permeate the letters. Lucinda Smith and Hannah Emery, the two matriarchs, opposed the fact that their children lived hundreds of miles away. For Lucinda, her daughter's departure from Maine was a second blow. Her daughter Laura had left fifteen years earlier, and the family had been unable to visit her.[22] Shortly after the Emerys' arrival in Illinois, Lucinda wrote, "I think you may conclude now to come a little nearer home to settle down in business." Later she sent an admonishment: "I wish you could be satisfied to remain somewhere within two or three hundred miles of us, for a few years at least, untill [sic] your Mother Emery and I have gone to our resting places."[23]

Lucinda Smith's correspondence has a haunting quality that attests to the precarious nature of life in the 1850s. The letters highlight her anxiety for her children as she fretted over Caroline's health and her spiritual preparedness: "I have great many fears about you. Your going to a different climate at the sickly season" [sic].[24] Such fears were well founded. Cholera, tuberculosis, and various other "fevers and agues" raged all around them the first summer in Illinois. Caroline noted in a letter to her brother John that she would like to see him and his wife Malina, but if they visited "you must stand [a] chance to get the chill and fever which is so aggravating that you would want to die. This is a bad place for children they die off fast."[25] Lucinda thought it equally important to be concerned for her daughter's spiritual preparedness. "I entreat you at the same time to watch against the encroachment of Sin and keep your Heart with all diligence that you at last may give a good account of your stewardship." Later she asked, "But tell me if you can where true enjoyment is to be found, aside from the possession of a good conscience void of offence (as much as possible) toward God, and Man and the pleased hope of an Eternity of rest in the kingdom of Glory hereafter[?]"[26]

The summer of 1855 brought a welcome addition to the Emery family. Cyrus and Caroline's first child was born July 17, and extended family members mirrored the Emerys' happiness. Cyrus sent letters to both Lucinda Smith and his brother Salter Emery, requesting that they give him advice about what to name their daughter. Lucinda asked that she be named "*Lucinda Clark*, but am not particular ..."[27] and Salter replied, "We have talked it over about the names and have concluded to let you find a name that will suit you and we will be suited for the tribe of Emerys have got most all the names we have about here. So give *Sis* some *odd* name and that will suit all hands."[28] Cyrus and Caroline seem to have taken the advice of both. They named her Eva Lucinda, a combination of originality and family tradition.

Cyrus and Caroline Emery settled into life in Illinois with relative ease because of his success as a craftsman and salesman. His lucrative business pursuits peddling tinware and books allowed them to begin building a house when their daughter was a baby. They anticipated filling this house with their children, with the books they ordered periodically from Lyman Crown in Boston, and with pictures of family in Maine. Once Caroline Emery's melodeon arrived from the east in the fall of 1856, they also filled their home with the music she loved to play and sing.

But within a few short months the Emerys' lives changed profoundly. By the late fall of 1856 Caroline Emery was ill with tuberculosis and pregnant. Her health failed rapidly after the birth of Caroline Ernestine Emery (Carrie) on January 2, 1857. Helpless from one thousand miles away, Lucinda Smith poured out her anxieties for her daughter in a stream of frantic letters. She wrote to Cyrus upon news of Carrie's birth:

> I rejoice with you both, that you have another precious treasure added to your stock of household treasure and enjoyment for I would not wish you childless, but my object in writing so particular at this time is to call your attention to the present state of her health. This second drane [sic] upon her constitution in this short time will be likely to prove a disadvantage to her health unless she has special care. Men who have been healthy are not aware of the tendency of disease to press the spirits down and while in this state we cannot relish food, and without proper nourishment we sink and die, and who can be to these two babes what she can be to them[?][29]

Doctor Smith sent recipes for "Hot Drops," "Spiced Bitters," "Nerve and Bone Ointment," and "Composition Powder." Caroline's situation did not improve, and in March her mother wrote:

> Should I follow the impulse of my own feelings–I should at once sit me down and weep to think we are so far separated that I can not at once fly to you to give you aid, but this will not do, as it would unfit me to exercise my reasoning powers in trying to fix upon the best course for you to take.[30]

The Smiths prepared a box of Catholican and other medicines to send to Caroline for her cough. To Lucinda's great disappointment these medicines never arrived. She was also concerned about her daughter's spiritual health in this time of crisis. Every letter speaks to her own faith in God and her hope that her daughter could find strength and solace through prayer. In a society where death was common and often sudden, the need to be prepared to leave this world and meet one's redeemer was an overriding concern of many Christians.

> My dear – dear Caroline
> Can it be possible that all this time you have been growing weaker and the remedies we hastened to send you have not reached there … Do try my daughter to cast your care on the Lord and believe that he does care for you and he will support you, and you may yet live many years to praise him … O breath[e] your silent prayers to him, in faith, and he will comfort you. Tell me if you do find support in him when Cyrus writes again.[31]

When Cyrus wrote again he delivered the news that Caroline had died on April 24, 1857, leaving him a young father with two small daughters. Lucinda responded to her son-in-law's letter with a mixture of love, empathy, and criticism:

> My dear son,
> … When I think of the agony you must have endured these few weeks past, it seems as if I should fly to meet you, and clasp these Motherless babes to my stricken heart! … Oh, I do hope that you will seek and find, consolation in *Christ*, in this distressing hour. When I think of what she must have suffered during the past *cold winter* it seems as if I could hardly bear it– could I have been with her, and borne part of her burdens, she might have lived longer. She ought not to have been without help One day since last Nov. [emphasis hers].[32]

Lucinda Smith's own steadfast faith provided comfort through the tragedy of losing her daughter, and she hoped in the wake of the crisis that she would soon see her granddaughters. Counseling Cyrus on the pragmatism of moving back to Maine, Lucinda wrote: "You[r] Mother and myself think you should sell your property there, and take your children this way, where your friends can assist you in taking care of them. You may have an attack of fever as it is so common to that climate and you can provide all that is necessary for your comfort here."[33] With his customary independence, Cyrus never seems to have considered returning to Maine permanently; however, he obviously needed someone to take care of his children and to provide stability for his family. Leaving his daughters in the care of family and friends in Illinois, he made the long journey back to Sanford, Maine, where he married Martha Ann Rose on July 19, 1857, less than three months after Caroline's death.

Her mother's death marked the beginning of what Eva remembered as an unhappy childhood. In later life, she noted that her stepmother Martha "was a handsome woman and wonderful to those she liked," but Eva did not consider her stepmother easy to get along with or like.[34] Martha Emery was stern, authoritarian, and unaffectionate, at least with her older stepdaughter. Although Eva did not remember her own mother's presence in her life, Martha never took Caroline Emery's place in her affections. From Martha's perspective, this headstrong, precocious, and creative stepdaughter must have been a mystery and an aggravation.

But Eva and her father developed a rapport and mutual respect founded on their similar temperaments and interests. They shared a common appreciation for history. When Eva was young, visitors to the Emery household regaled the children with stories that she remembered as heroic tales of conquest for the establishment of a new nation. The Black Hawk War in 1832 was one example. Prophetstown is situated near the northwestern Illinois-Iowa border, close to the Mississippi River in the heart of what was once Sac and Fox Indian country. Many of Prophetstown's residents in the 1850s were veterans of the war that ended Black Hawk's control of the region. Not surprisingly, these pioneers eagerly recounted their exploits. "In those days," Eva explained, "Colonel Seeley, an old officer of the Black Hawk war, used to sit by the fireside now and then and tell of Black Hawk and his warriors, and of skirmishes in the prophets town. With wide eyes and open ears … [I] drank in every word."[35]

Her father had a gift as a raconteur, and the Revolutionary War provided endless material for storytelling in the Emery family. His maternal great-grandfather, Titus Salter, "captured the powder from the British fort [at Portsmouth, New Hampshire] that was used … in the battle of Bunker Hill." Caleb Emery, Cyrus's paternal great-grandfather, had fought in the French and Indian War and was a colonel in the Revolution.[36] "All of this gave me an early love for American history," Eva explained. "It instilled a love of romance and adventure in me that has never left me."[37] Coupled with the tales of early Illinois history and her Uncle Crown's books, her father's storytelling and his deep enjoyment of history fostered an atmosphere of respect for literary pursuits within the Emery household.

Her father's political affiliation, his strong views on moral issues, and his success as a craftsman and entrepreneur also served as important models for Eva as she grew into womanhood. An anti-slavery advocate and a devoted Republican, Cyrus was traumatized when he heard the news that Lincoln had been assassinated. He reported that when he "realized the magnitude and horror of this report" he was "so sick [I] was obliged to lay down." Indeed, despite a fatal accident that befell his six-year-old daughter Iroline May on April 15, 1865, Cyrus seemed much more affected by the president's death. It was Eva in fact who annotated his "Reminiscences" to include the circumstances of "little May's" death.[38] Cyrus was also a longtime supporter of prohibition, having joined the Sons of Temperance as a teen in Maine and continued his temperance activities when he reached Illinois. He was very proud of his role in the 1876 election when Prophetstown went dry.

Cyrus built a lucrative business hauling scrap metal and rags, crafting and peddling tinware, and selling household brushes door-to-door; and he managed to turn a profit in the midst of the economic upheaval caused by the Civil War. He patented a number of inventions with friends, including the "package tie [which] consisted of a disk and cord attached to an envelope." In paying for the patent Cyrus received a one-half interest in the royalties which, over the life of the patent, brought him twenty thousand dollars. Cyrus's enthusiasm for invention and his independent, honest, and outspoken nature made him a respected figure in Prophetstown. Following her father's example, Eva would one day write forceful poetry on the moral evils of both slavery and alcohol, and she often exhibited a stubborn independence and an originality of thought like her father.

Eva began writing poetry at an early age inspired, she later commented, by a manuscript of poems left by her mother. Urged by her father to continue her efforts, she also found an eager and supportive audience among her teachers at the local Prophetstown school. Decades later, Eva wrote her son Everett, "I know the little encouragement my father and teachers gave me did much to make me enjoy literary work. I used to have a poem [ready] every Friday afternoon at school, the teacher always called for it."[39] At the age of fifteen her first poem, "Dreamland," was published in the Prophetstown *Spike* and then reprinted in one of the larger city papers. Eva reported years later that the favorable review it received from the editor "was like manna in the wilderness, as water to a parched traveler in the desert, for my plan of being a writer had previously met only derision and opposition." Under the pseudonym "Jennie Juniper" she was soon writing stories and poetry for other newspapers in Illinois, a number of which paid her a small sum for her work. All monies received, she explained, "I invested in books, as I did every cent I could lay my hands on."[40]

Eva also established contact with Grandmother Smith through correspondence and the sharing of poetry. Although she never met her grandmother, they built a warm relationship on a foundation of letters. The point cannot be emphasized too strongly: epistolary writings linked Lucinda Smith with her daughter Caroline and, together, their letters linked each of them to Eva. When Caroline died, her daughters were left with few fragments of her life. Cyrus Emery wrote that when he left Illinois for Maine in search of a second wife, many of Caroline's possessions disappeared including "books and most of her jewelry, clothing and many other things too numerous to mention … [They] were stolen from our home."[41] What remained was the melodeon that Caroline loved to play, the many books given to the Emerys by Lyman Crown, the cherished letters that Lucinda Smith had written to her daughter, and a few of her schoolbooks and writings. Eva once commented, "my mother's poems made a great impression on my youthful mind, and her schoolbooks … with Caroline Trafton, 1853, on the flyleaf were a precious heirloom."[42] Eva's relationship with her mother was mediated entirely through her grandmother's letters and the remnants of Caroline's school work; in turn, her relationship with her independent, indomitable grandmother was sustained with the letters and poetry they exchanged when she was young. The written word, in books, letters, and poetry provided her with intellectual nourishment, solace, inspiration, heroes and heroines.

By 1870 the Emery family had grown substantially to include six children, and there is little doubt that Cyrus Emery felt the strain of providing for all of them. Because of the demands of this burgeoning family, Eva, at fifteen, became "a bread winner instead of merely a bread eater," by teaching for twenty-five dollars per month at the Prophetstown primary school which she had attended. Although her wages were meant ostensibly to assist the family, Eva saved most of the money with her father's blessing; perhaps he intended it to be used when she married. She had other ideas, however; with a determination strengthened by her poetry writing and voracious reading she proclaimed her desire to go to college. It was a dream, she wrote, "that grew out of [my] mother's schoolbooks."[43]

Eva's announcement of her intention to pursue higher education met the kind of ridicule and disbelief that one would expect from the middle-class parents of a daughter in the 1870s. Her father called her idea "foolishness." He informed her, "colleges are for rich men's children." Confiscating her savings, Cyrus refused to hear any more about her college plans.[44]

Her father's decision was "a bitter blow" and seems to have been a surprise. He had been supportive of her literary efforts, so she probably assumed that he would approve of this ambitious educational goal as well. The "grit, firmness and endurance" the phrenologist discovered years later kept Eva from giving up in the face of family opposition. Instead, she quit her position at the Prophetstown primary school and found another opportunity teaching at a country school in Morrison, Illinois, while continuing to make college plans. To realize her dream she saved as much of her salary as possible. Later she noted, "I [was] determined to go to college – how or where, I did not know, but I felt that in spite of all opposition the way would in some way be opened so I could realize my ambition."[45]

The path that opened may have been partly a result of family tragedy. In the fall of 1874 two deaths struck the Emery household. Five-year-old Laura became ill and died in late September. Nineteen-year-old Eva tried to understand this inexplicable death, relying on the Christian promise of everlasting life. Her grief was palpable, and she memorialized her little sister with a twelve-stanza poem published in the Prophetstown newspaper. In the midst of the family's suffering and within weeks of Laura's death, baby Leonard also fell ill and died. Martha Emery was particularly devastated by the loss of her young son, and her grieving may have heightened the undercurrent of unhappiness that Eva experienced with her stepmother. Whether because of her own drive and persistence or because of the resignation and despair that permeated the Emery household in that autumn, Eva overcame her parents' opposition, though she never overcame her stepmother's objections, and entered college the following March.

At nineteen, then, Eva literally fled Prophetstown for Oberlin College in Ohio, having saved enough for one year's preparatory training she knew she would need. In 1909 she wrote a dramatic reconstruction of that flight for the Oberlin Alumni Magazine. Vividly she portrayed the pain of her departure and the roles various family members played in what was one of the most important events in her life. She wrote that she would "never

… I practically ran away–to Oberlin." Though unnamed, the voice that screamed behind her "you needn't ever come back! Your father will disown you," clearly was Martha's. The journey took Eva two days and nights, and she remembered being driven by "unseen irresistible forces" to Oberlin.[46]

When Eva left Illinois, she carried with her a stubborn determination to succeed, literary talents she attributed to her mother, and her father's example of independent thinking. The decision to reject a woman's traditional path and flee to Oberlin was one that would shape her literary pursuits and define her views on women for many years to come.

"The Gates Of Heaven":
Oberlin College
1875-1882

When Eva Emery left her home for Oberlin, Ohio, she continued to send in essays and observations to the Prophetstown *Spike*. One of her first commentaries confirmed that neither her independent spirit nor her persistence had suffered from the long and emotionally charged journey from Illinois. Perhaps anxious to reassure her father about the cost of her education, she wrote, "People are wont to look upon a college course as a great undertaking, involving too much expense for ordinary people to think of, but this, like all other things, varies according to the habits of the student." Instead of becoming a financial burden to her family, she reported to her hometown that she would put her "shoulder to the wheel" to earn her education.[1] "Self-help is the best help," she confidently asserted, and that belief along with infinite curiosity and eagerness helped her overcome many obstacles. Self-assured and resolute, she assumed that everyone who shared these traits could succeed. Oberlin provided a safe haven to test this worldview, and she often used familial imagery to describe the stability and nurturing she found among the students and faculty. In a telling metaphor, Eva wrote later that "as a mother, indeed, Alma Oberlin opened her arms, and took me in, and held me there, for seven years."[2] Oberlin's motherly embrace strengthened her belief in her own abilities while nudging her toward the realization that intellectual gifts and self-help alone could not break down all of the societal barriers that nineteenth-century women faced.

Eva's choice of Oberlin can be traced directly to two sources. One of her schoolmasters had attended the college and recommended it highly, and the Emery family had multigenerational ties to the Congregational Church, the religious affiliation of Oberlin. Other factors, such as a long abolitionist history, probably came into play as well. Oberlin College was the first coeducational college in the United States. It was founded on the Christian-egalitarian principle that all individuals were equal before God and, when Oberlin opened its doors in 1833, it opened them not just to white men and women but to blacks as well. Oberlin had much to recommend it to the young, dedicated, and bright woman from Illinois.

Eva also may have had practical reasons for her choice. Tuition was only twenty-five dollars per year (including room and board), which was considered to be low, and she would have the benefit of a classical education. At a time when other institutions were phasing out their classical studies programs for those based more on the elective system, Oberlin still offered a full classical course: Greek, Latin, mathematics, philosophy, science, and English literature. Given her love of classical literature and poetry, Eva must have found appealing this opportunity to continue and broaden her studies in such a challenging environment.

Arriving at Oberlin in March 1875, Eva became a librarian and then an instructor to pay for her expenses, all the while working on preparatory courses. She anticipated that it would take her seven years to finish: three of preparation and four years of college. She used the savings from her previous two years as a teacher to pay for the first year's tuition. Admiring her dedication, Cyrus Emery finally relented and sent the money she had earned between 1870 and 1872. In 1876 (at age twenty-one) she received a small inheritance from her mother's estate.[3] This gift from her much-loved and idolized mother must have felt like a blessing to Eva, a heaven-sent recognition of her will to persist.

College attendance was still a rare feat for women. Historian Barbara Solomon notes that in 1870 only seven-tenths of one percent of all women eighteen to twenty-one years of age attended a four-year institution.[4] Eva's cohort was the first generation of college-educated women, and those who strove to obtain the coveted prize were dedicated, determined, and often at odds with the wishes of their families. Eva's struggle to obtain her education, particularly the lack of parental support, paralleled that of another famous woman graduate of Oberlin, Lucy Stone. Stone, abolitionist, suffragist, charismatic orator, began teaching school at sixteen and saved her money, like Eva, for nine years in order to attend Oberlin until "at last even her father was convinced that nothing would deter her from her purpose."[5] Graduating from Oberlin in 1847, Stone went on to become one of the foremost leaders of the woman's rights movement in the nineteenth century. It is unknown whether Eva knew of Stone at the time she decided to attend Oberlin, but significantly, in later years both Eva and her husband Charles recalled that Lucy Stone was one of the ten most influential Oberlin graduates of the nineteenth century.[6]

The freedoms Oberlin accorded women in the 1870s were noteworthy. It is well to remember, however, that Oberlin's egalitarian Christian ethos did not extend to the realm of everyday society and culture; men and women were equal before God, but not in the classroom. In accordance with the notion that men and women occupied separate spheres, most classes would not have been coed, and free association between male and female students was restricted. Historians have coined the phrase "the cult of true womanhood" to define nineteenth-century traits of piety, purity, submissiveness, and domesticity, which white middle-class culture ascribed to its women.[7] At Oberlin, the administration and the students' parents could rest assured that all tenets of true womanhood were strictly observed. With this in mind it is perhaps understandable that one of Oberlin's most well-known graduates, Antoinette Brown Blackwell, labored without the approval of the college to realize her dream of becoming a leader in the church. Although she was ordained as a Congregationalist minister in 1853, Blackwell did not have the support of Oberlin's administration, which believed she had taken a decisive and unwelcome step outside her sphere.[8]

Yet the boundaries of "woman's sphere" do not seem to have placed a heavy burden on Eva's shoulders. Her literary interests sent her on a quest to become a woman of letters and a successful orator and, it seems, very little in the way of restriction stood in her way. She once wrote that "Oberlin opened the gates of heaven," and Eva found that college life in the 1870s permitted her to excel in areas where she had abundant natural gifts. Along with her major studies of Greek (both the language and the literature), she took courses in English literature, history, mathematics, Latin, French, and German. Boarding with the family of the college professor of Greek, Eva became proficient enough in the Greek language to read manuscripts in their original form. Frequently found writing and reading poetry, she eventually became the class "poet laureate" and excelled at oration.[9]

Eva launched her prolific student writing career almost the moment she arrived with the publication of a joyful, lilting spring lyric in the *Oberlin Review*.[10] The fact that she still needed to complete two years of preparatory work before she would officially enter Oberlin's class of 1881 did not deter her submission of poetry to the *Review*. She followed "A Vernal Lyric" with an ode to morning, another celebratory and hopeful poem that seemed to wash away any lingering anxiety caused by her traumatic departure from Prophetstown. The rolling trochaic tetrameter sets the mood:

Morning
Glancing o'er the golden gateway,
Comes a ripple of delight,
And the forest marshals straightway
Ev'ry phantom of the night.

Marching out a broken column,
Glide they down the gloomy west,
While in grandeur vast and solemn,
All the universe is dressed.

. . .

All the land is filled with praises,
Swelling from a thousand throats,
Buds and birds and trees and daisies
Pour the over-flowing notes.

Oh, how fair seems earth to mortals,
In this bursting out of Joy!
Seem we standing at the portals,
Of a bliss without alloy.[11]

Many of her future poems would follow this marching cadence, though as she became more sophisticated in her verse, she often experimented with variant foot, meter, and rhyming combinations. She published two more poems in the *Review* in the years prior to her admission to the class of '81, one on autumn and another about the crumbling, historic chateaux in Spain. Thus she set a pattern for much of her future poetry; she wrote frequently of the seasons, of weather, celebratory odes to God and paradise, and of people and places of historic note.

Once she was fully admitted to the college, she wasted no time in becoming involved in organized literary pursuits. In 1877 she joined the Ladies' Literary Society, one of the many student educational clubs at Oberlin and, upon the resignation of one of her classmates, she was elected to the editorial board of the *Oberlin Review*.[12] Representatives of the six Oberlin literary societies held places on the editorial board; all society editors were expected not only to produce the *Review* but also to contribute their own work. Eva's writings appeared sporadically at first, and then their numbers increased steadily over the next two years as she gained confidence in her poetic and literary work. She felt completely driven to write and, as she expressed it in her whimsical poem "The Pen Possessed," she was helpless to stop the flow of words. This rare instance of Eva's humor is a commentary on her obsession as a writer.

The Pen Possessed By a Literary Sinner
My pen has caught a wondrous power,
That's neither flesh nor spirit,
But stronger growing hour by hour,
My soul begins to fear it.

A thought comes to my busy brain,
In moments of abstraction,
Straightway that pen must make it plain,
To my entire distraction.

It writes and writes as if its steel,
Were concentrated knowledge,
And never can be made to feel,
It has not been thro' college.

It rings in rhyme, and doles out prose,
In rough-shod words and phrases,
Till this poor poet hardly knows,
The odds 'twixt blames and praises.

Now tell me man, and be my friend,
Before I meet destruction,
What shall I do to bring an end
To this mad pen's production?[13]

In the two years she was a contributing editor, numerous issues of the *Review* opened with her seasonal odes and tributes to historic characters, literary heroes, and God. In addition to her poetry, students at Oberlin also were frequently exposed to Eva's forceful, opinionated essays on numerous topics. Authors from the Romantic period in Britain, America, and Germany had a significant influence on her writing; her frequent discussions of the nature of intelligence and genius, her search for "the poet of the future," and discourses on imagination, originality, and sensitivity bear the stamp of Carlyle, Emerson, Fuller, and Goethe, among others. In Eva's writing, three major elements recur with consistency. First, she believed that students would reap the rewards of their education only through independent thinking, diligence, determination, and a desire to broaden their minds. Second, she argued persuasively and consistently that originality of thought coupled with a solid foundation in history and literature were the keys to success. Third, she often chastised her student colleagues for their intensity of action and their extremes in emotion, arguing instead that moderation in all things would lead to a strong moral and physical character.

One of Eva's first essays in the *Review* appeared in the November 1877 issue. Here she elucidated the first theme, that diligent reading and research would yield the rewards of cultural and historical understanding. Those rewards, she argued, included greater intelligence, wisdom, forethought, the development of moral character, and the "self-dependence" that characterized Margaret Fuller's writings. Her audience was her fellow college students, whom she upbraided for their carelessness, their "dip in the magazines, [and] a cram for an exercise." They should, she ordained, be taking advantage of every opportunity to read more widely and comprehend more broadly the vast quantity of literature that life held before them. "Here in the morning of our hopes we can infix in our very souls a taste and affection for the best in literature" she wrote. She criticized students' lack of diligence in inquiry and research, not just because their education would be less complete, but because a lack of historical understanding behind the literature rendered it meaningless. She argued, "Too often the choicest classics are rendered tedious through lack of outside reading suggestive of comparisons that vivify the thought as with a breath, a flash, of warmth, and fire." She sang the praises of the classics but noted that without "even a small amount of judicious reading on the history, nature, and character of Greek literature" readers would be lost amid "the technicalities of Socrates and Homer."[14]

Eva's criticism of students' reading habits extended to the structure of the academic curriculum as well. She often noted that the reading in which students engaged was flawed by design because it limited students to a set curriculum instead of encouraging them to venture more extensively into the unfamiliar or unique. Arguing that it would be "better to double the length of a college course alternating each year of study with one of general reading, than to press on as many do neglectful of genuine development," she pleaded for more innovation and imagination to accompany a solid background in the classics, philosophy, and history.[15]

The need to be innovative and original in one's writing and poetry is the second theme that appears in almost all of Eva's writing at Oberlin. The Romantic belief in the "potentialities of all things" and the gift of imagination permeate her essays. In March 1878 Eva reiterated a common sentiment that writing well and thinking well necessitated creativity. "We conclude that the average student may well claim the badge A.B. for the merit of being at least a skillful compiler, able to exclaim with far more truth than did Campbell: 'There's nothing original in me, excepting Original Sin.'"[16] Abhorring the lack of originality in most writers' work, their "limited vocabularies," and the "equally narrow conceptions of the great mass of living themes," she acerbically commented, "ninety-nine per cent of our so-called essayists never venture to make an observation until some other luminary has established a precedent."[17] She noted that without careful reading and purposeful thinking one could not hope to become truly literate or to produce sound scholarship. "Heaven defend us from the young man that is 'literary' and nothing else," she wrote. Concluding that nothing brilliant was possible from anyone's pen "however great the genius that guides it … without the preliminary drudgery of toil and thought,"[18] she neatly tied together her worldview: the joys that are unique to a life of the mind could belong to anyone who exercised diligence to the task at hand and who read, thought, and wrote with imagination and creativity.

Eva often encouraged beginning poets and writers, despite her railing against their laziness, but she seemed resigned to the fact that it was a rare person indeed who combined genius with ability. She also understood that changing the direction of the college curriculum was a daunting prospect. Wearily she noted that the nature of "a regular education is often unfavorable to originality."[19]

The third theme expressed in her writing, that of moderation in all things, could also be described as Eva's moral teachings to her fellow students. In these essays she combined observation, didactic teaching, and common sense to educate her peers, and their tone and content was similar to that of other *Review* editors. She wrote in November 1877 on the "neglect of repose," chiding her colleagues on the flimsiness of their theory that burning the midnight oil would actually put them ahead. "Every now and then we chronicle the sad fact that Mr. or Miss so-and-so has left college on account of ill health."[20] Ill health, she stated emphatically, had nothing to do with it, nor did over-study. Lack of common sense and lack of sleep were the culprits. She turned next to the practicality of women's clothing, in an era when women and men were debating dress reform. "Girls be sensible," she exhorted, "follow your English sisters, put on over-coats and boots," instead of the long skirts and thin shoes that were fashionable in the 1870s. "There is not a man in Oberlin that goes as thinly clad as some of our delicate maidens."[21] Eva encouraged moderation in emotion and sensitivity;[22] and she advocated self-abnegation and prudent fiscal behavior for those who were self-supporting at Oberlin;[23] finally, she argued for self-restraint for those who had "untamed restless spirit[s] … The one that compels himself to endure restraint, has stamina a thousand fold compared with the one that never realizes there is any restraint."[24] In a firm and determined voice Eva made the case for reasonableness, common sense, and moderate behavior. One of her poems also expressed this idea: in "Life" she answered the question of why we are put on this earth. Her answer, resoundingly, "We as mortals do but linger/ Here to form a character."[25]

Eva's penchant for didacticism and the influence of Romantic literature are clearly evident in her essays, but one must turn to her poetry to understand the effects of the Latin language and the Greek classics on her writing. Her passion for all things Greek inspired her to write about Greek poetry itself, "the music of the human heart," and to laud the work of Heinrich Schliemann who, in 1870, believed he had uncovered the lost city of Troy.[26]

> Schleimann, true heir of all the Greeks,
> Heroic in Homeric faith,
> The buried past revived speaks,
> And Delphi's shrine, prophetic, saith
> Thy name shall live, linked with the land
> That bore the gods, that tuned the lyre,
> That bred Achilles and his band,
> And stole Promethean fire ...[27]

Her enthusiasm for Schliemann is mirrored in many other exuberant odes, and her poetry generally addressed historic themes and characters or evoked the atmosphere of ancient Rome and Greece. She occasionally peppered her poems with both Greek and Latin phrases and allusions to classical literature; indeed, her "Lyra Hellenica," is sprinkled with poetry in Greek, and she wrote the class of '82's song, "Octoginta Duo," in Latin. She did not believe it was necessary to provide a translation.

Eva's study of Homer's *Iliad* and *Odyssey* and her reading of Hesiod's poetry led to experimentation with epic forms in her own work. "The Fall of Anahuac," in which she describes the bloody conquest of the Aztec empire in 1519, was published in the August 1877 *Review*. In 160 lines of rhyming hexameter, the meter most commonly found in epic poetry, she detailed the gruesome battle that ended Montezuma's reign, the despair of the Aztec god Quetzalcoatl, and the horrific deaths of the Tabascan Indians. It is a sweeping and graphic story. Eva assumes her readers are familiar with the central characters and the history of events; it helps to know, for example, that Huitzilopochtli was the Aztec god of war. She tells her readers at the outset "my theme is one of conquest, and my time, the twilight age of chivalry," but though she recounts the carnage with some sympathy for the Aztecs and criticism for the victors–"And o'er the ruin red when deeds of carnage cease/ Oh, mockery of Christ, they raise the Cross of Peace"–the epic never waivers from a sense of inevitability that Cortes will triumph. "O Clio," she penned,

> close the page, we guess the truth too well,
> Thro' famine, fire, and sword, the valiant city fell;
> In dumb unspoken woe, when hope of aid is past,
> Still, still she will not yield, defiant to the last,
> And when invading feet the hollow pavements tread,
> Behold a charnel-house, a city of the dead.[28]

The poem ends not with the Spanish defeat of the Aztec in 1519, but with a reference to the 1846 Mexican-American War. With the stroke of her pen, Eva wiped out Mexico's history of bloody conquest and the Anglo-European imperialism that brought about the demise of an empire. All is to be forgiven and forgotten, it appears, and Mexico, personified as the queen to America's king, should accept her subjugation and marry the enemy.

> Awake, O, Mexico, awake fair sister-land,
> To-day is stretched to thee our young Republic's hand,
> Four hundred years of strife, four centuries of shame,
> Bid thee unite with us thy once resplendent name;
> Uplift thy head, O, Queen, let all thy banners rise,
> And sweep with stripes and stars our two united skies,
> Prepare the bridal wreath, Columbia waits for thee,
> Be thou the home of Art, be thou our Italy.[29]

The central theme of this poem, the imperialism of Anglo-Europeans and their conquest of native peoples, is one to which Eva would return for the rest of her writing career, and "The Fall of Anahuac" exhibited her propensity for siding with the conquerors.

The theme of conquest, and the skill to write an epic poem, arose from Eva's deep appreciation of and background in the *Iliad* and *Odyssey*. She wrote in later years, "Classic lands and letters were more real to me than America and the English language,"[30] and her desire to write of monumental encounters between east and west, white colonizer-explorers and native peoples, gods and goddesses, drew much from the *Iliad*. Her writing is also reminiscent of the historical fiction of Sir Walter Scott. The pages of *Ivanhoe*, *Rob Roy*, and *The Bride of Lammermoor* had inspired her as a child; she noted once that she had read all of Scott's novels "and wished he had written twice as many more."[31]

Themes of victorious conquest and vivid battles occurred in another poem that Eva wrote while at Oberlin. The issue was slavery, and she crafted a poem in honor of Charles Sumner, whose controversial speech on the Senate floor in the midst of "Bleeding Kansas" in 1856 resulted in his receiving a near-fatal beating at the hands of fiery Representative Preston Brooks of South Carolina. The northern outcry over the event helped spur the abolitionist cause and further divided North from South. In Eva's poem, slavery is the "mighty monster" and Columbia its victim. Sumner emerges as Columbia's champion:

> No light-armed skirmisher was he,
> But armed for war and victory,
> Steel clad he came and down the list
> Spared not one bold antagonist:
> Against the castle grim he sent
> An avalanche of argument,
> Until its towering bastions fell
> And crushed the very citadel.[32]

The battle of Agamemnon and his men at Troy and Ivanhoe's rescue of Rebecca no doubt provided literary fuel for her fires of indignation. A skilled orator, Eva delivered this poem at Oberlin's 1881 Junior Exhibition. According to the audience, Eva's oration was "the best *literary* exercise of the day … We should hesitate to tell which was the better, the poem or the presentation; her whole expression seemed so to harmonize with her thoughts, her feeling."[33]

Eva's passion to write about a wide variety of history and historic characters grew out of her reverence for classical and Romantic literature and the epic form. She was fascinated by stories of interaction and conflict between peoples, whether they were Greeks and Trojans, Normans and Saxons, or whites and native peoples; that fascination led to many tales of encounters between Native Americans and missionaries, colonizers, and explorers as she sought to understand the essential elements of American history. In the future she would take up the theme of conquest and use her adoration of the *Iliad* and Romantic literature to write a chronicle of one of America's greatest epics, the Lewis and Clark Expedition.

Eva's personal experience as a woman living in the nineteenth century provided additional inspiration, often indignant inspiration, for other poetry and essays. She prided herself on an understanding of modern life based on historical literacy, coupled this with a keen sense of what she believed was right and just, and used her pen to expound on the plight of contemporary woman. The roots of this critique of women's place in American society grew from her broad foundation in literary studies, but larger discussions of social and moral reform, the efficacy of women's political participation, and changes in the availability and content of education for women also influenced her. Like most middle-class white women in the 1870s and 1880s, Eva believed in the primacy of women's attachments to the home. She, like her contemporaries in the early women's rights movement, believed in women's economic, legal, and political equality while at the same time arguing that women's unique role as wives and mothers granted them moral guardianship over society.[34] Many women in the late nineteenth century, including Eva, found their moral cause in the temperance movement.

Eva's support for temperance was no doubt influenced prior to her arrival at Oberlin by her father's opinion. Family tradition, and Oberlin's religious affiliation and support for Christian reform causes at home and abroad, inspired and sustained her belief that thousands of women were being victimized by the ravages of alcohol. Her poem "The Sixty Thousand" was a reference to an 1873 uprising of Ohio and Michigan women who were successful at closing down over one thousand saloons.[35] Published in the *Oberlin Review* in 1879, the poem substituted the sixty thousand women temperance activists for sixty thousand drunken men on their way to hell. The poem's steady cadence is reminiscent of a funeral dirge:

> In this land of boasted freedom,
> In this kingdom of the brave,
> Silently a spectral army
> Marches onward to the grave.
> Hark! I hear their muffled footsteps,
> Like a distant, dismal knell,
> As our sixty thousand drunkards
> Tread the path that leads to hell.

Hark again! that sound of wailing
Borne along the midnight air –
'Tis the cry of helpless orphans,
'Tis the widow in despair.
Still the sound is ever steady,
Tramping, tramping thro' the gloom,
Pass our sixty thousand drunkards
To the portals of the tomb.[36]

Eva's concern for the women and children who were victimized by alcoholic men was common among a broad constituency of women. While the movement appealed particularly to white, middle-class, Protestant reformers, temperance also drew in women from a variety of class and ethnic backgrounds and from all regions of the country. Founded in 1874, the Women's Christian Temperance Union (WCTU) emerged as an organization that allowed many women to participate politically for the first time on issues that affected them as wives and mothers. Significantly, men were not allowed to join the WCTU and, as historian Sara M. Evans argues, this created "a free space within which women experimented and pushed their traditional self-definitions past the boundaries of domesticity and into the broadest demand for full political participation."[37] Many women like Eva first participated as activists within the ranks of the temperance movement and took their passion and ideas for social and political change to the women's club and into the fight for suffrage.

Whether it was her advocacy of temperance or her intellectual understanding of the role of women in shaping history that first brought Eva to critique the place of women in American society, it is clear that she began a more formal study of women's sphere while at Oberlin. Like her other writings, Eva's essays on women drew inspiration from Thomas Carlyle and Margaret Fuller, especially his *Past and Present* (1843) and her *Woman in the Nineteenth Century* (1845). These two authors, along with her extensive reading in classical literature and Romanticism, formed the literary basis for her understanding of women in American society.

One of her college essays, "The True Lady," is both a treatise on the value of labor, reminiscent of Carlyle, and a discourse on the value of women's broader participation in nineteenth-century American society. Drawing from Carlyle and poets Whittier and Longfellow, Eva used domestic images of women in poetry to make her claim that "in work alone shall we find our high estate," and that "true feminine dignity" comes from labor that is challenging physically, mentally, and morally. "The True Lady" celebrates domestic attachments. The women Eva selected for discussion were Whittier's Juno "molding her golden butter in a milk-house," Longfellow's Evangeline presiding over the hearth of the farmer of Grand-Pre, and Priscilla from "The Courtship of Miles Standish" carding wool. The essay incorporates a theme that is present in most didactic literature of the late nineteenth century, namely that women are fit only for a domestic life, to be carried out with self-abnegation and good works. In the midst of the domestic imagery, however, Eva struggled to define a larger role for women. She urged women to develop logical and critical thinking skills, to not be "slaves to passion" but develop "into fairer proportions, conversant with art, science, and letters." The mark of Carlyle's *Past and Present* is undeniable: "All true work is sacred." Work is exalted, especially the labor done with one's hands, and only through labor will one find what is noble and worthy.

Eva's unpublished essays are undated, but there is a progression to them that suggests that her "Women of Genius" was written after "The True Lady." In "Women of Genius," there is no hesitation in the sentiment that women need opportunities beyond hearth and home. Her voice is strong and sure. Taking issue with the idea that women were not the intellectual equals of men, Eva explored the idea that women were capable of genius, and many of her thoughts resonated with the words of Margaret Fuller. An article in the *Atlantic* by Harriet Preston had provided the impetus for the essay. To Preston's observation that "[while] it is worthwhile to make arrangements on a large scale for the careful and costly training of boys … it would be foolish and extravagant to make [these arrangements] for girls," Eva responded that although it was difficult to find exceptional women in the past, it was not impossible. The fortunate few whose intellectual accomplishments set them above the rest were women whose education had received attention. She argued, "Let someone pick out a score of rare American girls with all the care of selecting a cadet for West Point and give them the careful and costly training of Margaret Fuller and we shall find her not the rare exception." She maintained that the barriers preventing women's full participation in society were neither just nor logical, noting "It is a bitter motto with the world that genius must surmount all barriers to *prove* itself genius." Eva concluded her response with the astute observation that "when our girls have had college advantages 200 years who will be likely to say that the number of women worthy of such an outlay will not be in proportion to the number of men …?"[38] To a young woman coming of age in the progressive atmosphere of Oberlin, Preston's ideas seemed "decidedly behind the age."

Margaret Fuller's assertion that "plants of great vigor will almost always struggle into blossom, despite impediments" found a ready audience with Eva, who admired Fuller's espousal of "self-dependence" and her modeling of a life based on study, critical thinking, and writing.[39]   In an 1881 *Review* essay, Eva paid tribute to Fuller, who, she argued, was unique among literary critics and among women. Praising Fuller's many talents and the impact she made on others, Eva reverently noted "as genius kindles genius, so at her altar many a torch was lit and many a kindred soul awoke to high resolve."[40]

Eva's poetry and essays about women demonstrate the beginnings of her political awareness and suggest the profound impact that her studies at Oberlin had on her understanding of herself and the meaning of womanhood in Victorian America. She found many a kindred soul among her classmates and in the pages of the history and literature she so enjoyed. Her reading, writing, and oratory also provided the seeds of her later participation in the Oregon Equal Suffrage Association, her continued and passionate support for prohibition and missionary work, and her advocacy of educational reform. Like many of her contemporaries in the nineteenth-century movement for woman's rights, she worked from within the boundaries of women's sphere to enlarge it; that is, her critique of women's place was not the more radical plea for rights based on justice but for rights based on women's experience as homemakers. She believed that because of women's unique moral qualities as wives and mothers their access to education, to meaningful labor, and to the political process would transform society for the better while stimulating and improving women's own minds and lives.

Oberlin College's dedication to open access for men and women students and the administration's desire that graduates go on to serve their communities in the arts, ministry, and education had as profound an impact on Eva as her study of classical and Romantic literature. Oberlin not only gave her a place in which she could explore new ideas and hone her writing skills, it also provided a milieu of progressive, ambitious, and intelligent friends. Eva tried to answer for herself "After college, what?" by exploring her options as a writer, a teacher and possibly as a missionary. A classmate, Carolyn Eldred, undertook a missionary assignment in Japan in 1878. In the course of their correspondence, Eva bombarded her friend with many questions about the Japanese people and their culture, partly because she herself was considering teaching in an international setting.

Her choice of what to do after college took a slightly different turn, however, when she encountered another of her classmates, Charles Henry Dye. Dye arrived at Oberlin in 1878 from Fort Madison, Iowa, where he was born and raised. Of Danish descent, Charles, like Eva, had Revolutionary War heroes in the family lineage. The Revolutionary government had paid Grandfather Andrew Dye for his military service with Ohio land. Once in Ohio, Andrew and his wife Sarah Minor Dye helped found the town of Troy, where they lived out the rest of their lives. In 1839, four years after his father's death, their son Henry and his wife Jane Mickelwait Dye moved from Ohio to the newly opened Black Hawk Purchase in Iowa, eventually settling in Fort Madison, where Charles Henry was born on August 23, 1856.[41]

Little is known about Charles's early life. Prior to his arrival at Oberlin he had been a student at Denmark Academy in Fort Madison. His decision to attend Oberlin probably was influenced by his church affiliation and possibly by its reasonable tuition. A member of the Congregational Church, Charles, by all accounts, was a thoughtful, articulate, intelligent, socially progressive, and deeply spiritual man. His Christian faith was deep and sustaining.

Charles's career as a student had much in common with Eva's. He was a classical studies major and, like Eva, participated actively in the Home Oratorical Association. In 1882 he won second prize for his oration of his essay "The Russian Revolution," delivered with "genuine earnestness and manly vigor."[42] A member of Alpha Zeta, Charles served on the editorial board of the *Review* in 1882 but unlike Eva he did not often submit his own writing. Charles and Eva both struggled to pay tuition and their room and board and taught school in the summers to make ends meet. Eva, in fact, had experienced a serious interruption in her academic career. She left to teach school in nearby Macedonia during the winter of 1879 in order to earn enough money to continue her studies. She returned to Oberlin in April, only to leave again in May for five months in order to recuperate from illness.[43] While Charles's brief periods of teaching did not cause him to lose academic ground, Eva's leave of absence resulted in her unwilling inclusion in the class of 1882 instead of her original class of 1881.

Their meeting was the beginning of a forty-seven-year partnership that was remarkable for its equality, interdependence, and symbiosis. Their courtship remains a mystery, but its effect on Eva was certainly profound. She was known at Oberlin for her serious and stern demeanor and once noted:

> when I was in my sophomore year someone started the report that I had been seen to smile, but it was not believed, for I was known as the "saddest" girl in school. The report really was true. I had smiled, and I often smiled thereafter, for I saw that there was something beside sorrow in life. Love had come into my life – love and joy and laughter.[44]

Charles's affectionate and open nature was a perfect contrast to Eva's reserved and determined outlook, and they were certainly well suited on an intellectual level. Meeting each other in their sophomore year did not deter either from finishing their education. They graduated together June 28, 1882, and were married two weeks later by Oberlin's president, James H. Fairchild, on the eve of Eva's twenty-seventh birthday. Charles believed he would study medicine, and Eva intended to continue her writing.[45]

If one word were to summarize the character that Eva Emery Dye formed over the course of her first twenty-seven years, it would be "determined." Her childhood experiences and memories, her mother's writing samples, and her father's enthusiasm for history all led to her utter determination and devotion to become a writer. Despite many obstacles, the seven years spent at Oberlin College fed her resolve and further opened a world of literature and history to a young woman who believed in the primacy of the "life of the mind." Life at Oberlin also honed her social and political views on a wide range of topics, and gave her a voice to express herself as an advocate for women's rights and temperance. Finally, Oberlin introduced her to a man who would be her partner, in spirit as well as in name. As she faced the new challenge of marriage she did so with a man who respected her intellect, admired her energy, and believed in her abilities as a writer.

Wife, Mother, Writer:
A Time of Transition
1882-1890

The years Eva spent at Oberlin helped to develop her skills as a writer, provided the education necessary for her both to embrace and to critique American history and literature, and honed her ability to make her voice heard on a wide variety of subjects. Her college experience also more clearly defined Eva's strong and determined character. The next phase of her life, the early years of marriage and motherhood, shaped her in an equally profound way. Marriage brought a loving and enthusiastic husband whose financial and emotional support enabled her to continue to write. As evidenced by diaries and letters, theirs was an egalitarian and complementary partnership that allowed each their independence. Motherhood in turn provided motivation and inspiration for much of her writing and influenced her evolving opinions on women's rights and social reform. The four children born to Eva and Charles between 1884 and 1897 softened the rather sharp edges of Eva's personality while enhancing her self-confidence and provided a stable emotional base for much of her later success.

After their marriage in July 1882, Eva and Charles began an eight-year journey to find a permanent family home. Sidney, the seat of Fremont County, Iowa, situated near the Missouri River on the southern Iowa-Nebraska border, was the first stop for the newlyweds. Sidney was a developing community of approximately one thousand people that offered rooming houses, a drug store, several churches, an imposing two-story brick high school, and the county courthouse.[1]

The completion of the railroad in 1867 linked Fremont County to eastern markets, a vital connection for an economy driven by farming and one that brought people and commerce to small communities such as Sidney in the 1870s and 1880s.[2] By 1885 the county employed nearly two hundred and fifty teachers and celebrated the publication of the first issue of the *Fremont County Herald*, which was produced in Sidney. Upon their arrival the Dyes roomed at a boardinghouse on the main street until their house in Hiatt's

Addition was ready. They attended the Presbyterian Church, where "the preacher's name was Dye, too," and Charles continued in the teaching profession that had paid his tuition and room and board while he was in college.[3]

This profession offered stability as well as new opportunities to Charles as he sought a path that would enable him to use his organizational skills and classical education while appealing to his commitment to public service. Despite the mention of a medical career on the eve of graduation from Oberlin, he never seems to have pursued that avenue seriously. In Sidney he served as principal of the public schools while also teaching high school.[4] Administrative tasks were his forte, and the experience he gained served him well in later years as president and secretary to numerous causes and organizations. In addition to his professional duties, Charles also wrote an editorial column for the *Fremont County Herald*. The "Sidney School Column" conducted by Prof. C. H. Dye was a public forum for ideas on the education of children.[5]

While Charles created a niche for himself in public school administration, Eva added to her store of literary and historical knowledge with Margaret Fuller's model of self dependence to guide her. Between 1882 and 1886 Eva focused on homemaking and did not continue teaching but did persist with her studies. One of the few comprehensive journal entries Eva penned while in Sidney attests to her voracious reading of an eclectic array of material. The list is especially impressive in light of the fact that the high school library's collection was the only one at her disposal. Eva consumed the works of Washington Irving, George Eliot, Henry James, Sarah Orne Jewett, Bayard Taylor, and Goethe. She also read widely in English and American history, including all five volumes of Catharine Macaulay's *The History of England from the Accession of James I to the Elevation of the House of Hanover*, J. T. Headley's *Life and Travels of General Grant*, and her favorite, Justin McCarthy's two-volume *History of Our Own Times*. In the margin of her journal she wrote, "When I finished this History of Our Own Times I felt I could rule the world."[6]

Just as at Oberlin College, Eva's "ruling the world" entailed not just reading but actively disseminating her opinions. She addressed the importance of a well-rounded education and the vital role that teachers played in a child's development in one edition of Charles's "Sidney School Column." Her thoughts are reminiscent of those she had addressed in the pages of the *Oberlin Review*. Here she reiterated her opinion that literature could only be brought to life through a historical and factual context, and she insisted on dedication to the task at hand and originality of approach. Teachers, she argued, had a greater influence over a child's literary tastes than did parents. She urged teachers to be "true missionaries" and engage a child not just in the story itself but also in the history behind it. "Tell him something about the piece, something about the writer," she expounded, "and the moment interest is aroused he reads with spirit and with understanding." She praised the McGuffey readers for teaching morality and "a model of pure English," and claimed that students would eagerly embrace quality reading if teachers would tell them that there were more of these "gems" of literature by the same authors awaiting them. She urged teachers to educate themselves on the lives of authors and then to learn and teach enthusiastically the history, action, and setting behind plays and ballads. Arguing that children would not read dime novels and other "rotten corruption" if they could find meaning in classical literature, Eva concluded with a sentiment about her commitment to ensuring the cultural literacy of Americans: "Give [children] the best and you have given a key to self education worth all the teachers in the world."[7]

Self-education had a direct purpose and outcome for Eva and Charles in the 1880s. Always motivated to read and study on their own, both pursued advanced degrees from Oberlin College while living in Iowa. Prior to 1898 the master's degree was granted to any graduate of Oberlin "who has been engaged in [three years of] literary or scientific pursuits, and has sustained a good moral character."[8] Charles earned his degree in 1885, presumably because of his full-time administrative work. Despite Eva's continued reading and writing and resuming her teaching career whenever possible, it would take her until 1889 to earn the degree. Her new responsibilities as a wife and mother and the fact that her teaching career was interrupted undoubtedly made it difficult to satisfy Oberlin's requirement for three years of professional work.

Eva's poetry and essay journals, begun in her sophomore year at Oberlin, mark the course of her literary pursuits through the mid-1890s and are a testimony to the changes wrought by marriage and motherhood. What is contained in the leaves of these books—and what is missing—provides a revealing glimpse into her thoughts and feelings and her motivations, priorities, and constraints. The births of Emery Charles Dye in June 1884 and Trafton Mickelwait Dye in January of 1886 marked the end, for several years, of Eva's prolific poetry and essay writing. The almost complete absence of records between 1884 and 1888 suggests that she devoted her time to her husband and children. Her journal, overflowing for years with lengthy odes, pages-long essays, and scraps of ideas for future work, was nearly silent, except for a few important items. But these journal fragments and a few clippings from scrapbooks demonstrate the depth of her commitment to pursue a literary life and bear witness to the energy with which she undertook the task of communicating her ideas.

Eva's didactic essays, her reading lists, and many of her published poems speak to the driven and serious side of her character that thrived on study and the self-education she so highly recommended to everyone. Yet her poetry had always been the place from which more personal emotions flowed, and one of the few poems that exists from her early married life illustrates hopeful anticipation and a lightness of spirit that is not evident in any of her writings before her marriage. Composed one month prior to Emery Charles Dye's birth, this poem celebrated spring and new life in May of 1884.

> The air is all a flutter,
> With a thousand wings,
> And the fragrance seems distilled
> of a thousand springs;
> Bees o'erladen humming by
> Laugh at you and we,
> Songsters carol in the sky,
> Hide in bush and tree,
>
> In deep, dim woods the May-bells
> Ring their jubilees,
> For a voice instinctive tells
> To buds and blooms and trees
> That June the Queen is winging
> Down her royal flight,
> All palpitating, bringing
> Feasts of red delight.[9]

But parenthood brought new responsibilities and many changes to their lives over the next few years, and Eva's customary energy and enthusiasm, once used solely for avid study and active writing, was now put to the task of raising her children. Charles wrote one of the last complete and conspicuous notations in her journal some time before 1888. With a historian's detail and careful lettering Charles inscribed his and Eva's marriage and the births of Emery and Trafton. Under the heading "Family

Record of C. H. and E. L. Dye," Charles meticulously wrote not only names and dates but the fact that he and Eva were married at "No. 15 S. Professor St. (the residence of E. H. Chapman)," and that "Pres. James H. Fairchild of Oberlin College was the officiating minister." He noted who was the "attending surgeon" for his sons' births and the street address in Sidney where they were living at the time. Significantly, the Family Record is the only example of his writing in her journals, and it set a precedent for their evolution. The journals became not only the record of her literary efforts but also the history of their family.[10]

In January 1886, when Emery was a year and a half old, they welcomed Trafton Mickelwait Dye. His unique appellation was a pairing of maiden names from Eva's and Charles's mothers. Within a few months of Trafton's birth the Dyes left Sidney, moving approximately one hundred and fifty miles southwest, to the town of Franklin, Nebraska. Charles became the principal of Franklin Academy, and Eva taught Greek and Rhetoric in the Ladies Department of the academy.[11] It was unusual for a married, middle-class woman in the 1880s to resume her teaching career while still raising small children, and the reason for Eva's return to the classroom is unknown.

Actually, little is known about the two years that the Dyes spent in Nebraska, but it must have been a crucial time of soul-searching for Charles. During this time he decided to forego a future in education and turned his sights instead on the legal profession. Contract law perhaps offered a challenge that the administrative tasks of managing a school did not, and it is also possible that the financial constraints of a growing family made it imperative that he find a more lucrative profession. The Dyes left Nebraska for Iowa City in the fall of 1888 so that Charles might attend law school at the State University of Iowa for one year in order to establish himself as an attorney.

The nine months the Dyes lived in Iowa City were busy and productive. Eva managed to carve out the time to begin the kind of research and writing that would establish her as an essayist and historian while teaching at Iowa City Academy and coping with her young sons.[12] She published an essay on Iowa's Amana Commune, taking her first step away from purely literary and poetical works and venturing into history.[13] Founded by German Inspirationalists in 1855, the Amana Colonies were cooperative communities with a highly structured religious and social order. Eva was intrigued with the settlers' persistence and fascinated by their communal labor organization. Always interested in the pioneering spirit, especially when it coexisted with religious zeal, Eva set a precedent in this essay for her future research on the Whitman and Spalding missions in the Pacific Northwest.

The essay on the Amana Colonies was her first published historical narrative, but the "Historic Capital of Iowa" was the piece that introduced her "charming style"[14] and knack for ferreting out historical detail to a wider audience. Published in the *Magazine of American History* this essay described early political life in Iowa City before the capital was relocated to Des Moines.[15] Interspersed throughout her history of the first governors and the development of the early legislature are picturesque vignettes of early settlement narrated in an oratorical style.

The essay is disjointed. Eva assumed readers would possess extensive knowledge of Iowa governance and politics; in addition, she ventured widely from political history to a tale of the bell cast for the Presbyterian church in 1841 and the history of the opening of the Mississippi and Missouri Railroad in 1856. What is apparent is that Eva was a consummate storyteller, and if she could have presented orally the information gleaned from newspapers and elder statesmen in Iowa City, she would have had an attentive and eager audience. For example, the story of the construction of the capitol building provided Eva the opportunity not just to present the facts but also to embellish for the sake of the readers' interest.

> From the 'Old Capitol Quarry,' till then untouched, save in the crude age of Indian art, stone was cut and hauled to the top of Capitol square, where busy workmen piqued the curiosity of the squirrel above and the lurking red man below, with the steady click of hammer and chisel. Slightly varying from the original plan by Father Mazzuchelli, the blocks of gray limestone shaped themselves in Doric symmetry, aspiring columns rose on the porticos, and the dome curved its fair calyx above the oaks of ages.[16]

Her essay received many favorable reviews. The *Iowa City Republican* claimed that "this historical contribution will rank as one of the very best ever published in regard to this city," and the *Burlington-Hawkeye* called it "a most delightful account of the establishment of the 'seat of government' in Iowa City."[17] This validation gave her the confidence to continue as a writer who could successfully blend traditional historical detail with decorated facts. "The Historic Capital of Iowa" set the style and tone for all of her future chronicles.

In June 1889 she completed her master's degree from Oberlin and Charles his law degree. His degree provided both flexibility and uncertainty for their immediate future, and Eva's gave her the determination to continue as a writer. The next month Charles left Eva and the two boys in Iowa City while he and a colleague headed northwest to Madison, South Dakota. There they hoped to build a thriving law practice in contract and commercial law.

Once Charles found adequate housing, Eva and the boys joined him. When Charles wrote to Eva before her arrival, he emphasized the need the people had for a good lawyer and believed his practice would be profitable. As staunch a temperance advocate as his wife, he noted that "two of the best attorneys had the delirium tremens this spring and all of their hair came out."[18] Other attorneys urged Charles and his partner not to settle in Madison because of the city's problems with alcohol, but Charles enjoyed the challenge. "We will show them that beer guzzling does not make lawyers and that honest hard work pays if the Lord will recognize honest effort."[19]

But Madison disappointed the Dyes. Family lore attributes the Dyes' departure from Madison to the cold and dreary winter they experienced in 1890.[20] While the weather may have been part of the reason, Eva noted years later that "the farmers had lost their crops and my husband grew heartsick over the fact that about the only law business he could get there was foreclosing mortgages."[21] One of the Dyes' friends was the Reverend Oramel Lucas, a Congregational Church minister in Oregon City, Oregon; he encouraged them to relocate to the Willamette Valley.[22] They left Madison in July 1890 for Oregon and never returned to the Midwest.

Against this backdrop of uncertainty and relocation, the completion of academic degrees, career changes, and parenthood, Eva continued her prose and poetry writing and started a new project as well. The "story of the children," was incorporated into her journals. Eva started writing the children's story to record some of the "funny things" her boys said. "I want to begin to keep track of some of them for their future amusement,"[23] she noted on the opening page in December 1888. These entries are the only source to shed light on her relationship with her young children, and they also provide subtle and significant glimpses into her relationship with Charles. Her literary endeavors and the story of the children must be viewed as essential parts of the whole. In fact, they are literally bound together because she interspersed her poems, fragments of essays, and finished works throughout the children's story. These writings illuminate her fundamental beliefs about motherhood in American society and provide a window through which to view her support for temperance and suffrage.

Eva recorded her children's exploits with care and detail. Although written over one hundred years ago, her tale of Trafton's third birthday is one with which any parent could identify. As a snapshot of a woman's busy domestic life in January 1889, it is priceless. "He celebrated the day," she wrote, "by sticking the broom in the stove and setting it on fire. I heard a great glee in the kitchen and reached there just in time to see Traffie's torch burst into a blaze." Later in the day while Eva was working in the kitchen she noticed "the children were very still." She found them under their bed applying "a liberal supply" of some of Eva's medicinal lotion to their faces. After being interrupted by a caller to the house, she returned to the boys' bedroom to find them bouncing on the bedsprings after having removed the bedding. "Last in their playing tonight Traffie knocked a kettle of hot lard on to the floor where the grease is still soaking as I shall not touch it tonight."[24] If she found the children's actions wearisome Eva did not note it, nor does her matter-of-fact tone reveal it; instead she recorded the day's activities with minute and affectionate attention and saved a page within the story for tracings of the boys' hands.

Many of the stories from the years when Emery and Trafton were small are similar to the tale of the birthday. Both boys were precocious, rambunctious, articulate, endlessly curious and, in most instances, Eva found them delightful. She proclaimed their imaginations "wonderfully active," their questioning natures "ingenious," and their minds "very keen."[25] At the ages of four-and-a-half and three, Emery and Trafton started kindergarten. Eva noted that they "are pretty young but they are greatly interested in the children's games."[26] Perhaps the necessity of getting her own work accomplished was one reason for putting them in school at such young ages, but it seems her desire to have them interact with other children and to begin school was more important to her. She proudly recorded a year later that they "have this winter (1889-90) read the First Reader through."[27]

Eva's respect for and devotion to Charles is also illuminated in fleeting glimpses throughout her journal, and the strength of their partnership is evident in the items she chose to record. While Eva did not devote pages of material to Charles in her journals, it is obvious, even through the veil of nineteenth-century decorum and reserve, that she adored her husband and he reciprocated. Under the heading "Talks with Charlie," she preserved some of Charles's conversations with her as he prepared Sunday school lessons. "Mr. Dye often expresses to me the most beautiful ideas," she wrote. Eva was impressed with the depth of Charles's faith and his unswerving sense of morality and justice. In one typical instance he told her that spiritual truth and insight came only through "a certain degree of renouncing self-will" and using one's ability "to see things in their true moral relations."[28] According to Charles, spiritual inspiration was directly linked to one's moral depth, and this belief sustained his support for temperance and provided energy for his lifelong activities in the Congregational Church.

Charles often read the newspaper at the breakfast table, and one morning he offered commentary on Emerson. Eva wrote in her journal, "Charlie said 'Emerson says America is only another name for opportunity.' Trafton looked up with an interested gleam in his eye and said, 'Did he, papa? Did he say it?'"[29] Eva respected Charles's opinion on a broad range of political and literary topics and his ideas often found their way into her poetry and essays. Trafton was not the only one intrigued by what Charles and Emerson had to say that morning in January 1889. Five months later when Eva's article on the capital of Iowa appeared the subtitle read "America Another Name for Opportunity."

Marriage and parenthood brought many lighthearted moments to Eva and Charles, and their relationship tempered their naturally serious demeanors. Eva's early life had been marred by the loss of her mother and the difficult relationship she had with her stepmother. Affection and laughter seemed missing altogether from her childhood, and seriousness, reserve, and firmness would characterize her personality for the rest of her years. With her children, though, came the opportunity to experience contentment. "Our children are our greatest delight," she once exclaimed, and humorous incidents between Charles and the boys often provided the occasion for a notation in her journal.[30] One day she mentioned,

> Emery went to church with his papa and heard a sermon on the text "Come unto me all ye that are weary and heavy laden and I will give you rest." His mamma asked him when he came home what the preacher talked about: "Mamma," he said "Come unto me and I'll give you a good nap."[31]

The Dyes eventually had two more children, but their third child did not arrive until 1896. A brief reference in Eva's journal suggests the ten-year gap between the two sets of children was unintentional. She wrote, "Emery wanted a little brother. Parents talked of adopting one. 'No,' Emery stated. 'I want one born in the house.'"[32] Emery eventually got his wish. Everett Willoughby Dye joined the household on August 9, 1896, followed by Charlotte Evangeline Dye on November 11, 1897.

In January of 1898 Eva underscored the difference Charles and the children had made in her life. "This is the happiest winter I ever have known," she wrote, "with papa and the big boys … and the dear little babies, Everett and Charlotte."[33] With appreciation and affection she also summed up her relationship with Charles: "To me there has never been anyone in the world so beautiful as my own husband therefore I have always wanted my children to look like him."[34] Charles was in many ways the model for all that Eva hoped their children would achieve, and she found his steadfast character and able intellect a source of strength. She viewed herself in equally important terms. Motherhood reinforced values Eva had originally expressed while at Oberlin: self-reliance and the development of a healthy "moral character," along with dedication to lifelong learning. Raising children of her own deepened and strengthened these commitments and provided new ways for Eva to understand herself and American society.

With motherhood came the opportunity to transfer those values to her children and to shape their character, but it also brought a new opportunity to see herself not just as an individual but as an interdependent family member. In defining a role for herself as a wife and as a parent she seized on the concept that upon mothers rested the fate of future generations. Mothers, she believed, had the authority and the responsibility to educate, instill moral values, uplift society, and ultimately transform the world. She expressed these beliefs best in her journal in 1885. Under the heading "The Mothers of Great Men," Eva listed the mothers of Washington, Lincoln, Napoleon, Goethe, and Byron. She then noted, "What we may hope for the future. That the multiplication of educated and intellectual women will multiply the number of eminent mothers and sons."[35]

Eva's belief that motherhood was both defining and important to the progress of society was not unique in the nineteenth century. Her ideas had a tradition dating from the post-Revolutionary period when women sought to understand their relationship to a new Republic. American women had made significant contributions during the Revolutionary War—in Revolutionary boycotts, petitioning campaigns, the quartering of soldiers, and the maintenance of farms and families during the crisis. And in the wake of evangelical ferment in the 1830s evolved the belief in women's unique ability to maintain piety and virtue from within the private sphere.

Denied the rights of citizenship, women bridged the gap between the domestic and public spheres by asserting their importance as mothers to future male leaders. Women used these ideas to define their civic responsibilities and moral authority, and as the basis for their involvement in voluntary associations during the mid-nineteenth century.[36]

Eva's journey through motherhood increased her attachment to the temperance cause and provided an avenue for her support of woman suffrage. Ten years had passed since the publication of her poem "The Sixty Thousand," her first public endorsement of temperance. During those years the Woman's Christian Temperance Union (WCTU) had grown from a fledgling organization of a few thousand to a national force with chapters in every state. Frances Willard, as national leader, inspired Eva and many other women with her broad-based reform initiatives, including labor legislation, health and hygiene measures, "social purity" campaigns to eradicate prostitution and raise the age of consent, prison reform, and many other city welfare reform measures.[37] At all times the WCTU based its critique of American society in the home and women's attachment to it, and taught women how to be engaged and intelligent citizens. Now a wife, mother, and homemaker, Eva found much to admire in the WCTU; she subscribed to its tract, the *Union Signal*, and published her own poetry in its pages. She also read Willard's autobiography, *Glimpses of Fifty Years* (1889), with avid attention.

The year 1889 proved to be a watershed for Eva. With the children in school and her master's degree in hand, she resumed publishing her essays and poems. Her essays included those on the Amana Colonies and Iowa City, and a prize essay on Longfellow from her college days reprised in the *Dakota Educator*. Woven in with the essays and numerous poems were new pieces that addressed the constraints of women's domestic life and their lack of public power. The writing was overtly political and heavily influenced by the platform of the WCTU and literary works such as Edward Bellamy's *Looking Backward* (1888).

Looking Backward was a futuristic novel set in the year 2000 that explored the benefits of economic collectivization and the harmony of political and social affairs that Bellamy claimed would be its natural result. It was a tale of a new society energized by a transformed social order where "virtuous, industrious citizens, contribut[ed] fully to the economic and political systems while enjoying an elevating intellectual culture."[38] Women were prominently featured in Bellamy's story, and they reaped the rewards of collectivized kitchens, nurseries, and schools. Women were no longer slaves to a domestic life; instead they were equal partners with men in the workforce, in politics, and in designing a social order where intellectual, educational, and cultural pursuits were valued and explored. Most importantly, women had a vital role to play in constructing and maintaining the new society. Women would be the "wardens of the world to come, to whose keeping the keys of the future are confided."[39]

Looking Backward struck a chord with many activist women who saw within its pages a manifesto for social change.[40] Eva, too, found support in it for her belief that women used up the best years of their lives in domestic drudgery when they instead should be serving as intellectual role models for their children. In response to Bellamy's book and similar ideas espoused by Frances Willard, Eva put forth her own idea of a collectivized laundry in an essay entitled "Blue Monday Must Go," published in *The Housekeeper*.[41] In ever-practical prose, she moved quickly from brief admiration of Bellamy's and Willard's futuristic views to a discussion of "the possible improvements of to-day." She argued that if one hundred families hired one man to wash their laundry for fifty cents per week, this public enterprise would be self-sustaining and beneficial to all parties. "The tubs of water, the fire, the steam, the lifting, the rubbing" would disappear and in its place, she claimed, mothers would be "the companions of their sons and daughters, their highest inspiration and guide." She was troubled by the vast numbers of women who were too worn out from "the complexity of [domestic] work," to be good mothers and stated emphatically that "if the Americans would be a strong and healthy race, the mothers of Americans must not be drudges shut away from free exercise of happy thoughts in open air and sunshine." [42] Eva's ideas prefigured those of Charlotte Perkins Gilman, whose *Women and Economics* (1898) argued for dramatic changes in the gendered division of labor and an end to the drudgery of domestic work that diminished women's abilities as wives and mothers.[43]

The concept of a public laundry was not the only focus of "Blue Monday," and it was in the expansion of her ideas on the progress of women that her views dovetailed with those of the temperance and suffrage movements. She argued that women must change the division of labor in the household as able "students of domestic economy" using the "courage and confidence" they had attained over the previous twenty-five years. "Women have begun to realize their own executive power … And it has reassured them."[44] Women, precisely because of their womanly virtues and their ties to the home, would lead the way toward a new society but only if they were freed from the mundane to participate fully in social change and only if they recognized and cultivated their own ability to lead. Eva's writings echoed those of Catharine Beecher. Beecher's *Treatise on Domestic Economy* (1841) and *The American Woman's Home* (1869) were widely read in the nineteenth century and espoused household efficiency and the importance of women's domestic realm to American society. According to historian Kathryn Kish Sklar, Beecher "saw the home as an integral part of a national system, reflecting and promoting mainstream American values." If Eva read Beecher's work is unknown; however, she certainly would have agreed with Beecher's assertion that

> the woman who is rearing a family of children; the woman who labors in the schoolroom; the woman who, in her retired chamber, earns, with her needle, the mite, which contributes to the intellectual and moral elevation of her Country ... [is] accomplishing the greatest work that ever was committed to human responsibility.[45]

It was but a small step for many women from the recognition of womanly virtues as necessary to the well-being of the nation to the assertion that women deserved the right to vote. While more conservative members within the WCTU prevented the addition of suffrage to the national platform in 1876, just six years later the organization endorsed a Department of Franchise designed to assist activists in their state suffrage campaigns.[46] Thus the year Eva married, the link between the temperance and suffrage movements was officially forged, and by the time she began publishing her poetry in the *Union Signal* in 1890, Elizabeth Cady Stanton and Susan B. Anthony were at the helm of the newly united National American Woman Suffrage Association (NAWSA).

As suffragists gathered support among temperance advocates, settlement house workers, labor activists, and other reformers toward the end of the nineteenth century, they revised and reconstructed long-standing arguments about why women deserved the right to vote. For decades suffragists had claimed that women were citizens with the same inalienable rights as men and, as such, justice demanded they be enfranchised. It was a claim based on Enlightenment definitions of the individual and predicated on the belief that women were similar to men in their capacity to reason.[47]

This so-called "justice" argument coexisted with the claim that women were inherently different from men, and that they would use their knowledge and abilities gained in the private sphere to change the public sphere for the better. In the face of increasing immigration, the instability of the economy, the growth of cities, and the rise of widespread political corruption and vice, the belief in individual rights took a secondary role behind the argument that the vote was a practical means to civic housekeeping. During the years from 1890 to 1910 the concept that women would use the vote to transform American society in their domestic image was a powerful organizing tool, and suffragists found much support for this argument, especially among white, middle-class women.[48]

In her poems, Eva espoused both views of women. She believed women were the moral gatekeepers of society and would transform American economics, politics, and culture, yet, at the same time, in the spirit of Enlightenment individualism and rationalism, she searched for and celebrated independent, self-reliant women as historical role models. Two of her poems from 1890 illustrate the dual nature of her claims about women. The first, "Only A Woman," published in the *Union Signal* in May, demonstrated the powerlessness of disenfranchised but worthy women and suggested many areas where women would make a difference if allowed to vote.

> Only a woman, no power hath she
> To grasp the law's deep mystery.
> Only a woman, she cannot feel
> The public pulse of woe or weal.
> Only a woman, devoid of mind,
> Weak, feeble, senseless, halting, blind,
> Mothers and teachers, pride of our schools,
> Rank them with aliens, criminals, fools:
> Send them back to the harem's veil –
> The land's too free when votes prevail.[49]

Arguing that wives, mothers, and teachers deserved to have a voice in how society was run, Eva selected schools, women's participation in the labor force, and the closing of saloons as areas where women's lives were directly affected by outdated laws and male behavior.

> Only a woman, she holds no land,
> She pays no tax, she takes no stand
> For schools and bonds; she cannot wake
> To mighty matters now at stake.
> Hers it is to sweetly trust
> That only man is wise and just;

Her own God-given right to think
Is but a snare on ruin's brink;
Casting ballots is dangerous sport;
The ship of state might fail of port
If wives and mothers had a say
On schools and bonds election day.
Those working women? who should heed
The tiresome call of squalid need?
Let them work or let them wed,
Let them look to men for bread.[50]

Her choices clearly reflected issues of central concern to both temperance and suffrage activists, and with scorn she dismissed anti-suffrage arguments that the enfranchisement of women would bring about the downfall of American social and political order. In closing she also made it clear that she fit squarely within the ranks of the white and middle class. Women like Eva Emery Dye, as they added their indignant voices to the suffrage movement, often aired their own class and race prejudices. In so doing they reiterated a common complaint that many suffragists voiced: if *all* men, especially blacks and immigrants, were legally enfranchised, then why not women?

Only a woman, tired and faint,
Be she beggar or be she saint,
Let her go home and scrub and sew,
And ask her lord what she would know.
Make way for men, good, bad, black, white,
But keep the women out of sight![51]

Eva's "A Woman Led the Deed" went even further to suggest that America itself would not have survived without women's civilizing and moral influence. She wrote this poem "one February afternoon when the babies were asleep," and it was a testament to the power women exercised in American history.[52] Beginning with Columbus and continuing through the colonial settlement of Massachusetts and Virginia, she attributed the successful outcome of each period in history to women's leadership.

Long, long ago Columbus sought
The proud old court of Spain,
And begged a fleet to find a world
Beyond the western main.

With long delays they wearied him,
With doubt and mockery,
Until a queen her jewels pledged
And sent him o'er the sea.

Long, long ago our pilgrim sires
Fled o'er the ocean wave,
To found a home on freedom's shore,
Or find a freeman's grave.
On Plymouth Rock a woman's foot
First touched the hallowed sod.
On Plymouth Rock a woman's voice
First rose in praise to God.[53]

One of the stanzas addressed the issue of slavery and lauded the "gifted pen" of a woman who "rang out the tocsin call." Though unnamed, her reference is clearly to Harriet Beecher Stowe, to whom Eva accredited much of the anti-slavery spirit and the success of the abolition movement. The last stanza was a call to arms against alcohol and a rallying cry for her WCTU comrades:

Long, long ago a demon came
To wreck the peace of home
And up and down fair freedom's land
His bloodstained vassals roam.
But hark! He halts, a woman's voice
Hath bid the demon fly.
For God and Home and Native Land
Shall slay him by and by.[54]

From the settlement of America to the resolution of the slavery question and the much hoped-for victory over demon rum, Eva boasted of women's accomplishments as the civic and moral custodians of society. Indeed, she portrayed them not just as upholders of the social order but as the founding mothers who made American society possible. While one may question some of her historical claims, it is clear from her writing that Eva believed in women's ability to be agents of change and leadership. "A Woman Led the Deed" would become her battle cry for a later effort to commemorate Sacagawea, and much of her later work and speeches attest to the energy and enthusiasm with which she wrote women into the historical and literary record of western society.

The 1880s marked a time of transition and growing maturity for Eva Emery Dye. Using the literary skills she had developed while at Oberlin College, she broadened her areas of interest to include historical topics pertinent to the Midwest. She also reflected on her personal values and her experiences as a wife and mother and used her understanding of women's sphere to critique the social and political place of women in American society. Firmly believing that womanly virtues would transform the public sphere, Eva was part of an older generation of activists who often defined themselves as inherently different from men. Perhaps most significant to her future success, Eva's relationship with Charles and their children brought stability and affection to a serious and dedicated woman who had previously known much hard work but not much joy. The next few years would unfold as some of the busiest, most productive, and most satisfying of her life.

The Literary Missionary
1890-1900

Eva Emery Dye arrived in Oregon City on July 13, 1890,[1] accompanied by her husband, her two young sons, and a vision of pioneer America. Journeying through Sacramento, Eva first encountered the history of the West in the form of statuary in the capitol rotunda.

> It was night when we arrived and the first glimpse I had of this Pacific coast was the magnificent statue of Queen Isabella of Spain, with Columbus kneeling at her feet … the soft glow of electric lights lent an enchantment to the benignant face and the spotless marble.[2]

Symbolic of Euro-American conquest, the figures represented a vision of America's history that was not simply representative of individual accomplishment and initiative but was illustrative of American preeminence and progress. To Eva's mind, the nation's brief history was epic in scope, to be celebrated and communicated with enthusiasm and energy.

The marble figures in Sacramento impressed her for other important reasons, and encapsulated in this one moment are significant themes that would reappear in all of her future writings and speeches. From her poetry and essays written while at Oberlin to her first published efforts in the 1880s, it is clear that she believed women played a significant role in the shaping of American history, just as she saw Isabella as the focal point in the statuary. Subsequently, her major historical works *McLoughlin and Old Oregon* (1900) and *The Conquest: The True Story of Lewis and Clark* (1902) featured women prominently. She deliberately and energetically included women in her writing, conscious that their presence in male tales of adventure made her work singular.

Significantly, Eva was quick to note that this was a "group of statuary from the hand of an American sculptor."[3] She thought it was vital that Americans should immediately begin crafting their visions of America's past in history, fiction, and art. It was her perception that America had not yet produced the poet or author or artist who could do justice to its stories, and on the eve of a new century she had a sense that time was running out. Much of her drive and enthusiasm can be attributed to her desire to be an American Homer and to capture America's stories before they were forgotten. In a brief "Introduction to History," written prior to her arrival in Oregon, she noted, "Some future historian will distill from the crude records of our west the pure essence of courage and romance, of poetry and endeavor."[4] The task fell naturally not to a professional historian but to Eva herself, and she ingeniously and successfully distilled sweeping tales of the West into her curious blend of historic chronicle, fiction, biography, and romance.

The decade of the 1890s also held other opportunities, in addition to her writing, for Eva to express her views on public education and cultural enrichment. Together with her husband, Eva founded the Willamette Valley Chautauqua Association in 1894. For the next thirty-four years Chautauqua was the most popular cultural entertainment in Oregon and a forum for the Dyes' educational and intellectual pursuits. It was also an important venue for the discussion of women's equal rights. Promoting educational betterment and the arts, Chautauqua activities tied Eva's belief in an educated citizenry to her desire to "civilize" the Pacific Northwest.

The 1880s had witnessed a tremendous growth in Oregon's population and economy, and many migrants had come from the Midwest to take advantage of opportunities in the international grain trade, lumber, milling, and the salmon industry.[5] Oregon also boasted a mild climate and lush valleys that were particularly well suited to farming. By 1890 Oregon's population had grown to 313,767, an increase of nearly 80 percent over the decade.[6]

According to family history, the Dyes arrived in Oregon City virtually penniless and "were forced to borrow the silver dollars each of their sons had received as gifts from their grandfather" in order to stretch their finances.[7] The year spent in Madison had not been a profitable one, and Charles was hoping he would be more successful in rapidly growing Oregon. He opened his law practice at Sixth and Main streets in Oregon City, and Eva secured a teaching position at Barclay School. She noted later,

> I secured a position as teacher, and I don't mind telling you that the last dollar of our carefully hoarded savings was gone

before I received my first check as teacher. Never before or since in our experience was a check so welcome as was that one.[8]

Oregon City was, in 1890, a small town on the falls of the Willamette River and a center for the milling of paper, grains, and lumber. Once projected to be the commercial heart of Oregon, by the 1850s it had lost its place to its northern neighbor Portland, which possessed the deep-water ports that ships required.[9] Until 1852 Oregon City had been the first territorial capital, and it was the first town in the region to organize a library, a temperance society, and a debating society.[10] These three early cultural milestones undoubtedly made it particularly appealing to the Dyes. Geographically the city was arranged in unique terraces, a town of three levels, rising from the east shore of the Willamette River. One history of the city describes the effect.

> Occupying the first of these benches, between the river and the cliff, is the business section of the city. A hundred feet above, on the second terrace, is the residential district. Two hundred feet above this is the third bench, stretching eastward toward the green foothills of the Cascade Range and the rigidly symmetrical slopes of Mount Hood. Streets so steep that they seem to stand on end connect these three levels.[11]

In fast-developing Oregon City, Charles's skills in real estate and contract law were in much demand, and the Dyes' finances soon recovered. Eva wrote, "Mr. Dye had got a foothold in the practice of law before the first year was up, so I resigned my position as teacher and went back to my first love—writing."[12] Charles in fact did remarkably well as an attorney and soon became Deputy District Attorney and City Attorney. Eva remarked to a friend in 1906 that her husband "has had a $3,000 a year practice now for some years and sometimes has doubled that."[13] His success enabled her future achievements in two important ways. It meant that Eva never had to seek employment outside of her own writing again, and his income provided for crucial domestic help so that she could spend much of her day writing.

Oregon City was the final destination for many travelers who had come overland on the wagon trains of the 1840s and 1850s, and it abounded with stories of adversity, accomplishment, and endurance. The town's elders, many of whom were first-generation pioneers, were eager to tell their version of the settlement of the Pacific Northwest. Just a month before the Dyes moved to the area, pioneers had "rejoice[d] over achievements earned in the face of death itself," when they celebrated the Eighteenth Annual Reunion of the Oregon Pioneer Association.[14] Veneration for the founders of the region was a common sentiment, and from her home atop the bluffs in Oregon City Eva soon learned that one of the central characters in the history of the Pacific Northwest was Dr. John McLoughlin.

The day Eva arrived in Oregon City, she later claimed, was the day she realized there was "beautiful historical material lying around like nuggets."[15] John McLoughlin and the men of the Hudson's Bay Company reminded her of Greek heroes, and she felt that their struggle to survive and prosper on the frontier was an epic in the making. She exuberantly noted, "Indians and missionaries, fur-traders and frontiersmen loomed like Agamemnon and his men, their deeds more kaleidoscopic than the wanderings of Ulysses. Oh, could I but be their Homer!"[16] With enthusiasm she began her research on McLoughlin's life.

Eva's childhood enjoyment of Sir Walter Scott, and her delight in the works of Washington Irving and Henry Wadsworth Longfellow while she was at Oberlin College, provided the literary stage on which the actors in *McLoughlin and Old Oregon* played. Scott and Irving were especially important in shaping the content and style of Eva's work. Scott was well known for his "Waverley" novels, both in Britain and America, and Irving's historical fiction was the first of its kind in America. Eva enthusiastically followed in their footsteps.

Eva modeled her idealized heroes and heroines on "the pulse of sympathy, the throb of a great heart, the charm of culture,"[17] she found exemplified in works such as Longfellow's *Evangeline* (1847). This poem is a fictionalized account of villagers' forced abandonment of Nova Scotia during the French and Indian War. Scattered "far asunder, on separate coasts," the French-Canadians settled mostly in the colonial South and became the foundation of the Cajun population.[18] Eva was attracted to the romance of the peasant girl Evangeline and her lover Gabriel, and the tragic tale that ensued when they were separated on the coast near Fort Gaspereau in 1755. Evangeline spent many years in search of her lover only to find him again on his deathbed.

Longfellow's heroine is patient, kind, self-sacrificing, and willing to spend years wandering the prairies and mountains in a futile attempt to find her betrothed. As one literary critic has noted, Longfellow's hero and heroine were "the reflected images of Adam and Eve sent out to wander the North American continent."[19] Along with the Christian symbolism,

Eva saw much in the character Evangeline that reminded her of *The Odyssey*. She likened Evangeline to loyal Penelope, the long-suffering wife of Odysseus, who waited twenty years for his return. "There are lives in 'Evangeline,'" Eva wrote, "that will be classic as any in Homer."[20]

Other important figures in *McLoughlin* originated with readings she had enjoyed while at Oberlin College. Her desire to write about Indians may have been sparked by Longfellow's *Hiawatha* (1855) and Irving's *Astoria* (1836). Eva believed Longfellow had captured the quintessential noble savage in Hiawatha's transformation from young brave to demigod. The impression *Hiawatha* left on Eva was profound. *Hiawatha*, she wrote, "has the Indian repetition, Indian thought, Indian sentiment and Indian expression;–it will live as a memorial of Indian legend and Indian life."[21] In turn Irving's anthropological descriptions of the "hospitable" and "worthy" Chinooks and Clatsops, the predatory nature of the "terrible" Blackfeet, and his portrayal of the Nez Perces as "a hardy, laborious and somewhat knavish race," instilled a lasting imprint on Eva's imagination. Interactions among native peoples and between whites and Indians were a central focus of *McLoughlin* and her later work, *The Conquest*.[22]

Astoria furnished other ideas and inspiration in method and subject matter. Irving recounted the exploits of John Jacob Astor and his attempts to bring Americans into the fur trade in the Pacific Northwest between 1810 and 1812. His work provided much background material for the era just prior to McLoughlin's tenure at Fort Vancouver, and Irving's thorough use of available diaries and letters gave validity to his account.[23] His attention to historical details and fascination with the Pacific Northwest provided inspiration for Eva in her first attempt to write book-length historical fiction.

Finally, Sir Walter Scott's many historical novels supplied the background necessary for her to write confidently of the "feudal" structure of the Hudson's Bay Company and the Scots influence of its chief factors and traders. Fort Vancouver was to her "a rude stronghold of central Europe in the middle ages," where McLoughlin and his assistant, James Douglas "dispensed hospitality after the fashion of Saxon thanes or lairds of a Highland castle."[24] Her description of McLoughlin's early years is another good example of her appreciation for things Scottish. Of John and his brother David she wrote,

> They played in those hills, rugged as Scotia's rock-ribbed
> Highlands. They caught a military presence from the soldier

grandsire who had brought a Highland regiment with him to America to colonize these seignioral [sic] manors. Here Scottish books were read and Scottish tales retold. Here the bagpipe droned and the kilt hung in the old colonial closet.[25]

Scott, Longfellow, and Irving provided Eva with necessary examples of style, method, and theme as she wove her tale of the early Pacific Northwest. As popular authors of the British Romantic period and its cousin the American Renaissance, they motivated Eva in her effort to develop American national literature to rival that of Britain and Europe. Long before she encountered Oregon and its history, Eva had found within the leaves of their books the inspiration to write stories she believed would be of national significance.

McLoughlin and Old Oregon (1900) explores old Oregon much more than it does the life of John McLoughlin. The story she recounted extended far beyond the world of the Hudson's Bay Company to include the history of the first missionaries and the first Overland Trail migrations to Oregon. In its wide-ranging focus, the final product lacks the cohesiveness of biography and assumes a great deal of prior knowledge on the part of the reader. Its strengths lie in the extensive use of primary sources to enhance the narrative and in Eva's ability to derive from those sources personalities and warmth that brought her characters to life.

McLoughlin opens in 1832 with the story of Nathaniel Wyeth, an American who attempted and failed to set up a fur-trading fort on the Snake River to rival the dominance of the Hudson's Bay Company. On a second journey to the region in 1834, Wyeth brought the Reverend Jason Lee, who settled among French Canadians and their Indian wives in the Willamette Valley. Eva insisted that the significance of Wyeth's story was that he brought Lee, thus providing the first missionary presence in Oregon. The following chapters celebrate "The Coming of the Whitmans" and "The Wedding of Jason Lee." McLoughlin appears in the background as a benevolent and watchful parent, helpful to the missionaries and concerned about their safety, but the focus of the narrative is clearly on the Christian– and American–entry into the region.

The structure of *McLoughlin* is chronological, covering the years 1812 to 1848, with half of the forty-three chapters focusing on the years 1839 through 1841. It is not until well into the text, when McLoughlin returns from an

1839 meeting of the London Council, that the reader learns of his early life and education, his employment with the North West and Hudson's Bay Companies, and his marriage to Margaret McKay.

Born in 1784, McLoughlin was a French Canadian of Scottish and Irish descent who was trained as a physician but ultimately gave up medicine for the fur trade. Employed first as a trader for the North West Company's depot at Fort William, McLoughlin quickly moved up the ranks to become the fort's chief trader.[26] He emerged as an important leader in reconciling North West Company men to their employment with the Hudson's Bay Company when the two merged in 1821. His organizational and diplomatic skills did not go unnoticed, and Sir George Simpson eventually appointed McLoughlin chief factor of the Columbia Department in 1824. The territory McLoughlin commanded was vast, extending "from the present northern boundaries of California and Nevada to the Alaskan border, and from the Rocky Mountains westward to the Pacific."[27] Within this landscape he managed a meandering network of trading posts, including forts Vancouver, Colville, Langley, McLoughlin, Boise, and Hall.

McLoughlin was an imposing man, well over six feet tall, with flowing white hair and a disposition that commanded respect. The Native Americans called him the "White Headed Eagle," and he was esteemed for being a just and fair leader with the Indians and white traders. Under his leadership the residents of Fort Vancouver grew enough food to become self-sufficient, built saw and flour mills, and engaged in extensive trade networks with a variety of Native American tribes in the area.

In the history of Oregon, McLoughlin is known for his many charitable acts toward American citizens. He provisioned, outfitted, and extended the hospitality of Fort Vancouver to many weary visitors, including an array of trappers and traders, and in particular the missionaries Jason Lee, the Whitmans, and the Spaldings. His assistance to Americans through the years eventually brought about his separation from the Hudson's Bay Company in 1846 because Sir George Simpson viewed this aid as a threat to Company profits and sovereignty. Forced into retirement, McLoughlin lived out the remainder of his life in Oregon City, the town he had platted and planned in 1842.[28]

Although *McLoughlin* is a tale of men, from trappers to traders, and Native Americans to missionaries, Eva highlights the roles of women throughout the story. While the chapter that introduces McLoughlin is entitled "McLoughlin's Early History," the central characters are his wife

Margaret and daughter Eloise. In Margaret's biography and that of other pioneer wives and mothers, Eva found heroines that helped her to understand the history of the Pacific Northwest.

Margaret was once the wife of Alexander McKay, the explorer who accompanied Alexander Mackenzie on his crossing of the continent between 1789 and 1793. McKay eventually met John Jacob Astor and became a partner and explorer for Astor's South West Company expedition to the Columbia. Margaret McKay was his widow, part Indian, French, and Scottish; she married McLoughlin shortly after news of McKay's death came in 1811. Margaret's heritage and the loss of her first husband provided the recipe for romance that Eva exploited. Noting that "no white woman could go into the Indian country, but Margaret could go because she had Indian blood," Eva saw in Margaret the self-effacing, efficient, and patient wife who combined "the manners and mind of the whites with the daring and pride of the Indian."[29] Margaret McKay represented all that was good in white women and "noble savages," and Eva could not have found a more perfect wife for McLoughlin. In the marriage of John and Margaret McLoughlin she encountered all the elements of a good story: romance, cross-cultural interaction, and the excitement of frontier life.

Like the chapter on McLoughlin's early life, which puts Margaret in the foreground, "The Coming of the Whitmans" opens not with Marcus Whitman and Henry Spalding but with their wives Narcissa and Eliza.

> When Wyeth was returning defeated to the States he met a vision in the mountains, a beautiful woman with golden hair and snowy brow, riding like Joan of old to conquest,–Narcissa Whitman. With her rode Eliza Spalding, a slender, dark-eyed devotee, who back in the States had knelt in a lonely wayside inn to consecrate her heart to Oregon. Two brides were on that wonderful journey, farther than flew the imperial eagles of Rome, to their life-work on the Columbia.[30]

Eva's portrayals of Narcissa and Eliza are not the sophisticated character analyses that a twenty-first-century reader would find balanced and complex. Instead the women are archetypes, cast as long-suffering, kind, patient, and dedicated to spreading Christianity among the native peoples.[31] Eva did not address Narcissa's ambivalence about her missionary role, nor did she mention the sheer drudgery and weariness of life at the missions even though loneliness, fatigue, and unhappiness were frequent concerns in Narcissa's letters to her family.[32] Even Narcissa's appearance changed for *McLoughlin*; Eva transformed her from a woman with auburn hair into a fairy-tale beauty with "golden hair and snowy brow." Thus Eva created paragons of virtue sent out into the wilderness as helpmates to their heroic husbands. The picture that emerges is one of seamless collaboration and cooperation between white women and men, and the only conflicts in the pages of *McLoughlin* are the Anglo-American conquest over native peoples, and the struggle of white people to survive in a hostile environment.

Despite the fact that Eva's historical figures are uncomplicated, they are still interesting, and their liveliness is one of the most successful aspects of *McLoughlin*. Unlike the characters in Longfellow's *Evangeline*, who "exist at several removes from life itself,"[33] Eva's actors tell stories, write letters, converse, and overcome despair, destruction, and illness. Although many of the conflicts in their lives were unexamined, her historical actors were very much a part of the history that unfolded around them.

To enliven her characters, Eva strategically incorporated available diaries and letters when recounting the Whitmans' mission life. She quoted at length from Narcissa's letters to her husband in 1842 while he was enroute to Washington to convince the American Board of Missions that he should be allowed to continue his work at Waiilatpu, as well as from letters to her mother describing the influx of immigrants to the mission just prior to the Whitman Massacre in 1847. A May 1840 conversation between Marcus and an Indian regarding the treatment of their wives is recounted nearly verbatim.[34] In all cases original letters from Narcissa to her family members attest to Eva's accuracy.[35] Thus excerpts from primary sources lent veracity to Eva's derivative story and illuminated the Whitmans' personalities.

Eva's commitment to writing a story that utilized as much factual material as possible resulted in extensive efforts to document her work. Stories and reminiscences from aging pioneers formed the majority of her authentication, and elders in Oregon were pleased to regale her with tales of the past. In addition, she wrote letters requesting historical reminiscences to brothers, sisters, children, and grandchildren of major characters in the book. For example, the tale of Whitman's exhausting journey to Washington in 1842 was enriched by a letter from Marcus Whitman's sister Harriet.[36] Similarly, she noted instances where "a gray-haired grandsire" had enhanced her understanding of McLoughlin or his assistant, James Douglas.[37] Eva also had available the transactions of the Oregon Pioneer Association, which reprinted quantities of diaries and letters of early settlers, including letters from Narcissa Whitman. Finally, in 1890 she would have had a number of early histories of the region at her command, including volumes of the works of Hubert Howe Bancroft, Elwood Evans' *History of the Pacific Northwest: Oregon and Washington* (1869) and W. H. Gray's *History of Oregon* (1870). The last of these was perhaps the least appealing to Eva. Gray was known for his virulent dislike of the Hudson's Bay Company.[38]

Eva's use of extensive historical materials does not overshadow the fact that she intended to write fiction, and this is most apparent in her portrayal of Native Americans. Although she recognized and highlighted the differences among, for example, the Chinook, Cayuse, and Flathead Indians who form a large part of her tale, she still essentially divided all native peoples into two groups: the good or noble Indians, and the bad and vengeful ones. Those who assimilated to mission life or who were educated in eastern schools were worthy, and those who undertook to rid their land of white encroachers were evil.[39] The influence of Homeric conventions is recognizable in her use of formulaic adjectives, and these conventions flatten rather than deepen her character sketches. Thus the repetition of the "faithful" Flatheads, the "knightly" Cayuses, the "stately" Walla Wallas, and the "robber" Klickitats calls attention to diversity among Native Americans in the Pacific Northwest but does not move them beyond their typecast roles. Her descriptions of native peoples are also reminiscent of those found in Irving's *Astoria*. Eva for the most part considered the Indians childlike, and many of her native characters have the unfortunate habit of saying "ugh-ugh."[40]

In her treatment of the cultural conflict between the missionaries and native peoples Eva also failed to cast a critical eye on the missionaries' efforts to Christianize the Indians. According to her, the missionaries were not at all responsible for the Whitman Massacre, and the ensuing Cayuse War was justified retribution by five hundred settlers in the Willamette Valley. Whitman emerges as a beloved martyr and his wife is the Joan of Arc of the West.[41]

At the time, Eva's romanticized version of the history of McLoughlin and especially of the Whitmans did not seem out of place or contrary to peoples' understanding of the West. In the 1890s a common myth prevailed that Whitman had saved Oregon for the United States. Promoters of the myth argued that Whitman had gone to Washington, D.C. in 1842-43 to promote American acquisition of Oregon territory and westward migration rather than to save his mission. This heroic portrayal of the missionary encouraged other heroic tales. In the 1880s and 1890s several biographies of Whitman were published, all of which promoted the myth. The most popular of these were the Rev. J. G. Craighead's *The Story of Marcus Whitman* (1895) and the Rev. O. W. Nixon's *How Marcus Whitman Saved Oregon* (1895). It was not until 1900 that widespread doubt about the Whitman myth began to circulate among historians, and even this reassessment did not reach the general public for many years. Thus, during the time that Eva was writing about Whitman she was surrounded by similar accounts of his importance. It would have been surprising indeed for her take a critical view of events that other biographers and the general public celebrated as heroic.[42]

McLoughlin ends with "The Death of Dr. McLoughlin" in 1857, so his last years as Chief Factor and his retirement to Oregon City in 1846 structure the end of the story; however, the climax really occurs several chapters earlier with the Whitman Massacre and the Cayuse War. Significantly, the final scene of the massacre points out again that it was woman's plight that touched Eva:

> Narcissa, the snowy Joan, led all the host of women to the conquest of the West, an innumerable train that is following yet to this day. The snowy Joan led her hosts; and, at last, like Joan of old, she ascended to God with the crown of a martyr.[43]

As she did throughout the story, Eva highlighted the role that white women played, and if her drama were staged, as indeed the opera *Narcissa* was in 1926,[44] one could imagine the hushed silence of the audience as the curtain fell on Narcissa Whitman. Despite her praise of McLoughlin and Whitman, "the Father and the Martyr of the Pacific Northwest,"[45] the reader is left with the definite impression that it was women who made the settlement of the West possible. For Eva, women were inextricably linked to America's past and vital participants in epic conquest.

In her literary treatment of women, Eva continued and expanded on ideas that can be found in her earlier poetry and essays and in her support of temperance and suffrage. She believed in the primacy of mothers as arbiters of morality and justice and sought examples of worthy mothers in history and fiction. She searched for heroines that embodied civic virtue, unswerving devotion, determination, strength, and commitment. Margaret McLoughlin, Narcissa Whitman, and Eliza Spalding represented women she believed had triumphed over adversity and who had partnered with their husbands to conquer the West. In a speech to the Oregon Pioneer Association in 1895 Eva clearly laid out for the audience a central theme of *McLoughlin and Old Oregon*.

Joan of Arc saved France and crowned her king. Narcissa Whitman and Mrs. Spalding, the first white women that crossed the Rocky mountains, proved that women could endure the journey ... when man sank with fatigue and despair, a giant of courage rose in the heart of the faithful wife. She drove the team, she bathed the fevered brow; like a skilful general she covered the flying retreat before pursuing famine [sic]. It is the universal testimony that for quiet endurance the pioneer mothers surpassed the men.[46]

Despite its flaws, Eva's work placed pioneer women at the center of a mythmaking epic, and it is worth noting that her fictionalized account of Narcissa Whitman was the first of its kind. Romantic biographies of the Whitmans did not appear until the 1930s (coinciding with the Whitman Mission centennial), and other fictionalized accounts of Narcissa Whitman's life came even later in the forties and fifties. Despite his excellent overview of the literature on the Whitmans, historian Clifford Drury never included *McLoughlin and Old Oregon* in his discussion of twentieth-century romanticized history nor did he give Dye credit for inspiring the opera *Narcissa*, which he mentioned in detail.[47]

Eva finished her manuscript in 1894, originally calling it "King of the Columbia"[48] and began searching for a publisher. She received encouragement from Harper's, which was willing to publish the work as a serial in their magazine. This news was disheartening to Eva, who refused to divide her book. She wrote, "I worried and fumed over that for weeks. I just couldn't cut it up. It seemed to me like my whole life was wrapped in those pages."[49] There is no evidence to suggest that she ever tried to find another publisher and, when the Panic of 1893 grew into a major economic depression, financial backing for such ventures ceased. She put her book away in a drawer and soon had two young children to occupy her time. A friend's chance visit in January 1900 revived efforts to publish the manuscript. He took the work back with him to Chicago, presented it to A. C. McClurg and Company, and by April of that year, *McLoughlin* made its debut.[50]

Reviews of *McLoughlin and Old Oregon* were mixed, largely because of the confusion over whether it was history or fiction. The most scathing attack came from Frances Fuller Victor, author of *River of the West* (1870) and four complete volumes of Bancroft's works.[51] A meticulous researcher, prolific writer, and skilled historian, Victor seemed personally affronted and angry with Eva's "mingling of fiction with historical truth in a work which is likely to be mistaken for a wholly serious one."[52] Victor complained that Eva's characterizations of John McLoughlin were undignified and her descriptions of the mountain passes in Oregon and Washington inaccurate, and that information provided on Sir George Simpson's 1841 journey from Fort Vancouver was misleading. Even "in unimportant matters," Victor wrote, "such as representing Eloise McLoughlin as an equestrienne, we must say 'wrong again.'"[53] Fortunately for Eva it was Victor who was wrong in this instance. If the letters of Narcissa Whitman are accurate, the women at Fort Vancouver did ride horseback "as often as once a week for exercise, and we generally ride all afternoon."[54]

Eva once mentioned that Victor had been encouraging of her manuscript, to the point of offering to help her find a publisher,[55] but perhaps Victor had not had an opportunity to read the work before she committed herself. Clearly she did not view the final product as suitable history. We do not know if Eva was stunned by this unfavorable review of her work in the respected *American Historical Review*. Perhaps she accepted Whitman biographer William Mowry's point of view that Victor "quotes little peccadilloes where she draws a different inference from other people, and magnifies them as serious errors in your book."[56]

Other comments were more favorable. An anonymous reviewer in the *Oregon Historical Quarterly* noted, "This book is by far the best that the general reader can select for an introduction to the life of early Oregon," citing "Mrs. Dye's minute study, sympathetic assimilation, and unique strength in constructive imagination" as positive qualities.[57] Oregon historian John Horner wrote with enthusiasm, "Every step represents a delightful panorama."[58] The general public agreed with Horner and bought *McLoughlin* in sufficient quantities to necessitate a third edition by February 1901. A. C. McClurg and Company was pleased with the sales of Eva's book and encouraged her to continue writing on topics of western history. In selling their copyright and plates back to Eva nearly twenty years later, her publisher noted they had sold ten thousand copies of *McLoughlin and Old Oregon*.[59]

Historian Patricia Nelson Limerick has written, "The history of the West is a study of a place undergoing conquest and never fully escaping its consequences."[60] It is apparent that *McLoughlin and Old Oregon* failed to address the consequences or the conflicts embedded in the history of conquest and instead chose to focus on what one reviewer called "an exceedingly interesting series of pictures almost as vivid as real life."[61] To her credit, however, Eva grasped an idea that has driven much recent scholarship on the West: that the interactions between men and women, Native Americans and whites, and Protestants and Catholics made the settling of the West provocative and significant. The research and writing of *McLoughlin and Old Oregon* whetted her appetite for further exploration of America's founding myths, and she built on her heroic themes to create what she hoped would be her finest epic adventure, *The Conquest: The True Story of Lewis and Clark.*

While the manuscript of *McLoughlin* languished in a drawer between 1894 and 1900, Eva did not let discouragement win out over her pursuit of a useful and meaningful life of the mind. The Dyes went to Oregon to escape hard times and harsh winters in South Dakota, but one thing they missed from their experiences in the Midwest was a lively cultural and intellectual life. Eva wrote later, "Everything was so dreary, it seemed as though we could not live in Oregon City."[62] One of the cultural events they had enjoyed while in Nebraska was Chautauqua. With their extensive educational background and commitment to public service, the Dyes were well prepared to launch a similar enterprise in Oregon City.

Chautauqua was an annual extravaganza in many cities throughout the East and the Midwest, an assembly of noted speakers and large crowds who first gathered to discuss religious issues and to educate Sunday school teachers. Established in 1874 in upstate New York, the event took its name from Lake Chautauqua where the first assembly was held. Soon there were Chautauqua summer gatherings in Ohio, Iowa, and Michigan. Although it was organized with the intent of disseminating Christian morality and inspiration, the Chautauqua soon expanded to include lectures and study hours on American and world history, literature, politics, archaeology, economics, and even ornithology. Baseball games, musical performances, and theater were also incorporated into the programs, making the Chautauqua a community enrichment experience unparalleled in American history.[63]

Chautauqua Literary and Scientific Circles were an offshoot of the assemblies and provided people with the opportunity to form literary and religious study groups in their own homes. In the fall of 1893 one of Eva's friends approached her about giving private lessons on literary topics. In the midst of finishing *McLoughlin*, Eva declined but told her "if enough of the young people cared for a Chautauqua circle we would start one at my house." The response was overwhelming. A dozen participants grew to sixty until the Dyes believed they had enough interest to explore the idea of holding a summer assembly.[64]

In keeping with the Chautauqua's religious roots, the first people consulted about the idea of an assembly were the ministers of all the local churches, followed by Oregon City's business people. Eva approached Harvey Cross, attorney and former state senator, with her plan to create an assembly in Gladstone Park. Cross, the owner of the land, agreed to a fifty-year lease of the park grounds at no cost, a vital philanthropic gift that was one reason for the Chautauqua's subsequent success. The Willamette Valley Chautauqua Association (WVCA) was organized in June 1894 and held its first assembly in late July.[65]

Eva's participation in the Chautauqua extended far beyond the ideas she provided, and if the first year's assembly is any indication, her persistence kept the event from foundering on more than one occasion. She journeyed to California in May 1894 to secure three speakers from the Rev. J. S. Smith of the Pacific Coast Chautauqua. Later in the summer the Pullman railway strike paralyzed national travel, and none of the speakers could attend. Undaunted by this unfortunate turn of events, Eva traveled to Portland with Rev. Gilman Parker. There they met with ministers from Portland's churches, four of whom agreed to lecture on topics including "Abraham Lincoln and the Civil War" and "Wendell Phillips." Eva also engaged Oregon suffragist and writer Abigail Scott Duniway to speak on the closing night. Dr. George Wallace's speech on Phillips was memorable. The rain began pelting the large and attentive crowd, but he continued to speak through the downpour when the audience shouted for him to continue.[66] When the assembly closed on July 26 the profit stood at fifty-nine dollars. "It became evident," Eva noted, "that the Willamette Valley Chautauqua had come to stay."[67]

The first year's assembly was noteworthy for the Dyes in another way. Having rented a house on J. Q. Adams Street for their first four years in Oregon City, they were in the process of building a new home on Jefferson Street during April, May, and June. They moved in just before the Chautauqua started. Eva later commented, "I remember yet how tired I was when it was all over."[68]

The WVCA soon expanded its base of speakers to include prominent individuals, especially William Jennings Bryan, newspaper editor Henry

Watterson, and humorist Bob Burdette. Bryan spoke at the assemblies in 1896 and 1897 attracting a huge crowd of over six thousand eager listeners at his first appearance.[69] Some of the nationally known speakers were suffragists, and the link between the WVCA and the struggle for suffrage began early. A Women's Congress was held during the 1896 Chautauqua, and Anna Howard Shaw Day was the "most successful one of the assembly." She spoke again at the assembly in 1898, and local suffragists, including Eva and Abigail Scott Duniway, were familiar orators and organizers on behalf of the vote for women.[70]

The Willamette Valley Chautauqua became the most successful and largest assembly on the West Coast,[71] and this achievement has been attributed to the persistence, dedication, and vision of its founding members, most of whom were Oregon City attorneys, bankers, and local educators. The Dyes participated actively during the WVCA's thirty-year existence, with Charles frequently serving as vice president and president and Eva as secretary. Her position involved hiring the speakers, editing the daily Chautauqua newspaper that began in 1894, and composing editorials and press releases for Oregon's newspapers.

In later years, as the Chautauqua's focus drifted more toward entertainment than education, Eva combated this trend with her popular "Symposium," an hour-long lecture and study session held each day during Chautauqua. Although it seems to have begun as a generic lecture series with speakers obtained through Eva's extensive knowledge of local authors and educators, it quickly evolved into a forum on topics of interest to women. She wrote to a friend once that the Symposium presented "from 2 to 4 speakers, mostly women," and had become "practically a Woman's Club compressed into ten or 11 days, always crowded."[72]

The Dyes were indefatigable in their support of Chautauqua, and inspiration came from their delight in literature, history, and politics and an unending desire to share that enthusiasm with fellow Oregonians. More specifically, Eva's dedication to Chautauqua can be traced to her early love for Greek culture and her determination to seek out and celebrate the heroic. In describing what was unique about the Willamette Valley Chautauqua Eva once explained,

> the baseball and other grand stand games, races, and exhibits of the Boys and Girls Clubs. It follows more the pattern of ancient Athens where an audience of 20,000 would sit for days in an open air theatre witnessing the presentation of from

twenty to thirty dramas, the greatest project in adult education the world has ever known.[73]

It was not just the aura of ancient Greece that inspired Eva, however. She also believed that the assemblies helped to identify leaders in the community who expressed and cultivated heroic ideals, and she used language to describe them that was befitting Greek gods. Willis Hawley, president of the Chautauqua for ten years, also president of Willamette University and later a congressman, was a well-known figure in Oregon City. Eva once wrote that he could often be seen "bounding like a champion athlete, a yard and a half at a step, up the State House steps, into the library and out again, away to the college and the classroom, or into the athletic field, ever the leader."[74] As president of the Chautauqua, Hawley presided over the events, and Eva noted enthusiastically, "not only his six feet of manhood impresses with a sense of mastery, but his wonderful voice carries command." His favorite subjects to deliver as Chautauqua lectures were constitutional, political, and economic history. According to Eva he was known all over the Northwest for his scholarly addresses "and for his clean record, one that all men honor." Eva's portrayal of Hawley as "the greatest man Oregon has yet produced" was in keeping with her notion that Chautauqua created and sustained public virtue.[75] She believed it fostered a selfless commitment to community service as well as the integrity and honor that were necessary qualities for living and historical heroes.

If the initial inspiration to bring the Chautauqua to Oregon arose from Eva's literary background and reverence for all things Greek, then the energy to sustain years of interest and momentum certainly came from the Dyes' commitment to public education. Like Bishop John Vincent and Lewis Miller, the two founders of the New York Chautauqua, Charles and Eva shared a belief "in education as an inalienable right."[76] Eva in particular saw the Chautauqua as a great opportunity, welcoming all to its ten-day summer programs to explore new religious, political, and literary ideas as well as to experiment with the arts and "physical culture." In Eva's estimation, the assembly had something to offer everyone.

> College men and women, long cut off from old privileges, come here to renew their youth; aspiring men and women who never had any advantages come here to get inspiration. Worn-out farmers' wives, grown old with toil, count as the season comes,

on the lectures of Chautauqua. They bring their notebooks and study and study hard.[77]

Eva saw a direct link between the Chautauqua and higher education, believing that the assemblies inspired people to attend college. Viewing her own collegiate education as an invaluable asset, she was eager to help others to educate themselves. Of the Chautauqua she once noted, "It is an educational force especially among the young that few realize. Where none went away to college before, now we have scores, the result of its influences."[78]

Historian Donald Epstein would have agreed with Eva's assessment. According to Epstein Chautauqua assemblies did two important things. They "led directly to the founding of University Extension services and summer schools," and they encouraged an open-minded discourse on wide-ranging topics from speakers of varying religious beliefs and ethnic backgrounds.[79] The Willamette Valley Chautauqua was no exception to the national rule, and the Dyes' active support for thirty years was instrumental in bringing educational enrichment to thousands of people on the West Coast. Eva once mentioned that "next to my literary work my heart is bound up in this Chautauqua assembly,"[80] and even through the 1920s when the Chautauqua was a financial burden and an exhausting organizational task, the Dyes and their allies worked tirelessly to keep it going. The Dyes viewed the Chautauqua as a mission to bring cultural and educational opportunities to the Pacific Northwest. Always appreciative of the missionary spirit, Eva bridged her literary interests and her commitment to public service with the Chautauqua.

Eva Emery Dye was forty-five years old when *McLoughlin and Old Oregon* was published in 1900 and at the beginning of a writing career that would not end until shortly before her death in 1947. The notoriety that came with *McLoughlin* and her extensive work on behalf of the Chautauqua brought her many more opportunities to explore the history and literature of the Pacific Northwest. She soon became a noted speaker and often-consulted expert on the history of the West. Her success only made her more determined to continue writing and more convinced that there were other epic stories of American conquest waiting to be told.

Envisioning the West: Sacagawea, Lewis and Clark, and *The Conquest*

1898-1902

In 1880 young Eva Emery wrote an essay aptly describing her sentiment that America needed a poet or writer who could eloquently and proficiently recount its epic past.

> In the race of Progress we have leaped beyond the Greeks, we have left the splendor of the Orient, we have crossed the seas and laid the corner-stone of a new world and a new time. ... Mountains lift their peaks, rivers roll in grandeur, and our plains stretch away unmentioned yet in history. A great new life is ours, the best of many lands, a liberty unsung in any tongue, an age unfettered by the chain of tyrant kings. No song immortal has bodied forth our western world, no poet has stood on high and grasped the grandeur of our empire.[1]

Twenty years later Eva Emery Dye still believed that no one had "grasped the grandeur of our empire," so she set out to tell the tale of American conquest herself. She agreed with western expansion as envisioned by Thomas Jefferson; she was excited by the opportunity further to explore and write about early American history; and, most importantly, she sought to promote heroic stories. By the time A. C. McClurg and Company published *McLoughlin and Old Oregon* (1900), Dye had already chosen the topic of her next book. She plunged into the research and writing that resulted in *The Conquest: The True Story of Lewis and Clark* (1902) with a clear sense of purpose.

The Conquest is credited with popularizing the history of the Lewis and Clark Expedition and Sacagawea in particular.[2] Dye created a mythic tradition that transformed the historical Sacagawea into a compelling cultural construct, which is evident from the many fictionalized accounts of Sacagawea's life that followed and the numerous monuments erected to honor her and Lewis and Clark. Dye's vision of America at the turn of the twentieth century was embodied in her portrayal of Sacagawea, and her writing has drawn criticism along with praise from those within and outside of the historical profession. While the impact of Dye's work was obviously substantial, historians have not examined the history of her ideas or placed this book in the overall context of her life.[3] Most importantly, few scholars have thoroughly assessed the volume in light of its shaping of popular perceptions of the Lewis and Clark Expedition.

In August 1896 the Dyes had just concluded a successful and busy second year of Chautauqua in which presidential candidate William Jennings Bryan had spoken to a huge and enthusiastic crowd in Gladstone Park. Charles, then forty, was ending two years of service as deputy district attorney for Clackamas County, and his law practice was flourishing. On the heels of her participation in the 1894 Women's Congress in San Francisco, Eva, at forty-one, began her activism in the Oregon woman suffrage movement as Clackamas County's campaign coordinator. She also continued to gather and write histories of Oregon's pioneers and hoped that her manuscript on John McLoughlin would eventually find a publisher. At mid-life, Eva and Charles were financially stable and becoming influential leaders in Oregon City. At home they also enjoyed the increased independence of Emery, age twelve, and Trafton, age ten.

To these many challenges and successes the Dyes added two more children. Despite the births of Everett and Charlotte in 1896 and 1897, Eva's research and writing became more focused, intensive, and prolific between 1896 and 1902. Far from disrupting her work, contentment with family life fueled her determination to proceed.

Eva found the task of caring for young children demanding and felt isolated at home while the children were small, yet she reveled in their development and enjoyed their company. In January 1898, when Charlotte was two months old, Eva penned an unusually long entry in her journal that attests to the difficulties she faced.

> Feel like myself for the first time since baby came. Can actually answer the doorbell. Sometimes I have felt I c[oul]d not go—was tired and house not in order and babies needed me. …
> Actually made a call. Took baby Charlotte in my arms and hauled little Everett in his wagon over to Mrs. Latourettes. Tipped Everett out in the road. Got him in again but finally

c[oul]d not get over or around a stone and left him and went on
with baby and came back after him. He was crying. It is not
easy to get out with two babies.[4]

Because it was "not easy to get out with two babies," Eva used many
hours at home writing lengthy and affectionate entries about her children's
development. Despite her fatigue she clearly enjoyed the second opportunity
she was given to experience motherhood, which is evident from an early
journal entry about her youngest. "She has such a knowing way of looking
at me as I wait on her," Eva wrote, "just like a little woman. Her little
cheeks, not much larger than silver dollars getting rounder and plumper
every day, and I kiss and kiss and kiss them."[5]

Dye wrote little when Emery and Trafton were very small; however,
when Everett and Charlotte were young her literary efforts continued
apace. She always maintained that her children were not a burden to her
writing; in fact, she once commented, "When my children were in sight, I
always wrote better. If I didn't know where they were I simply couldn't
do anything, and it is a singular fact that some of my best work has been
done when there was considerable noise around me."[6] She was assisted in
large part by the emotional support and financial generosity of Charles,
whose income provided domestic help, and by her older sons. She once
noted in her journal that Emery and Trafton were "the best boys to help
mamma I ever saw. They are better than any hired girl any time. They
wash dishes, scrub, build fires, get wood, set table, and even get a meal if
necessary."[7]

In Dye's private writings we see the image of a completed family, and
perhaps because of her satisfaction, 1898 proved to be an important turning
point for her literary and historical endeavors. Although she was
disappointed that her manuscript on John McLoughlin was still
unpublished, she continued writing. She noted in her journal that "while
[Charlotte] was a nursing babe," she composed a series of vignettes on
early Oregon settlers and Native Americans.[8] Gleaned from the materials
she unearthed while researching the life of McLoughlin, *Stories of Oregon*
(1900) sold as a primer for Oregon grade schools. Publishers Whitaker
and Ray sold four thousand copies of her text and would have sold more
had not the plates and the last run of three thousand books been destroyed
in the 1906 San Francisco earthquake and fire.[9]

While Charlotte (nicknamed "little Eva") was still an infant and Everett
a rambunctious toddler, Dye used the hours while the children napped

and played to write an essay that would be extremely important for her future career. Her article, "The Hudson's Bay Company Regime in the Oregon Country," was included in Frederic G. Young's *Semi-Centennial History of Oregon* (1898). This essay, which focused on John McLoughlin's assistance to Americans and America's "right" to possess Oregon, celebrated the achievements of Anglo-Saxon conquest in the West. The romantic style is unmistakable in her description of the merging of the North West Company with the Hudson's Bay Company in 1821.

> Britons spilt British blood at Winnipeg. Parliament called a halt among these contentious children,–"Britons may fight Frenchmen, Indians, Americans, anybody but each other. Come, compromise, marry," said motherly old England, "marry, and I will give you a wedding present." So the hoary old Hudson's Bay Company proposed to the blooming young Northwest Company [sic]. It was plainly a wedding of capital and labor. The Northwest Company had nothing but her hands, her courage and her splendid exploration. Behind the Hudson's Bay were the money-bags of nobles and the Bank of England. Representatives of each went to London to fix up the wedding dowry.[10]

Although the flourishes of Dye's pen were broad and sweeping, her thesis–that the Oregon story was part of a broader history of America's dominion over the wilderness–was one that resonated with other Oregon historians.

Frederic Young was a colleague who shared Dye's vision of history. At the turn of the century Young was a professor at the University of Oregon, trained in economics and sociology, and chairman of the fledgling history department. He believed in and promoted the new scientific and professional approach to history that was becoming vogue in universities throughout the country. Like Dye, Young saw the history of the West as an important piece of a larger story, part of America's manifest destiny. He revered Oregon's pioneer history but only as a means to understanding American progress. According to historian Amanda Laugesen, Young believed Oregon's pioneers "were at the heart of a process of nation-making," and significant for the role they played in a dramatic epic. In a 1900 article for the *Oregon Historical Quarterly* Young wrote, "The passage from the Atlantic slope to the Pacific of these first American households bearing the first embers of western civil-ization [sic] must ever stand as a momentous event in the annals of time."[11]

Dye's more romantic approach to American history may seem at odds with Young's desire to apply a scientific, objective, and rational methodology to the study of Oregon's past. Yet both believed that history was a tool to educate citizens and teach patriotism. They also shared a passion for the research and collection of documents that would help elucidate the history of the region and the nation. Young's inclusion of Dye's essay in his 1898 work, therefore, provided an entrée to other university-trained historians whom she respected and admired. They in turn welcomed her participation and accepted her efforts to promote the understanding of Oregon and American history.

The degree to which Dye was accepted by the historical establishment was evidenced by an invitation she received late in 1898. On December 17, she attended the founding meeting of the Oregon Historical Society. Among the other twenty-five participants were Frederic Young, who was appointed secretary and became the first editor of the *Oregon Historical Quarterly*, and Harvey Scott, the powerful editor of the *Oregonian*, a historian and the society's first president.[12] Scott, himself a veteran of the Oregon Trail, and a man who believed Oregon should use its history to promote business, became an important supporter of Eva's next book and a personal friend of the Dyes. She later reported that she had been asked at the meeting to serve on the society's board of directors but had declined the offer because of the demands of her young family.[13] It was the only time she acknowledged that her children's needs conflicted with her emerging public role.

In late 1899, Whitaker and Ray accepted *Stories of Oregon* for publication, and by the next spring A. C. McClurg and Company offered to publish her manuscript on John McLoughlin. Almost overnight Dye achieved the kind of success about which she had long dreamed. Her notoriety in Oregon brought demands for public speaking and more writing, and soon her schedule reflected the important place her career occupied in the Dye family. She worked from nine o'clock to noon at her typewriter and returned there again from one o'clock to five every day. It is perhaps through the eyes of her youngest child that one can best understand the impact her work had on her family. In an interview with a reporter, Dye recalled one day when "small Eva danc[ed] up to her father in the garden, inquiring: 'Where's Miss Dye?' 'Here's Miss Dye!' said her father, as he caught her up in his arms. 'No,' insisted the 3-year-old, 'I mean the one what types.'"[14]

In her search for heroic topics to celebrate in western history, Dye recognized early in her research on Dr. McLoughlin that the Lewis and Clark Expedition was an epic event. She also surmised, correctly, that its history had not been widely recounted, especially in historical fiction. Timing, however, was everything. The extensive research she had done to document *McLoughlin and Old Oregon,* the many contacts she had made with early Northwest settlers, and the confidence she felt among other Oregon writers and historians all contributed to her ability to undertake her next project. At century's end, she was ready to write her "*Iliad* of the West."

The first published indication of her interest in Lewis and Clark came in the 1898 essay for Frederic Young's book. In addition to recounting the history of the Hudson's Bay Company, Dye noted the role of two explorers she believed were even more significant to the founding of Oregon than McLoughlin. She wrote, "It was not the Hudson's Bay Company, not even the Northwest Company, but Lewis and Clark, that first scaled the Rockies and traversed the wilds of Idaho." It was not the British, she argued, that deserved the credit for the exploration of Oregon, "but the private secretary of an American President and officers of the United States Army, that first ran the gauntlet of the swirling Dalles, and measured the Columbia to the sea."[15]

Frederic Young and Harvey Scott shared Dye's interest in Lewis and Clark. Some of Young's first articles in the newly established *Oregon Historical Quarterly* argued for the importance of the explorers to America's national history. Claiming that there were "four or five links in the chain of our right" to the Pacific Coast, he concluded that "the Lewis and Clark expedition was not merely one of a series of events forming the basis of our claim to Oregon, but it was the event that carried the others in its train."[16] Meanwhile others such as Harvey Scott and Portland businessman Henry Corbett promoted the idea that Oregon should host an exposition commemorating the centennial of the expedition to rival the Louisiana Purchase Exposition in St. Louis.

Historian Carl Abbott notes that the first news articles about a possible exposition appeared in 1899, but they attracted little support. In December 1900, however, Portland's business community decided to explore the idea further, and Harvey Scott and the Oregon Historical Society came together to endorse "a commercial exposition to be held in conjunction with the centennial of Lewis and Clark's exploration of the Oregon Country."[17] Dye was aware, therefore, that the story of Lewis and Clark was a potential best-seller.

The timing of these events was significant for Dye's decision to write about Lewis and Clark, but it was not the only reason she was interested in the explorers. Dye's ideas also reflected her appreciation for the vision of Thomas Jefferson, in particular his democratic principles and desire for an "empire of liberty."[18] She called Jefferson "the great apostle of popular sovereignty" and was impressed with his abolition of entail and primogeniture in Virginia.[19] She believed that his commitment to national expansion arose from his desire to create a democratic empire where merit, talent, and virtue would reign. In turn, she saw his efforts to protect the West from Spanish and French encroachment as heroic. The Louisiana Purchase thus heralded the beginning of a new era of American power. She wrote that America was "on July 3, 1803, an infant Republic hugging the Atlantic, on July 4, a world power grasping the Pacific!"[20] Viewing white settlement of the West as only the beginning of American conquest, she credited Jefferson with the same ideas. Thus, according to Dye, Jefferson "sent Lewis and Clark to open up a road to Asia," and he "more than any other, had the vision of to-day [sic]."[21]

John Palmer Spencer, in his forthcoming essay on the historiography of the Lewis and Clark expedition, argues that *The Conquest* was a result of Dye's admiration for Theodore Roosevelt and his imperialistic foreign policy in the 1890s. He notes that, "*The Conquest* and books like it were not simply backward glances at the favorite themes of Roosevelt the historian (that is, manliness and Anglo-Saxon conquest); they may as well have been polemics for the policies of Roosevelt the president."[22] Dye's publishers certainly saw the connection between her book and the president. According to her, A. C. McClurg wanted the book dedicated to Roosevelt "but there was not time to wait and fill the advance orders piled up for that Christmas." Interestingly, Dye wished it had been dedicated to editor, friend, and booster for the exposition, Harvey Scott. In the rush to get the book out for the 1902 holiday season, the dedication was omitted.[23]

Dye was definitely influenced by the political times in which she lived, and she commented years later, "Everything Roosevelt says is worthwhile."[24] America's expansion overseas during the McKinley and Roosevelt administrations provided opportunities for cultural, economic, and military intervention, though many Americans disagreed over whether expansion should occur by force or more peacefully through the efforts of evangelizing Christian missionaries and by flooding overseas markets with American products and technology. The Spanish-American War had just ended when Dye began her research, and America's attempts to squelch

Philippine independence made many Americans uneasy about the future and nostalgic about the past.[25] What drove Dye to research and write epic stories of heroism was a deep need to respond to this uneasiness and nostalgia. It was not so much the politics of her day but the mood of the Progressive era that shaped her writing. She wrote, "Hero-worship is characteristic of youthful, progressive people. Whole nations strive to emulate ideals. The moment that ceases, ossification begins."[26]

If Dye's work is a backward glance at a bygone era, it was Jefferson's ideal America that she worshipped and the heroes she celebrated were cast in Jeffersonian attire. Historian Merrill Peterson notes that at the turn of the twentieth century Jefferson was again in vogue as a cultural hero largely because of the publication of more personalized accounts of his life. Sarah Randolph's *Domestic Life of Thomas Jefferson* (1871) and James Parton's *Life* (1874) had earlier helped mold the image of Jefferson as the Virginia gentleman.[27] In Randolph's account, especially, he appeared as devotedly domestic, chivalrous, and honorable. Parton, in turn, featured Jefferson the philosopher-statesman, the artist and scientist, and the educator. We do not know whether or not Dye read these works; however, the chapter highlighting Jefferson in *The Conquest* examines Jefferson the man rather than Jefferson the politician. Dye recounts Jefferson's fascination with science, his "old-style Virginia dinners," his tending of plants, and his love for Monticello, which she called "his little principality." She thought highly of his classical education, noted more than once his extensive travels, and believed, wholeheartedly, that he was "an object of adoration to a people."[28] For Dye, it was the virtue, chivalry, and courage of Jefferson, George Rogers Clark, Meriwether Lewis, William Clark, Daniel Boone, and many others featured in *The Conquest* that made the history of the post-Revolutionary period an American epic. "'The Conquest' is more than a story," she stated, "it is a continuous pageant across the continent, a vision of demi-gods battling for the future United States."[29]

Dye's research began in the spring of 1900 with her reading of available texts on Lewis and Clark. She first encountered Paul Allen and Nicholas Biddle's edition of the Lewis and Clark journals. The Biddle-Allen edition, as it is known, was a condensed and paraphrased version of the expedition writings published in 1814. The entries are presented in one voice, and lack the individual personalities of Lewis and Clark and the other diarists. Of this edition Dye wrote, "At that time the only record available was the Biddle text. And I almost *died* over that, almost fainted away, it was so dead, so perfunctory."[30] Soon after she discovered an 1893 history of the expedition, edited by Elliott Coues. This four-volume work was a reprint of the Biddle text, but included maps and extensive footnotes on flora, fauna, geography, Native American history and culture, and genealogies of the expedition members.[31] Coues was a better reference than Biddle, but still Dye was dissatisfied with the published sources.

As she had with *McLoughlin*, Dye decided that to make her heroes come to life she needed to know her subjects more personally. As one critic put it, Dye sought out "persons who had direct, collateral, or imaginary association with the exploring party."[32] She was fortunate that there were grandchildren and nieces and nephews of her subjects still living and able to supply her with documents and reminiscences. The Coues edition contained a "Tabular Statement of the Living Lineal Issue of William Clark" complete with addresses as of 1893. It is probably from this list that Dye was able to contact Clark descendants and make plans to visit them in St. Louis, Detroit, Louisville, and New York.

In March 1901 she undertook her first lengthy journey to the east. She was gone for three months, when little Eva was just three-and-a-half years old. Charles's widowed sister Mary Gilmer and her daughter Bessie came to live with him to take care of the household and children. Dye's trip included a visit to the University of Wisconsin, where she met Frederick Jackson Turner. While there she also examined the Lyman Draper collection of manuscripts on George Rogers Clark, William Clark, and Daniel Boone. From Madison she traveled to St. Paul to meet with historian Olin Wheeler, whose work and interest in Native Americans captivated her. Dye's journey also took her to the Newberry Library in Chicago, to the Library of Congress, and to numerous historical societies.[33] While in Washington D.C., Dye met the widow of Elliott Coues. Of the challenges Coues faced in annotating Biddle's narrative, Dye wrote, "He did the best he could, of course. His wife told me all about it."[34]

Dye met many historians in the course of her trip, but Frederick Jackson Turner deserves special note. His enthusiasm for the history of the frontier West and his knowledge of George Rogers Clark were invaluable to her. She noted that Turner "was a great inspiration to me,"[35] and she claimed he agreed with her that "in about two years there will be a Lewis and Clark furore."[36] Whether she was familiar with Turner's famous lecture "The Significance of the Frontier in American History" (1893) is unknown; however, she certainly shared his central ideas that "the frontier is the outer edge of the wave—the meeting point between savagery and civilization" and that the conquering of the wilderness by Anglo-Europeans explained

American development and institutions.[37] Western pioneer history, in Turner's estimation, became the key point of entry for understanding America. Dye praised him lavishly–"the best most competent informed man on Middlewest history"–and was highly appreciative of the University of Wisconsin and the State Historical Society of Wisconsin.[38]

In St. Louis and New York, Clark descendants welcomed her into their homes and their family history. William Hancock Clark and John O'Fallon Clark, grandsons of William Clark, assisted her in particular with family memorabilia and letters and suggestions about where to find additional information.[39] In a letter to C. Harper Anderson, nephew of Meriwether Lewis, Dye noted the helpfulness of the Clark relatives:

> At Detroit, next, I was met by William Hancock Clark, oldest living grandson of General Clark. We went over to Canada and found the family of Drewyer, the hunter of the expedition … The true name is Drouillard. Col. Clark gave me letters to all his relatives, more than I could visit.[40]

Paralleling her experience researching John McLoughlin's life, Dye exuberantly noted, "my contact with sources was like peeping into a gold mine glittering with treasure – as yet unexploited."[41] Proud of her extensive collection of materials, she claimed that "altogether I have more than any one else in the world, now, and have every reason to believe that I shall have the most complete history of the great explorers ever written."[42]

In Philadelphia, Secretary Isaac Hays of the American Philosophical Society (APS) denied her access to the original journals of Lewis and Clark. He believed that all the information she would ever need was in the available sources and was unwilling to grant permission to "outsiders" when the society had not yet published the Lewis and Clark journals in their entirety.[43] Late in the fall of 1901, Dye began planning her next trip east and wrote an emphatic letter to the Oregon Historical Society (OHS) requesting an endorsement of her work for the APS. She argued in her letter that her work would only have credibility if she was permitted to do "original investigation" and that published works, especially the Biddle edition, were "utterly inadequate to my needs." She inquired of the OHS board of directors, "Now what can you do to help me?"[44]

While Dye was awaiting an answer, she also learned that the APS, inspired by the upcoming Louisiana Purchase Centennial Exposition, had engaged Reuben Gold Thwaites to edit a new edition of the original journals. In February 1902 she wrote to Thwaites, congratulating him on his new appointment. She also informed him that she had many letters in her possession from the families of Lewis and Clark and added that she had "personal acquaintance with the children, grandchildren, nieces or nephews, of Lewis, Clark, Drouillard, Shannon … Bratton, Gass, Floyd, and am on the track of Ordway and Pryor." She offered to let Thwaites borrow or copy many items from her now extensive collection in exchange for an opportunity to examine the original journals. In a tone similar to the one she employed with the OHS board, she did not mince words. "Having spent two years in the study of Lewis and Clark, I have had ample reason to wish for a complete copy of the original journals. Now, how soon will this be available?"[45]

By the time Dye embarked on her trip in April she had in hand letters of introduction from the OHS board to the State Historical Society of Wisconsin, where Thwaites was engaged in his painstaking work, and to the APS. Her book was nearly finished except for some aspects of the expedition she was hoping to verify in the original journals. She wrote later, "The Conquest was practically written before I ever read the original journals that might have made it a better book."[46] In the end, it was perhaps Thwaites who benefited most from the exchange of ideas and documents, for it was her relationship with William Hancock Clark and Mrs. Jefferson Kearney Clark that paved the way for a remarkable discovery.

Both Dye and Thwaites were looking for the missing journal of Sergeant John Ordway, a text that had vanished after Biddle's use of it in 1814. Dye had written to Lewis's nephew, C. Harper Anderson, in the fall of 1901 that "in the most surprising way a lady away off in Michigan has put me on track of the Ordways."[47] When Dye met Thwaites in Madison, they undoubtedly discussed the Ordway journal and its possible location. She was intrigued with the possibility that she and Thwaites were closing in on the missing journal, so with letters of introduction in hand both from her previous year's acquaintance with John O'Fallon Clark and William Hancock Clark and from Thwaites, she went to visit Mrs. Jefferson Clark in New York City,[48] where she met Mrs. Clark and her niece Julia Clark Voorhis. Legal control of William Clark's estate rested with Voorhis and her daughter, Eleanor Glasgow Voorhis, an arrangement that became an issue later for Thwaites.[49] Dye reported,

> I was most cordially entertained. Valuable heirlooms were exhibited, silver and paintings, but no manuscripts were to be found. "We have none," [Mrs. Clark] said. The same report

came from other members of the family—in Philadelphia, Washington, D.C., and Louisville—until I came to St. Louis, where John O'Fallon Clark emphatically declared the manuscripts must be in the hands of his aunt, Mrs. Jefferson K. Clark, in New York City. "I sent them there myself," he said. "They had lain for years in my grandfather's old secretary. I cleared them out and shipped the whole to the Jefferson K. Clarks in New York City. I doubt whether they ever looked into those boxes."[50]

Dye stated later that she returned to Madison and informed Thwaites that Mrs. Jefferson Clark had in her possession a "'Lewis and Clark Journal' wrapped in buckskin."[51] What actually occurred was that Mrs. Clark had provided her with a list of memorabilia that seemed to have little significance to either Dye or Thwaites, though it included a journal. But back in Oregon, the list intrigued her. Correspondence between Dye and Thwaites resumed in autumn 1902 when she reminded him of the "newspaper list of documents and relics in possession of Mrs. Jefferson K. Clark." She had come to believe that the Lewis and Clark journal on the list was the missing Ordway journal. She wrote, "We know the Ordway journal is not in the Philadelphia lot, so this is likely to prove to be it and really ought to be published with the others as John Ordway's record of the great journey." Thwaites replied, "That is a joyful suggestion of yours, as to the possibility of the remaining MS. in Mrs. Clark's possession, being the missing Ordway Journal."

Dye's persistence prompted Thwaites to action. He mentioned that he was "trying hard to get a reply from Mrs. Clark, and have written to the Major [William H. Clark] also."[52] Thwaites finally made contact with Mrs. Clark but then could not obtain her cooperation and that of Mrs. Voorhis. He remarked that his "search for the Ordway journal stimulated Mrs. and Miss Voorhis into a closer scrutiny of their family treasures."[53] By the time he was able to view the contents of the boxes, the owners were already negotiating with potential publishers. They had, he said, "golden dreams concerning [the collection's] cash value."[54]

At long last, in October 1903, Mrs. Clark invited Thwaites to her home in New York.[55] There he found an amazing collection of materials: four of Clark's expedition notebooks, which were copies of Lewis's; one of Clark's field books, which, according to Thwaites, was "the only one of the kind that I know of in existence"; the military "order[ly] book frequently referred to by Lewis and Clark in their journals"; many letters between

Lewis, Clark, and Jefferson; and approximately "fifty maps made by Wm. Clark varying in size from six inches square to 1 x 9 feet in extant."[56] It was, according to historian Paul Cutright, "the most important discovery of Lewis and Clark material since Coues's rediscovery, a decade earlier, of the original journals."[57]

Reporting to Secretary Hays in August 1903, Thwaites wrote, "We have just discovered in New York some half dozen note books, chiefly by Clark, similar to those which are in the possession of the Society, together with a considerable mass of other material bearing upon the expedition."[58] The "we" was not identified, but Dye stated, "No doubt I was the one that traced the real Lewis and Clark records, and Mr. Thwaites might have given me credit but such a thought never occurred to me. Those records might have been stored to this day if some one had not happened to be vitally interested." She also claimed to have mentioned the discovery to Frederick Jackson Turner and noted proudly, "Professor Turner, the famous Frederick J. Turner, told me I had 'turned up something' when I traced these things."[59]

After protracted negotiations with Julia Clark Voorhis and her daughter, Thwaites was able to use this collection for his edition, and the papers, maps, and a number of portraits eventually found a home at the Missouri Historical Society.[60] Dye never received credit for her part in the discovery, but Thwaites devoted the lengthiest acknowledgement in the *Original Journals'* introduction to her:

> Mrs. Eva Emery Dye of Oregon City, Oregon, has contributed
> most liberally from the surprisingly rich store of historical
> materials which, with remarkable enterprise and perseverance,
> she accumulated during her preparation for the writing of *The
> Conquest*; her persistent helpfulness has laid the Editor under
> unusual obligations.[61]

The assistance Dye received from the Clark family made a significant impact on the content of her book. *The Conquest* is divided into three books. Book One, "When Red Men Ruled," covers the period from Lord Dunmore's War (1774) until Jefferson's recruitment of Meriwether Lewis to lead the expedition, and describes the numerous Indian wars waged in the name of American expansion. Book Two, "Into the West," details the

Louisiana Purchase and the entire period of the Lewis and Clark Expedition. Book Three, "The Red Head Chief," examines the aftermath of the expedition and Clark's career as governor of Missouri territory and superintendent of Indian Affairs. *The Conquest*, therefore, opens with George Rogers Clark in 1774 and ends with William Clark's death in 1838. The book is, in effect, a collective biography of the Clark family. All events are filtered through the Clark lens, which is an unusual perspective for twenty-first-century readers. Scholars of Lewis and Clark have tended to emphasize the former because of Lewis's eloquent writing and observations, his relationship to Jefferson, and the many intriguing questions related to his tragic death. It is apparent, however, that Dye believed the Clark brothers' story was more interesting than that of Meriwether Lewis.

George Rogers Clark, the hero of Book One, is featured as a young and promising surveyor and scout during Lord Dunmore's War. The story progresses through the early settlement of Kentucky County and his key role in the founding of Harrods Town, his victory over the British at Kaskakia (1778) and Vincennes (1779), and disappointment over his inability to capture the fort at Detroit. Dye in fact believed Clark was so anguished over Detroit that "for the first time the over-wrought hero gave way to intoxication to drown his grief,—and so had Clark then died, 'Detroit' might have been found written on his heart." Throughout the story, Clark is the gallant fighter of both Indians and the British. Dye describes him as "invincible," "bold," "prescient," a man with a "Napoleonic eye," and a "leather-armoured knight from the beleaguered castle in the wood."[62]

Dye's hero falls in love with Donna de Leyba, the sister of the Spanish governor of Upper Louisiana. Although it is unknown if this story is true, the romance serves to make Clark more interesting and more human to readers. It also provides another opportunity to feature the virtues that Dye believed were most important for her heroes: pride, courage, strength, and self-abnegation. Clark casts aside the unfortunate de Leyba when her brother's cowardice brings about the end of Spanish rule in St. Louis. Dye wrote,

> On his way to the Government House, he saw the lovely Donna at her casement. Her hair was dishevelled, her eyes wet with tears. She extended her hand. Clark took one step toward her, and then pride triumphed. "Never will I become the father of a race of cowards," and turning on his heel he left St. Louis forever.[63]

The role that Clark plays in *The Conquest* is that of empire builder in a hostile land, and Dye credits him with opening the Ohio valley to settlement.[64] His status and his legacy are passed on to his younger brother William and friend Meriwether Lewis. Although Lewis and the younger Clark are present throughout the beginning of the book as precocious and observant children in patriotic families, they first appear as key figures in the story during the 1790s. At that time they were young soldiers in the service of General "Mad Anthony" Wayne, and when the older Clark retired from public life at the turn of the nineteenth century, he passed the scepter of power on to his brother. Dye wrote, "It seemed almost as if William took up the life of George Rogers where it was broken off, and carried it on to a glorious conclusion."[65]

The biographies of the two brothers also allowed Dye to explore Native American culture and history, a topic that fascinated her. The elder Clark's role as Indian fighter carried her through portrayals of the Shawnees, Delawares, and Wyandots as vicious savages bent on the destruction of Kentucky and the Ohio valley. Book One breathlessly describes George Rogers Clark leading the charge in one battle after another against the British and the Indians. In contrast, William Clark's career as Indian Agent presented a less sanguine approach to the problem of white settlement on native lands. Dye featured Clark as a troubled peacemaker among the tribes. Unable to protect the Indians from white encroachment on their lands or prevent depredation by other tribes, Clark is a weary buffer on the frontier. She wrote, "Could the influence of one man have availed against armies of westward pressing trappers, traders, and pioneers, the tribes would have been civilized."[66]

Although she was sympathetic to their plight, Dye concluded that the removal of Native Americans from their tribal lands was inevitable. Her writing reflects prevailing views among whites and the tenor of federal Indian policy in the late nineteenth century. White reformers argued that the reservation system of the 1870s isolated Indians from the benefits of white culture and perpetuated tribal identities, savagery, and poverty. Their sentiments were institutionalized with the Dawes General Allotment Act (1887), which provided for individual land allotments for Native Americans. The philosophy behind the Dawes Act argued that private land ownership and U.S. citizenship, together with education and church attendance, would "civilize" Native Americans.[67] With few exceptions most middle-class white Americans held the view that the new policy would save Native Americans from certain extinction; thus reformers perceived the Act as both necessary and benevolent. Through private land ownership, they claimed, Indians would finally be assimilated into the dominant culture and economy, reaping the benefits of American progress.

Throughout both *McLoughlin and Old Oregon* and *The Conquest*, Native Americans are depicted in rather stark opposites, reflecting her understanding that "good" Indians could be salvaged by the dominant culture and "bad" Indians were unredeemable. Dye portrayed noble Indians like the Shoshone as childlike, inquisitive, peaceful, and somewhat pathetic, while ignoble savages, such as the Blackfeet and the Sioux, are described as "profligate rovers,"–lawless, anarchical, vicious, and conniving. The latter were not candidates for assimilation; instead they were "bloodthirsty" and must be vanquished.[68] Dye was a product of her time, and while in hindsight we find her beliefs disturbing, she was not alone in adhering to less-than-progressive ideas about Native peoples. Her work perpetuated rather than challenged accepted contemporary notions of Native Americans.[69]

Dye's descriptions of Native Americans were also affected by the dictates of bookselling, and her publishers had a stake in the way in which she presented them. In an interview she commented that when visiting A. C. McClurg and Company prior to *The Conquest's* publication she "noticed a book cover design of a most melancholy Indian, and at the top of it 'The Conquest.'" She was later informed that "this was Mrs. Dye's subjugated Indian." The original ending for her book featured "a glimpse of the civilized Indian," as she put it; however, her publishers did not think it would sell as well as "the more picturesque savage."[70]

The Conquest depicted civilized and savage Indians not only in the sections focused on the Clark brothers' frontier careers but also in Dye's portrayal of women characters. Her search for a heroine began with the historically available white women and ended with the young Indian woman Sacagawea. The decision to use Sacagawea in a heroic role and the evolution of Sacagawea's character reveals much about Dye's understanding of race, gender, and white American culture at the end of the nineteenth century.

Because all events in *The Conquest* revolve around the Clark family it is not surprising that Dye's first choice for a heroine was Julia Hancock, the woman who would eventually become Clark's wife. It is Julia's portrait–provided by John O'Fallon Clark and eventually part of the Voorhis collection—that is the frontispiece to the first edition of *The Conquest*. Introduced in one of the closing chapters of Book One, "the maid of Fincastle" is featured in a fairy-tale wooded setting where Clark prevents his damsel in distress from getting her satin slippers muddy. Like all of the white women in the story, Julia is beautiful, virtuous, and domestic, a model of nineteenth-century true womanhood. In earlier chapters Rebecca Boone, Ann Rogers Clark, Lucy Meriwether Lewis, and even the ill-fated Donna de Leyba fulfilled similar domestic and supportive roles as wives, mothers, and sisters.

Julia ("Judith") Hancock was meant to captivate Dye's readers, but the would-be heroine played no part in the expedition itself, nor did her personal attributes or accomplishments render her as interesting or tragic as Narcissa Whitman or Eliza Spalding had been in Dye's earlier novel. Casting her as heroine became problematic. After sifting through "the dry old Biddle edition" of the Lewis and Clark journals, Dye finally found the woman she was seeking.[71] As she told the story later,

> I had Judith, the girl Clark left behind him when he went on the expedition. I then hunted up every fact I could find about Sacajawea. Out of a few dry bones I found in the old tales of the trip I created Sacajawea and made her a real living entity. … The world snatched at my heroine, Sacajawea. Judith apparently was overlooked.[72]

In Sacagawea Dye had found a character that embodied the spirit of adventure and was a powerful image of pioneer womanhood.[73]

Mothers were of particular interest to Dye. She had written journal entries and poetry in the 1880s on the "mothers of great men" and her support of social and political reforms for women was, as we have seen, based on her belief in the moral superiority of mothers as teachers. Her poem "The College Girl," written shortly after her arrival in Oregon City, is exemplary of her view that woman's highest calling was as a mother.

> What becomes of the college girl,
> The girl of mother-heart?
> At the cradle side she kneels with pride,
> Her willing hands by love are tied
> To life's divinest art.
>
> What becomes of the college girl,
> The girl of book and pen?

> She is training sons, the future great,
> Creating heroes for the state,
> A mother unto men.
>
> What becomes of the college girl,
> The girl of classic hall?
> In social walk or civic strife,
> In church or home or school her life
> Uplifts and sweetens all.[74]

Dye's writings on Margaret McLoughlin, Narcissa Whitman, and Eliza Spalding also make it evident that mothers as a force in America's settlement and expansion were key to her interpretation of the West. Dye's childhood experience of losing her own mother also may have played a subconscious part in her consistent choice of mothers as heroines. Regardless of the reasons, it is evident that Dye found irresistible the image of Sacagawea journeying with her baby on an eighteen-month expedition.

Dye brought Sacagawea to life in *The Conquest* by appealing specifically to her role as a wife and mother, and she highlighted the domestic touches Sacagawea brought to the journey. The narrative of Book Two is held together by the fact of Sacagawea's motherhood and her domesticating presence on the journey. Books One and Three have a similar thread running through them: the importance of families to the settlement of the West. As historian Jan Dawson has claimed, "Nowhere in *The Conquest* does Dye portray women or men as rugged individualists, standing outside networks of relatives and other dependents. The figures in the work are always responsible to and for others."[75]

One of the important functions Sacagawea fulfilled on the expedition, both on the actual journey and in Dye's account, was to assure the safety of the explorers through hostile territory. It was Sacagawea's motherhood, not just her femaleness that Dye highlighted. She wrote,

> The women crowded around Sacajawea and untied her baby
> from its elkskin cradle. They fed it and gave it little garments.
> That baby was an open sesame touching the hearts of all.
> Sacajawea, riding on her horse to the Columbia, found friends
> with every tribe … The Indian mother-heart opened to
> Sacajawea. Her very presence was an assurance of pacific
> intention.[76]

Sacagawea is almost always featured with her baby. Among the skittish Nez Perces, for example, Dye noted that despite Clark's attempts to calm the Indians, "not until Sacajawea landed with her baby was tranquility restored."[77] The expedition writings only mention that Sacagawea herself was reassuring to the Indians. The Biddle text notes, "Soon after the interpreter's wife landed, and her presence dissipated all doubts of our being well-disposed, since in this country, no woman ever accompanies a war party."[78] Dye's change to the original text subtly alters the facts of the event and reminds the reader of Sacagawea's maternal role.

According to Dye, Sacagawea provided a comforting presence for the men of the expedition, thus like other pioneer women in *McLoughlin* and *The Conquest* she became the civilizing influence among a group of men. Significantly, it is motherhood that provides normality in a strange environment. Dye's musing on Sacagawea's state of mind creates a more complete character and enables the author to insert her own values about womanhood.

> All day the firelight flickered on Sacajawea's hair, as she sat making moccasins, crooning a song in her soft Indian monotone. This was, perhaps, the happiest winter Sacajawea ever knew, with baby Touissant toddling around her on the puncheon floor, pulling her shawl around his chubby face, or tumbling over his own cradle. The modest Shoshone princess never dreamed how the presence of her child and herself gave a touch of domesticity to that Oregon winter.[79]

In an effort to portray scenes of domestic tranquility, Dye ignores conflicts between Sacagawea and her husband. Touissant Charbonneau is often described in the expedition journals as lazy, cowardly, and inept. Lewis and Clark rebuke him on more than one occasion for beating his wife. Hardships that Sacagawea endured as a result of his abuse remain unexamined in *The Conquest* just as Dye failed to address conflicts between men and women in *McLoughlin*. Instead she mentions more than once that Sacagawea is fortunate to be married to a white man. When Sacagawea meets her kinswoman, Dye wrote, "as girls will, with arms around each other they wandered off and talked and talked of the wonderful fortune that had come to Sacajawea, the wife of a white man."[80]

In promoting an ideal image of womanhood, Dye's characterization also ensures that her heroine will embody youth and beauty. She also works to erase the line between what she views as Sacagawea's savagery and a more desirable civilization, for example in the scene in which Sacagawea first glimpses her Shoshone kinfolk. Biddle and Coues provide the following:

> On setting out at seven o'clock, Captain Clark, with Chaboneau and his wife, walked on shore; but they had not gone more than a mile before Captain Clark saw Sacajawea, who was with her husband 100 yards ahead, begin to dance and show every mark of the most extravagant joy, turning round to him and pointing to several Indians, whom he now saw advancing on horseback, sucking her fingers at the same time, to indicate that they were of her native tribe.[81]

Dye took this evidence and transformed it into a moment of youthful anticipation. It is the one scene in which Sacagawea's baby is not mentioned.

> Sacajawea, the little Bird-woman, could not wait. In her anxiety she begged to walk ahead along shore, and with her husband went dancing up the rivulet of her childhood. She flew ahead. She turned, pirouetting lightly on her beaded moccasins, waving her arms and kissing her fingers. Her long hair flew in the wind and her beaded necklace sparkled.[82]

Dye clearly wants to make Sacagawea as appealing as possible to her white readers. What might have been considered a "savage" gesture, Sacagawea's sucking her fingers, is changed to a more civilized and romantic image. Her flowing hair and pirouetting feet are reminiscent of a graceful ballet. Dye's account personalizes the factual history of this event while promoting an ideal of youthful pioneer womanhood with which the public could identify.

Dye's portrayal of Sacagawea serves as a bridge between the nineteenth-century journal texts and an early twentieth-century audience, and one way in which she secures the interest of her readers is to feature the cross-cultural connection between Sacagawea and the white explorers. Married to Charbonneau and mother of his child, Sacagawea is also part of a kin network that is reestablished when she is reunited with the Shoshone. Bound both to her native culture and to the white explorers, she is, as Dawson notes, "a liaison between whites and the West's Indian inhabitants."[83]

Sacagawea is also depicted as a princess; her brother is the chief of the Shoshones, and her "royalty" supplants any idea that she is merely a slave or a simple Indian girl. The princess motif seems important to Dye as an indication of Sacagawea's worthiness, but it is also used to suggest that she is equal in importance to America's most cherished female Indian ideal, Pocahontas. When Sacagawea views the Pacific Ocean, Dye wrote, "Sacajawea, save Pocahontas the most travelled Indian Princess in our history, spoke not a word, but looked with calm and shining eye upon the fruition of her hopes."[84] Sacagawea's departure from the expedition also allows Dye an opportunity to reflect on the Indian woman's role. Her words suggest that Sacagawea will outshine Pocahontas. She wrote,

> Some day upon the Bozeman Pass, Sacajawea's statue will stand beside that of Clark. Some day, where the rivers part, her laurels will vie with those of Lewis. Across North America a Shoshone Indian Princess touched hands with Jefferson, opening her country.[85]

Ethnohistorian Rayna Green argues that symbolic images of the Princess and her counterpart the Savage Squaw have been prevalent icons of the New World since the sixteenth century as Euro-Americans sought to understand "this earthly, frightening and beautiful paradise." Princess imagery evolved in the Revolutionary era to include a more classical and Caucasian portrayal of the "good" Indian woman, carrying "a peace pipe, a flag, or the starred and striped shield of Colonial America." When art met life in the form of Pocahontas and Sacagawea, the women were "defined in terms of their relationships with male figures. If she wishes to be called Princess, she must save or give aid to white men."[86]

Dye's heroine does not possess many of the elements of either stereotype— she is not the venal, primitive, crude savage of the Squaw, nor is she the Christian convert and sexually inviting image of the Princess. Thus Jan Dawson argues that in her characterization of Sacagawea-as-Princess Dye was perhaps "searching for new ways to understand the complex history of white settlement of Indian lands."[87] Dye may not have recognized these archetypes as described by Green, but it is clear that she believed Sacagawea's nobility assured her "goodness," and her helpfulness to whites is certainly a central part of the story.

In Sacagawea's exit scene Dye pulled together the key elements she used to create her character, and, it should be noted, this is the scene many critics highlight when arguing that Dye's portrayal is exaggerated. It is

Dye's editorializing that historians object to, and this scene is full of romantic embellishment.

> Sacajawea, modest princess of the Shoshones, heroine of the great expedition, stood with her babe in arms and smiled upon them from the shore. So had she stood in the Rocky Mountains pointing out the gates. So had she followed the great rivers, navigating the continent.
>
> Sacajawea's hair was neatly braided, her nose was fine and straight, and her skin pure copper like the statue in some old Florentine gallery. Madonna of her race, she had led the way to a new time. To the hands of this girl, not yet eighteen, had been intrusted [sic] the key that unlocked the road to Asia.[88]

In Dye's estimation, motherhood, domesticity, and royalty made Sacagawea a figure worthy of remembrance in literature and art.

Sacagawea's role as civilizing force for the expedition is provocative given the cultural milieu at the turn of the twentieth century. Dye's contemporaries, writers such as Charlotte Perkins Gilman and Theodore Roosevelt, defined concepts of womanhood and manhood and equated the white race with civilization and cultural advancement. Gilman's *Women and Economics* (1898) not only described utopian households in which white women no longer engaged in the drudgery of everyday tasks, but also was a treatise on the importance of white women to civilization. According to historian Gail Bederman, Gilman advanced the notion that white women, not white men, were the true conquerors of savagery and primitivism. "According to Gilman," she wrote, "civilization is intrinsically feminine. Had men not been feminized, they could never have become either human or civilized."[89] Gilman believed that white women had saved white men from certain destruction through centuries of mothering and maintaining the social fabric of communities. In contrast, Roosevelt's popular chronicles, especially *The Winning of the West* (1889-96), helped foster the idea that the frontier was a battleground between white American men and savage forces. His work equated manliness with civilization. For both authors, the supremacy of the white race was never in question, but they differed over whether it was white manhood or white womanhood that defined America's success.[90]

In the context of these influential works, Dye's depiction of Sacagawea is an intriguing variation on the interplay between race and gender. Sacagawea is neither white nor male and thus some might have thought her a poor choice for the role of civilizer. However, Dye uses Sacagawea's domesticity, the fact of her motherhood, and her connection to white men to create a sympathetic figure, and takes care to describe her in ways that would make her a natural protagonist for white readers. Dye's understanding of nineteenth-century white womanhood dominates her characterization of Sacagawea; indeed Sacagawea's Indianness seems to vanish along the trail. Like Gilman, Dye embraced the idea that women were intrinsically important to the nation's development, and she subsumed Sacagawea's race under a veneer of whiteness-by-association that made her a convincing emblem of civilization.

Historians seeking to understand Dye's portrayal of Sacagawea have distorted her motivations and overlooked the compelling domestic imagery in *The Conquest*. For example, Ronald Taber's influential 1967 article "Sacagawea and the Suffragettes" argued that *The Conquest* was written because Dye was a suffragist, and further, that she constructed her book as a promotional tool for the National Woman Suffrage Association. He noted that the Oregon Equal Suffrage Association held its twenty-fifth convention in 1898, and that during the meeting its members drafted an open letter in support of an equal suffrage amendment. Dye's signature was on the letter. Taber acerbically commented that Dye wrote *The Conquest* not because she was a "factual historical novelist," but because "Mrs. Dye was also a suffragette, and the women of that movement were ready to grasp at anything that would further their cause."[91]

David Remley followed Taber, arguing that "the guide myth was created by feminists interested in promoting women's rights, chiefly by Eva Emory Dye [sic] in *The Conquest: The True Story of Lewis and Clark* (1903) [sic]."[92] Sacagawea biographers Ella Clark and Margot Edmonds also noted that it was Dye's "keen interest in women's rights that led her to a study of Sacagawea."[93] In 1996 the Sacagawea-as-suffragette notion seemed relevant to historian Donna Kessler. She noted that *The Conquest* is "the most significant written work concerned with Sacagawea during the [Progressive] period" and that "Dye promotes suffrage, with Sacagawea becoming a model for independent American women."[94] All of these historians have evaluated the impact of *The Conquest* to explain its origins, thus confusing cause and effect. They also have failed to notice that Dye's "model American woman" hearkened back to nineteenth-century true womanhood instead of forging onward to equal-rights feminism. Dye was a suffragist, believing that votes for women would improve their lives, but she was also a conservative woman not yet ready to relinquish traditional notions of women's sphere.

If historians have misunderstood the roots of *The Conquest* and Dye's characterization of Sacagawea, they have also missed the mark when claiming that *The Conquest* exaggerated Sacagawea's role as "guide" to the expedition. Although Dye is often exuberant in her characterization of Sacagawea and romanticizes her role, it is worth pointing out that she generally remains true to the historical subject. She portrayed Sacagawea as helpful in finding food for the explorers and pointing out landmarks, useful in interpreting, clearheaded in a nearly disastrous incident with one of the pirogues, and an important insurance policy against hostile tribes. For all the criticism Dye has received, it is significant that the domestic imagery surrounding Sacagawea is more detailed and persuasive than the evidence that she guided the expedition.[95]

Dye never used the word "guide" to describe Sacagawea's role on the journey. In a chapter entitled "A Woman Pilot," Sacagawea points out Beaver Head Rock and other landmarks to Lewis, but that is the extent of her assistance. Dye wrote, "Sacajawea pointed to a steep, rocky cliff shaped like a beaver's head … 'This is not far from the summer retreat of my countrymen. We shall meet them soon, on a river beyond the mountains running to the west.'"[96] Despite the title of the chapter, the text, instead of featuring Sacagawea as pilot, features her reunion with the Shoshone. Interestingly, Dye's account of the reunion is actually much briefer than that found in Biddle and Coues. In short, she had plenty of material had she wanted to exaggerate or embellish.

On the return trip in 1806 Sacagawea traveled with Clark. Again, she is portrayed as helpful at pointing out landmarks familiar to her from childhood. Dye wrote,

> Out of Ross Hole Sacajawea pointed the way by Clark's Pass, over the Continental Divide, to the Big Hole River where the trail disappeared or scattered. … On her little pony, with her baby on her back, the placid Indian girl led the way into the labyrinthine Rockies.[97]

Later at the Three Forks Sacagawea was useful, according to Dye, for pointing out "the Yellowstone Gap, the Bozeman Pass of to-day, on the great Shoshone Highway."[98] Clark's journal told a more detailed story.

From the Biddle edition on July 6, 1806:

> Here the tracks of the Indians scattered so much that we could
> no longer pursue it, but Sacajaweah recognized the plain
> immediately. She had travelled it often during her childhood,
> and informed us that it was the great resort of the Shoshonees
> ... and that Glade creek was a branch of Wisdom river, and
> that on reaching the higher part of the plain, we should see a
> gap in the mountains ... and from that gap a high point of
> mountain covered with snow.[99]

There are several other examples of Sacagawea's recognition of
mountains, creeks, and plains in the expedition writings from July 6 to
July 13, 1806, that show that Dye was not exaggerating Sacagawea's
importance. When Dye gained access to the original journals via Thwaites
she may have read Clark's actual journals, which were not filtered through
the Biddle lens. On July 13 Clark wrote, "The indian woman who has
been of great service to me as a pilot through this country recommends a
gap in the mountains more south which I shall cross."[100] Given his remark
it seems disingenuous to criticize Dye for suggesting that Sacagawea led
the explorers through the mountains.

Finally, it is important to note that Dye's text never portrays Sacagawea
as a guide to the entire expedition. Her account follows that of the
expedition writings, and in both Sacagawea is useful for pointing out
landmarks in territory with which she is familiar. Dye wrote later, "I never
heard that any one considered her a guide of the whole expedition or for
an part of it except where she lived as a child. I have often criticized that
expression myself."[101]

If *The Conquest* presents a less exaggerated Sacagawea than critics or
historians suggest, it is true that Dye herself helped to construct the bridge
between the text and the legendary Sacagawea. She did so in interviews,
speeches, and writing after the book was published. Dye protested the
characterization of Sacagawea as savior or guide to the expedition, but
not too loudly, for in the aftermath of its publication *The Conquest* received
favorable publicity, positive reviews, and encomiums from an eager public.
All of this helped to sell books. Advance publicity argued for the book's
strict accuracy and "utmost enthusiasm," explaining to potential readers
that "the fictional form is adopted to lend interest to the telling, but it is
history of the truest and highest and most vital kind, history touched with
imagination."[102] The week before *The Conquest* was published the *Oregonian*

provided excerpts from the book and ran a lengthy story detailing Dye's travels to authenticate her story. They also reminded readers of the popularity and accuracy of *McLoughlin and Old Oregon*.[103]

Once the book was published, the appeal of her book–and Sacagawea– became obvious. Dye noted excitedly, "The Minneapolis papers first took her up, Helena quoted them, and Seattle and other cities, then the Chicago *Inter-Ocean* came out with an editorial in honor of the Pocahontas of the West."[104] The *New York Times* stated, "The story shows uncommon skill on the part of the author, combined with a thorough study of the original narrative."[105] Locally, the *Oregon Historical Quarterly* chose to focus more on Dye's style than the substance of her book. The anonymous reviewer pronounced,

> her spirit as an ardent hero-worshipper, her aptitude for biographical narrative, her keen zest for dramatic and historic conjunctions of time or place, her strongly feminine point of view so rarely applied to chapters of adventure, and above all her intense enthusiasm which fuses remotely related details into an integral whole – these make "The Conquest" a book useful to the student of history.[106]

Dye received many letters of praise, and they provided justification for future mythmaking. Teachers told her their students were reading *The Conquest* in preparation for the St. Louis Exposition. Enthusiasts formed reading circles throughout the Midwest in order to discuss her book. Historians and antiquarians in Ohio, Illinois, Iowa, and Kentucky thought her biography of George Rogers Clark and her history of the "opening of the West" were excellent.[107] Clearly her historical fiction had touched a chord with people who appreciated her heroic and patriotic version of history. It was but a short step from the acceptance of her characters to the legends that would make Sacagawea and Lewis and Clark icons in the American imagination.

As Dye's celebrity status increased she was asked frequently about her decision to write historical fiction. In a speech to the [Portland] Woman's Club Dye explained to her audience why she had written *The Conquest* as a story.

> I knew more people would read it. It would touch a larger public, and really do more toward diffusing a knowledge of the subject than a formal history would. Besides, I see things too

vividly to tie myself down to dead history. Living history is a romance, the people, the people in action is what we want to see. Most histories make me tired.[108]

As the first edition of fifteen thousand flew off the shelves, she must have felt satisfied that in selecting fiction over history she had made the right choice.[109]

Dye's exploration of the lives of Jefferson, George Rogers Clark, William Clark, Meriwether Lewis, and Sacagawea represented an indefatigable effort to create a story that had historical validity. Despite her contention that most histories made her tired, Dye's research speaks to the value that she placed on the historical record. Dye never credited herself with being a historian, and in fact stated that "I have never made investigations purely for historical purposes but for literary uses."[110] However, the historical materials she amassed and subsequently bestowed at the Oregon Historical Society, the energy with which she pursued all inquiries, and the importance she placed on having verifiable evidence to support her fictionalized account attest to her skills as an historical researcher. Early in 1901 she wrote,

> these chronicles of our fathers, how rich they are! How full of venture and endeavor! … Such a blossoming as the world has never known, lies here ungathered. The heroic past, the border warfare, the inveterate foe, and the dauntless hero, stand ready at the beck of the master than can fuse and fashion the immortal epic of a people.[111]

Dye wrote *The Conquest* to celebrate white American achievement and because she believed she had the literary skills and vision to write an epic of empire. Despite the part it would play in her own success, the chronicle of the Lewis and Clark Expedition found within *The Conquest's* pages occupies only one-fourth of the entire text—proof that she envisioned Lewis and Clark's epic journey as just one part of America's larger story of expansion. The book is an unabashed celebration of Frederick Jackson Turner's belief that the study of "successive frontiers … won by a series of Indian wars" explained American development and democracy.[112] And while Turner had white men in mind when he studied the evolution of American society, Dye turned nineteenth-century notions of savagery and civilization on their head by depicting an Indian woman as the humanizing force of the expedition. *The Conquest* transformed the historical Lewis and Clark into cultural heroes and made Sacagawea an American pioneer heroine. Embracing Dye's portrayal of the young woman, the public enthusiastically bought her book and supported her next enterprise, the creation of a Sacagawea monument.

Sacagawea, the Women's Club Movement, and Suffrage Activism

1903-1912

Nestled between the Foreign Exhibits building and the Palace of Agriculture at the 1905 Lewis and Clark Centennial Exposition lay the Sunken Gardens, a beautiful setting filled with gleaming white statuary, fountains, and a "spacious lawn, provid[ing] visitors a relaxing oasis."[1] Proceeding northwest from the main entrance through the Sunken Gardens, visitors could stroll to the Grand Staircase, which overlooked the waterfront of Guild's Lake; in the distance fairgoers could glimpse both Mt. Hood and Mt. St. Helens. The setting was spectacular by all accounts, but a statue draped in the American flag made the scene from the Grand Staircase even more inspiring on July 5, 1905, the day the statue of Sacajawea came to rest at the fair. The unveiling, scheduled for 3 o'clock the following day, was the culmination of two years of organizing and fund-raising activity on the part of Dye and several other Oregon women, especially her friend Sarah Evans. Together they seized an opportunity to celebrate their understanding of pioneer womanhood and turned it into a significant experience in community organizing.

The Sacajawea Statue Association was an offspring of the women's club movement and a bridge between women's cultural and political activities.[2] As such it was an important training ground for women to hone their leadership and organizing skills and carry them into Oregon's fight for woman suffrage after 1906. Dye's book *The Conquest* was the inspiration behind the statue association's effort to memorialize Sacagawea, and the association's project to commemorate "the Woman Pilot" was a turning point for women's participation in the Oregon woman suffrage movement. It transformed the campaign from the one-woman cause of Abigail Scott Duniway to the collective effort of many activist women.[3]

The history of the club movement in Oregon began in the late 1890s, as it did for hundreds of women's clubs throughout the nation. The first Oregon clubs to join the newly created General Federation of Women's Clubs were the Thursday afternoon Club of Pendleton (January 1894), the Neighborhood Club of LaGrande (January 1896), and the Portland Woman's Club (March 1896).[4] Often devoted to literary pursuits, music, and art, these clubs drew in women interested in self-improvement or "culture," as historian Karen Blair has described it.[5] Once formed, the Portland Woman's Club (called simply the Woman's Club until 1920) set the pace for organizing existing clubs into a state federation.

The impetus for forming the Woman's Club came from prominent women in Portland who were inspired by a rousing address given by Mrs. A. H. Stuart, a clubwoman from Olympia, Washington. According to club organizer and suffragist Abigail Scott Duniway, Stuart was not "just" a clubwoman but a "staunch pioneer co-worker in the [Washington] Equal Suffrage Movement." Duniway viewed Stuart's participation in Oregon club work as a "stroke of wise statesmanship," hoping that the formation of a woman's club would facilitate her efforts to secure equal suffrage in Oregon. Duniway planned to use the clubs as a forum for suffrage, commenting that she intended to "break the rules" of order at their meetings and offer "some motion, tending in our direction, from the floor."[6] What she undoubtedly did not anticipate was that club members would set their own agenda and would not necessarily be friendly to ideas about suffrage.

The seventy-eight charter members of the Woman's Club set to work defining their future. Quickly they decided that municipal housekeeping was their domain;[7] the first issue they chose was the creation of a free library in Portland. The women formed a library committee, chaired by Sarah Evans. When they learned that city statutes would not permit taxation for library purposes, and that the state legislature would not permit such a law for one city alone, they ingeniously decided a state federation of women's clubs could work to pass such a law, ultimately helping other cities acquire tax-based libraries.[8] Evans issued a call for a convention of Oregon women's clubs to be held in October 1899, and thirteen clubs enthusiastically responded. In addition to eleven literary or culture clubs, participants included the Portland Teachers' Association and the Portland chapter of the National Council of Jewish Women.[9] The Oregon Federation of Women's Clubs was formed, and joined the General Federation in January 1901. Evans was president of the Woman's Club in

1903 and held the same office in the state federation from 1905 to 1915. In the latter organization's first fifty years, no one but Evans occupied the presidency for as long a term.[10]

Oregon Federation members were, predictably, members of the middle and upper middle classes, who had both the leisure and the income to devote time and energy to such endeavors. They, like their eastern counterparts, had to come to terms with differences within their membership over future goals. Almost immediately tensions arose over the nature of club work, with some members resenting the intrusion of reform activities into their cultural and social pursuits. As was the experience in the General Federation, club members in Oregon were, as a group, late in supporting suffrage. It was not until 1912 and the final suffrage campaign that the Woman's Club, for example, endorsed suffrage.

Leaders in the state federation and in the Woman's Club especially tended to be more interested in reform than their members; most of the leadership supported suffrage from the late 1890s.[11] These women also were committed to a wide variety of causes, including temperance, education, and several organizations devoted to preserving Oregon's pioneer past. Approximately fifteen women in the Portland area served on the executive committees or were presidents of seven of the most influential women's organizations: the Woman's Club, the Oregon Equal Suffrage Association, the Daughters of the American Revolution, the Oregon Federation of Women's Clubs, the Women's Christian Temperance Union, the Willamette Valley Chautauqua Association, and the Sacajawea Statue Association. These organizations were the training grounds for Oregon's suffrage movement.

The ties between suffrage and club work in Oregon can best be illuminated with an examination of the work and lives of several women whose histories are part of the public record. Prominent as writers, speakers, and activists, Sarah Evans and Eva Emery Dye left a historical trail that enables us to uncover their role in Progressive era reform. While Dye is well known as a writer, her important role in political and social change in Oregon has not been explored. In turn, historians have completely neglected Sarah Evans's vital leadership of the club movement and in woman suffrage.[12] Their relationship with one another and with suffragist Duniway illustrates many of the possibilities for cooperation and conflict within women's organizations at the beginning of the twentieth century.

Sarah Ann Shannon was born in 1854 of Pennsylvania Irish ancestry. She grew up in Bedford County and graduated from Lutherville College in 1873. As an adolescent she served as her attorney father's able assistant, frequently discussing political and legal affairs with him.[13] This early influence was probably significant to her later political ambitions and interests. In 1873 she married William Evans, a man whose mining and iron manufacturing business took him to Vancouver, British Columbia, while his wife and their three daughters remained in Portland. Diminutive, with a wry smile that can be seen in photographs from her older years, Evans was a no-nonsense woman who "proved a rock against all arguments once she was convinced she was right."[14] Her correspondence with Dye reveals a fiercely independent woman with a keen mind and a knack for knowing how to get people to do what she wanted.

Abigail Scott Duniway was also a formidable woman, whose personality was shaped by a harrowing Overland Trail journey that left her mother dead and by poverty during her married life. Strong-willed, independent, and a capable writer, Duniway started a suffrage newspaper in 1871 entitled the *New Northwest* that drew from her experiences as a farmer's wife and as a milliner and teacher. From its pages she exhorted women and men to support women's rights in order to "elevate all humanity; to make the world better, purer and happier; to make woman, who is by nature and association the best friend of man, his political equal, and that thereby both may receive the equal benefit of the laws by which both are equally governed."[15] Founder of the Oregon suffrage movement and a leader in women's club activities, Duniway was a personal friend of Susan B. Anthony and among the pioneering generation of suffragists in the Pacific Northwest. Believing the temperance movement to be a divisive detraction from the goal of woman suffrage, she remained anti-prohibition throughout her life. This stance often put her at odds with the younger generation of activists who argued that temperance and suffrage were two sides of the same coin.[16]

Like Duniway, Evans was not an outspoken advocate of temperance, and she was committed to the principles of the Democratic Party at a time when most reformers were Republicans. Caught up in the Progressive reform fever in Oregon, she served as Portland's first market inspector from 1905 to 1930. While other women focused on ending prostitution or encouraged temperance, Evans's main passions were woman suffrage and ameliorating sanitation problems in the city. Portland health officer Dr. Esther Pohl frequently praised the work of market inspector Evans, "particularly her effort in securing the enforcement of the ordinance against spitting on the street, one of the surest ways to spread infection."[17]

Also like Duniway and Dye, Sarah Evans was a woman who did not suffer fools gladly. She often criticized the frivolous pursuits of elite women. On one occasion she angrily noted that the general empty-headedness of women "just make[s] me wild! There are so few who don't put their 'social duties' first, and so few who take things seriously."[18] Evans's leadership in the Woman's Club and in the Oregon Federation of Women's Clubs was part of her plan to use the organizations to further civic reforms she felt were worthy. Unlike others she railed against, she never viewed these organizations as purely a social outlet.

Dye and Evans undoubtedly met in the late 1890s, but they wrote their first letters to one another in 1902, just before Evans took over as president of the Woman's Club. These two women were an unlikely pair. Dye's literary interests were all consuming and any extra energy not used for her writing went into the Willamette Valley Chautauqua Association. She also devoted many hours to public speaking on the value of education and American history. Unlike Evans, Dye was a lifelong supporter of temperance and Republican values. Despite their personal differences and out of respect for each other's drive, determination, and ability to get things done, they forged an important political alliance in 1903. From a history class within the Woman's Club they decided to create a separate association dedicated to memorializing Sacagawea.

The Woman's Club created a number of committees that were designed to increase women's cultural sophistication in the arts, literature, and history. The Oregon history committee began reading Dye's work, *The Conquest*, early in 1903. Her heroine, Sacagawea, captivated the imagination of the clubwomen, and they conceived a plan to recognize Sacagawea's accomplishments at the upcoming Lewis and Clark Centennial Exposition. Three members of the history club subsequently met at the home of Mrs. Charlotte M. Cartwright and gathered enough money to pay for the stationary and postage required to call a "general meeting," which was subsequently held at the Oregon Historical Society. The women at the meeting ratified the plan to create a statue, and six were elected officers of the Sacajawea Statue Association. Members appointed Dye as president and Sarah Evans as secretary. At the meeting Cartwright contributed the first one hundred dollars and dues were set at fifty cents.[19]

The association's officers were a group of women whose family connections or personal activities linked them to the pioneer generation in the West. Dye's depictions of westward migration and her fascination with the heroic pioneer past garnered the respect and admiration of other women. Charlotte Cartwright was a first-generation pioneer whose mother had died shortly after their trek overland in 1845 and whose father had erected the first cabin on the land that would become Portland. She was a charter member of the Woman's Club and prominent in the State Pioneers' Association.[20] Martha Dalton shared similar women's club credentials with Cartwright and also was a first-generation pioneer, having migrated to Corvallis in 1852. Others had prominent relatives associated with the bygone romance of western migration: board members Mrs. E. W. Bingham and Mrs. S. L. M. Farmer were the "daughter of Isaac Stevens, Washington's first governor" and the "granddaughter of George Shannon, who accompanied Lewis and Clark to the Coast," respectively. Representing the wealthiest Portland residents was Mrs. J. B. Montgomery, state regent for the Daughters of the American Revolution, founding member of the Society of Colonial Dames, and wife of railroad magnet James Montgomery. She was also on the Board of Lady Managers for the St. Louis Exposition (1904).[21]

At the same time, Dye founded the Woman's Club of the Lewis and Clark Exposition to promote the exposition generally. Its membership was indistinguishable from the statue association, and the two merged in September 1904, becoming the Oregon City Woman's Club. The Woman's Club of the Lewis and Clark Exposition brought in members whose interests extended beyond the statue festivities and included those who wanted club programs in literature, history, and art. In May 1903 the club entertained William Hancock Clark, grandson of William Clark, who came to Oregon City as a guest of the Dyes to promote the exposition.[22]

Dye's idea to memorialize Sacagawea encouraged related efforts in historic preservation. John McLoughlin's home in Oregon City was sold in 1867 after his daughter and son-in-law relocated to Portland. It became the Phoenix Hotel and gradually fell into disrepair. Eventually known as a place of ill-repute, the home's original stately appearance diminished as Oregon City's mills grew up around it. The story of its dramatic move up Singer Hill to the City Park in 1909 and subsequent restoration has been well told by others, but the importance of the Woman's Club of the Lewis and Clark Exposition to its history has not.[23] Dye's *McLoughlin and Old Oregon* stirred interest in the old home and club members believed "the owners might donate the building for library use if the Woman's Club was able to raise money to have [it] repaired and outfitted." Their efforts began in the autumn of 1903 along with the Sacajawea statue project but even "wholehearted support by many leading citizens" could not overcome the difficulties of raising the necessary funds.[24]

Club women's efforts failed initially but were revived by Dye in 1908 when it appeared the house was destined for certain destruction. She and her husband—and many friends, in particular E. G. and Charles Caufield— founded the McLoughlin Memorial Association in 1909 and helped to raise the money needed to move and restore the home. Today McLoughlin House is a museum and a National Historic Site. The museum honors Dye's contributions to Oregon history with a dedication and displays of photographs and her writings.[25]

While Dye worked to generate interest in the McLoughlin house and the exposition, Evans became the organizational presence behind the Sacajawea Statue Association. Although Evans appears to have consulted her colleague about literally everything that pertained to their endeavor, her active role as secretary made their success possible. This tireless energy for details along with her many connections to other prominent Portland women made her a formidable ally or enemy for anyone involved in local politics. Beginning in October 1903, Evans also exhibited her talents as editor of a column called the "Woman's Page" (to distinguish it from the "Society Page") in the *Oregon Journal*. Throughout the next decade clubwomen in Portland turned to her page in the Saturday evening paper when they wanted substantive news on women's issues. Unlike most secretaries, Evans was never shy about taking credit for her efforts; in fact in much of the coverage of the Sacajawea Association's work it is hard to find anyone else's contributions acknowledged.

From the outset of their activities, the Sacajawea Statue Association's members made it clear they intended to celebrate pioneer motherhood, so board members' pioneer connections were important to the association's overall success. In their fund-raising efforts members could draw on the substantial nostalgia and respect that many Northwest residents had for the pioneer generation and for the pioneering spirit. In its appeal to donors, the association acknowledged the importance of the image they were creating: "It would be a beautiful and touching tribute for the women of today to pay, not alone to Sacajawea, but to the pioneer mother and to womenhood" [sic].[26] Sacagawea's participation in the expedition provided a story to which many women could relate. As first-generation immigrants themselves, or as women who had grown up hearing the stories of their parents and grandparents, Northwest women could sympathize with the tale of a young mother on a perilous journey.

Claiming they were recognizing the efforts of all pioneer women, the statue association only acknowledged Sacagawea's race as a helpful factor in "opening the West." Thus Dye noted, "What Sacajawea did, many Indian women, did, in succession, becoming the wives of trappers and traders, revealing the secrets of their country and giving over its trade and resources to the whites, opening the way to higher civilization."[27] Alternatively, Dye and her colleagues ignored her race altogether by celebrating her femaleness rather than her Indianness.[28] Dye's portrayal of Sacagawea in *The Conquest* relied on domestic imagery to create a heroine with whom women could empathize, and as Paula Baker has argued, motherhood and womanhood were "powerful integrating forces" that often cut across class and racial lines.[29] Women's shared experience of motherhood allowed Dye to claim that Sacagawea represented all women who had trekked westward with their husbands and children in the nineteenth century.

The Sacajawea Statue Association invited women to participate in a cause that was wholly woman identified, and women leaders in the organization were successful in promoting the idea that a positive outcome for their endeavor rested on women's shoulders. The association was governed entirely by women, and they ran a highly efficient political machine. Dye and Secretary Evans canvassed the state of Oregon for donations via letters and personal appearances. The association offered prizes for the first and largest donations from women's clubs, and Evans sent hundreds of letters publicizing Sacagawea and soliciting donations from all over the country, and to women in England, Cuba, Puerto Rico, Alaska, and the Philippines. Clubwomen, suffragists, and temperance activists all donated money toward an ideal cast in bronze. Also crucial was the association's decision to enlist a young woman, Alice Cooper of Denver, to sculpt the statue. Cooper was a student of famed Chicago sculptor Lorado Taft. Finally, Viola Coe, noted Portland physician and suffragist, and her husband Dr. Henry Waldo Coe donated twenty tons of copper for the statue from the St. Helens's mines.[30]

Although women led the statue association and solicited other women for donations, Dye and Evans quickly discovered that without the assistance of businessmen in Portland they could not be successful. Men provided necessary money and connections, and their support helped create legitimacy for the statue effort. The lessons learned in fund-raising and networking among men's and women's organizations served Dye and Evans well in the future.

Prominent men in Oregon and throughout the country assisted the statue association through their monetary and public support. The Improved Order of Red Men (IORM), a national, white, fraternal organization that held "noble" Indians like Sacagawea and Pocahontas in high esteem, proved to be of inestimable help in raising money for the statue and provided free publicity for the statue unveiling. The IORM also cancelled its own scheduled day at the Lewis and Clark Exposition in order to work jointly with the statue association at the fair on July 6.[31]

The IORM had a subordinate women's auxiliary, the Ladies of the Degree of Pocahontas. Evans was informed that the statue association need not send letters requesting donations to the Ladies "because they are under direct control of the Red Men," and would presumably do the IORM's bidding.[32] Thus the cooperation of the IORM meant the cooperation of their women's auxiliary; however, it could have easily gone the other way. An unwillingness to participate on the part of the IORM could have meant the loss of an opportunity to involve the Ladies of Pocahontas, thus severing ties with women rather than augmenting them.[33]

At the same time that Dye and Evans were soliciting the help of the IORM they were also forging ties with the Portland Commercial Club. Organized in 1893 to promote "the upbuilding of the State of Oregon and the Pacific Northwest" the Portland Commercial Club invited into membership men who were leaders in business and civic life.[34] In June 1904, when it became clear that fifty-cent donations would not begin to meet the statue association's financial needs, Evans met with Tom Richardson, the full-time publicity manager of the Commercial Club. He had never heard of Sacagawea but promised his enthusiastic help. Evans slyly commented, "He's the best card we have drawn yet. I have a little influence there that it would take too long to explain."[35] Whatever influence she had paid off beyond her expectations, for Richardson introduced the statue concept to Theodore Wilcox, president of the Portland Flouring Mills and chairman of the executive committee for the Commercial Club.

An introduction to Wilcox was a political coup for the statue association. It gave them an audience with some of the most influential and wealthy men in Portland. Before Richardson agreed to help, Evans had written to Dye that association members had discussed a campaign plan to canvass Portland for donations. The campaign would be launched by first approaching someone for a five-hundred-dollar contribution. "If we get it, it assures large donations from others and we want to get his name first. If we start in with a small donation that is the kind we will get all through," thus illustrating that she had learned an important fund-raising principle.[36] As it turns out, the man they had in mind was Theodore Wilcox.

Meetings with Wilcox produced positive results. On September 7, Evans reported that she had just returned from an interview with the Commercial Club leader: "The whole thing in a nut shell is the *statue is to be built and paid for and what we can't raise they will for us.*"[37] Wilcox believed "there are certain things in a city that always have to be done," and if the statue association was unable to raise the funds themselves then "a few people with means must step in and do them."[38] In a curious twist, though, he wanted the money to be credited to the wives of Commercial Club members, not the men. He said that "when the time comes that the deficiency can be approximated ... Mrs. Wilcox will be one to give you a generous donation, and I will give you the names of men *whose wives* will make up the balance."[39] [Emphasis hers]

Wilcox's enthusiastic support and his inclination to let the wives of businessmen take credit for the statue's success can best be explained with reference to the history of voluntary associations and to women's sphere at the turn of the twentieth century. Other than in overtly political causes such as suffrage and prohibition, women's roles were perceived to be privately oriented and therefore apolitical. Although many women participated in activities that blurred the distinction between the private and public spheres, most women and men viewed women's voluntary associations as appropriate extensions of women's domestic roles.[40] Thus, as Paula Baker has stated, "women's moral nature gave them a reason for public action, and, since they did not have the vote, such action was considered 'above' politics." Since men saw no reason to find women's activities threatening, "women reformers not only drew little visible opposition from men but often received male financial support."[41] Commercial Club members undoubtedly believed that the endeavor to create a statue was purely a cultural effort; that the statue was linked to the recognition of women's pioneer and female roles and rooted in domesticity; and that their wives' participation in such an event enhanced their own social status.

The self-interest of those involved in the fund-raising was an important aspect. As Sara M. Evans has argued, voluntary associations function well precisely because of the self-interest of their members.[42] Having the wives of wealthy men participate enabled the executive committee to maintain their claim that the money was raised by women and also gave elite women in the community prominence. Wilcox's plan was foreshadowed in October

1903 when Evans wrote to Dye that they needed some reward for women's participation and donations. "Outward glories," such as drawing the cord for the unveiling "might induce some rich man to give a big sum if he thought his wife would be it."[43] The history of men's participation in the fund-raising was never known to anyone outside the statue association.[44]

The support of the Commercial Club and the IORM were clearly invaluable to the statue association, but their actual monetary contributions can only be estimated—no account books survive. On the day of the unveiling the *Oregon Journal* ironically trumpeted "But the fund! There is where the real history begins! How was it raised?" The newspaper reported that most of the money had come in very small increments, and approximately two thousand dollars of the total seven thousand dollars had been raised from donations of one to twenty-five dollars. The newspaper also reported that the largest contribution had been two hundred dollars. Perhaps more important than the money raised from Theodore Wilcox was the valuable lesson Evans learned from him. In the psychology of fund-raising he told her never to plead for money. He firmly told her, "You don't want to *beg* this money. We'll make them think its a privilege to give it without asking."[45]

The association's leadership also developed skills in networking and lobbying that ultimately kept Dye and Evans from losing control over the statue concept. From 1903 to 1905 the association worked without the endorsement of the Lewis and Clark Exposition and outside the bounds of its authority because of the Fair Commission's decision early on that "no separate exhibit of women's work" would be implemented. According to them, "women … are placed on the same plane with men as competitors in every line – artistic, educational, industrial and economic."[46]

While the Fair Commission boasted of its egalitarian decision to put women on an equal footing with men, it is clear that women were represented in stereotypical fashion or not at all. For example, out of the hundreds of paintings and sculptures that adorned the art exhibit only five (including the Sacajawea statue) were done by women. Other women had prominence as restaurateurs, where their talents in domestic economy could be highlighted; one "mining queen," would be present "offer[ing] specimens of ore from her claims," and "there will be the charming souvenir girl, the candy girl, the grape juice girl and many others who have charge of selling booths, and who will alluringly tempt one to buy their wares."[47] Unlike the 1893 World Columbian Exposition in Chicago, where women's professional, industrial, and artistic works had been displayed on a separate but equal basis with men's, it was evident that women's achievements would be underrepresented at the Lewis and Clark Centennial Exposition.[48]

Because the Sacajawea statue would be one of the few pieces of women's art publicly displayed and celebrated, the statue association could not afford to take lightly the need to be taken seriously by the Fair Commission. The organization had to be the one that people identified with the Sacajawea statue in order to raise money successfully and publicize the unveiling. Two examples demonstrate the difficulties the association faced prior to the commission's endorsement of its work. The first threat to the association's autonomy came from one of Dye's friends, Edyth Weatherred, who borrowed Dye's motto for the association, "A Woman Led the Deed," for her own projects. Short of copyrighting their slogan, Dye and Evans discovered that they could not prevent other people from making use of their concepts.[49] Weatherred also left Evans stranded in Pennsylvania on their way to meet with sculptor Lorado Taft in Chicago. She traveled on without Evans and provided Taft with her own ideas for a statue. He was not able to undertake the project himself but suggested that one of his students, Alice Cooper, would be a good choice. Ultimately Weatherred and the first wife of renowned poet C. E. S. Wood sold statuettes of Sacagawea for their own financial gain.[50]

Second, a Portland sculptor named Barrett proposed to the Fair Commission in 1903 a stone fountain of Sacagawea for the exposition, an idea that had originally come from Dye. When Barrett's fountain design appeared in December, Evans wrote angrily, "I consider the whole thing a stolen design from us." She astutely noted that no one would be willing to support two statues and argued that the Sacajawea Statue Association ought to protest loudly to the Fair Commission. "If they have any money to give for a permanent monument—we are entitled to it," she wrote. If the Fair Commission let Barrett's design go forward, she asserted, "it will be just another setting down on the women."[51] Evans and Dye were upset for another reason. Barrett's conception represented an entirely different Sacagawea than that proposed by the association. In February 1904, visitors to Woodard and Clark's department store in downtown Portland could see his clay model. As Evans described it, "*It's a fright* … The figures are nude – sure a '*fig leaf*' and the figure on the horse is sitting side ways with her *naked legs crossed.*"[52] Clearly this was not at all what the statue association had in mind for its appreciation of pioneer womanhood. What disturbed Evans the most was the suggestion that Barrett's design was in fact their idea. She was "sick over the hideous thing for 99 out of 100 think it *ours*, I know it for I've stood around and listened to what is said."[53]

The threat to the statue association's ideal pioneer woman galvanized its members and led them to increase pressure on their constituents to contribute time and money to the cause; thus the crisis ultimately had a positive effect. Their efforts in 1904 to solicit large contributions from the IORM and the Portland Commercial Club reflected an urgency born of their fears of failure. Once they forged alliances with prominent Portland businessmen, Barrett's plans vanished, and the statue association received official recognition from the Fair Commission.

Two years after their efforts had begun, Dye and Evans finally reaped the fruit of their labors with the unveiling of the Sacajawea statue on July 6, 1905. Earlier in the year the statue association had decided to share the glory of the unveiling with the National American Woman Suffrage Association (NAWSA). As the NAWSA leaders planned their annual meeting they were invited to come to Oregon by Fair Commission chairman Jefferson Meyers and his suffragist wife, Dr. Annice Jeffreys Meyers. National suffragists were hoping that Oregon would be the next state to adopt woman suffrage in an upcoming (1906) referendum, so it was with much enthusiasm that the NAWSA arrived in Portland.[54]

The NAWSA convention ran from June 28 to July 5 in Portland's First Congregational Church, with the Sacajawea statue unveiling scheduled as their culminating activity on July 6. Suffragists made much of the connection between Sacagawea and votes for women. Sarah Evans, from her "Woman's Page" in the *Oregon Journal*, made explicit reference to this link on July 2.

> As Sacajawea welcomed with intelligent appreciation the
> civilization of the white men [so] should the women of
> Portland welcome the intelligent presentation of the higher
> ideals of right government these women have brought to them
> across the "shining mountains"[55]

The morning of July 6 a parade led by a platoon of police and national delegates from the IORM left the intersection of Fourth and Jefferson streets in downtown Portland and meandered its way through the business district. Following the fraternal organization were the exposition band; a float of Sacagawea pointing westward to Oregon country; delegations of citizens from Washington, Idaho, and Montana; a float depicting the Boston Tea Party (with a reminder: "But first of all the teapot bubbled");

local delegates of the IORM; carriages of well-dressed members of the Sacajawea Statue Association and wives of the IORM; and one more float, of George Washington crossing the Delaware. Finally, cadets from Chemawa Indian School in Salem marked the end of the parade.[56] The procession stretched nearly a mile and was flanked on both sides by a large and enthusiastic crowd cheering raucously when the floats passed by. At the exposition grounds the crowd swelled into the thousands as the time for the unveiling drew near. The *Oregon Journal* described the scene as "profoundly patriotic," a sentiment echoed in the many speeches that accompanied the lifting of the flag from the statue.[57]

At the unveiling all of the women most visible in the NAWSA and in the Oregon Equal Suffrage Association were present, and Susan B. Anthony, Abigail Scott Duniway, and Dye gave speeches. Anthony noted that Sacagawea's contribution to the expedition was a "patriotic duty" and "that if it were not for that brave little Indian mother, there would be no Oregon or Portland."[58] Duniway devoted her entire speech to "Pioneer Mothers" and echoed the ideas that without women the West never would have been settled. She made a radical claim for pioneer womanhood, arguing that without their civilizing influence men would have failed. "Sacajawea remain[s] as a historic reminder of a vanished era, when woman carried man on her shoulders – a feminine atlas." Finally, Dye's presentation speech demonstrated how powerful and political the image of pioneer womanhood could be.

> With women and wagons, Oregon was taken. Indians expected to see an army with banners when the white man came, but no, the mother and child took Oregon … And Sacajawea led them all, the dark-eyed princess of the native race, the child of Asia, beckoned the white man on, toward her ancient home in the Orient.[59]

Dye's suggestion that "the mother and child took Oregon" provided women with a positive and persuasive rendition of true womanhood.[60] Based on the belief that pioneer women were the creators of culture in the West, suffragists argued that women had an important claim to citizenship and equal rights. Suffragists' language at the unveiling reminded the sons of pioneers that, without women, the Pacific Northwest would be "uncivilized." Thus women's contribution to western settlement entitled them to the vote. Standing next to a cultural icon of pioneer motherhood draped in the flag, women made an unforgettable connection between women's domestic and cultural sphere and the public world of politics.

Many observers of the event and the NAWSA leaders remembered July 6 as the highlight of the conference.[61] The presentation of Sacagawea as the ultimate representation of pioneer motherhood was part of the suffrage movement's preoccupation with "civic housekeeping" and the good that women, especially through their maternal influence, would do in the public sphere once they attained the vote. Reminiscent of the themes of Republican Motherhood, the promotion of Sacagawea-as-mother struck a nerve with many women; like Dye and Evans many women believed that their maternal role would naturally lead women into the political and public sphere.[62] Evans provided a telling conclusion to these festivities that linked suffrage with motherhood and fused pioneer motherhood with patriotic citizenship.

> The picture will never fade from the memory of those who saw Miss Anthony and Dr. Shaw standing on the platform with the sun lighting up their silver hair like an aureole and their faces radiant with hope, as "The Star Spangled Banner" sung by an Indian boy raised a tumult of applause while the flag floated away revealing the idealized mother and babe.[63]

The Sacajawea Statue Association began as an effort to memorialize one woman and evolved into an important avenue for training its members in community organizing. Association members learned how to lobby the business community, raise money, and promote their ideas. Dye and Evans benefited especially, honing their leadership and networking skills and becoming well known as supporters of women's equal rights. For the executive board in particular, the events of 1905 were the catalyst that brought them fully into the political sphere. The association functioned as a bridge between the private sphere of women's cultural activities and the public politics of suffrage. It stands as a small but important representative of the alliances among Oregon women that extended throughout the club movement and into suffrage activism.

For Dye, joining the cultural with the political gave her a voice to express a long-felt frustration in her writing. Always walking a fine line between history and fiction in her works, she found a new way to understand this dichotomy after 1905. Her later works reflected the belief that those who called her work fiction did so because they objected to the presence of women in her books. In a speech to the Daughters of the American Revolution in 1906 she offered a radical critique of traditional history and historians.

the public demands women as well as men in its history. My books are true histories, but because women are in them the old style historians must needs class them as novels. Very well, call them novels, it is certainly novel to give woman any special mention now when the muster rolls of the pioneers said only "Mr. So-and-so and family." The names of the wives are lost and forgotten.[64]

Her effort to memorialize Sacagawea in *The Conquest* and at the exposition became symbolic of a larger effort to legitimate the history of women and provide recognition for their deeds along with men. The statue association's slogan "A Woman Led the Deed" was also a unifying motto that connected her historical romances to women's history and woman suffrage.

The years from 1900 to 1906 were the heyday of cooperation among women's associations dedicated to both cultural pursuits and reform. Woman suffrage had gone down to defeat in Oregon in 1884 and 1900; the movement had remained almost dormant after that. Consequently, relationships among women flourished in an atmosphere that was not overtly political. The depth of the ties forged in this intense period can be seen in the growing friendship between Dye and Abigail Scott Duniway and in the alliances created when suffrage was again put on the ballot.[65]

Duniway and Dye probably met shortly after the latter's arrival in Oregon City in 1890, but it was not until 1896 that their mutual interest in woman suffrage brought them together as friends and allies. In June of that year, Susan B. Anthony arrived in Oregon as the keynote speaker for the Congress of Women, an event organized by Anthony and Duniway to encourage more active participation of Oregon women in the suffrage movement. The meeting coincided with the reinvigoration of the Oregon Equal Suffrage Association (OESA)[66] and with Dye's appointment as Clackamas County Chair of the OESA, a position she held until suffrage victory in 1912. Dye also brought national suffrage leader Anna Howard Shaw to speak at the Chautauqua festivities in 1896 and 1898, and Duniway participated in these events as well.[67]

Duniway's biographers have never commented on a series of letters to Dye from Duniway in 1904 and 1905; this is surprising given the striking picture of their friendship the letters portray. Duniway was a woman who produced strong reactions in people–usually negative–but she appeared warm and loving in her letters to Dye. This correspondence developed in reference to their common bond as writers–Dye had recently published *The Conquest* and was working on *McDonald of Oregon* (1906), while Duniway had just finished *From the West to the West* (1905). Duniway urged Dye to write a candid review of her book, modestly claiming that "it makes no pretension to anything but *originality* and is therefore strictly web-foot-ish. I hope you didn't expect too much" [emphasis hers].[68] Dye apparently obliged with her review and predicted that Duniway would have "tremendous success."[69] Duniway believed that Dye was a better writer, and deferring to her friend's talents, she wrote,

> Now, Dearie: busy as you are, and faithful historian as you
> must be, just lie down of afternoons in your wrapper or
> lounging robe, and read my story carefully. Then go to work, as
> I know you can, and write a better one. Give your imagination
> rein and your historical knowledge of the times you depict the
> whip and the spur.[70]

Duniway's letters are signed, "lovingly yours," "lovingly," or "lovingly and cordially," closing phrases rarely used in her correspondence either to friends or family members. Dye reciprocated her affection.

Dye's emerging friendship with Duniway illustrates the cooperative ties among women's associations in the early years. An examination of the executive board of the OESA from 1900 to 1912 also reveals the depths of those connections. In addition to the bonds between members of the Sacajawea Statue Association and the OESA, Mrs. W. H. Games, recording secretary of the OESA from 1900 to 1904, was the 1902 treasurer of the Woman's Club; Lucia Fox Additon, one-time state Women's Christian Temperance Union president, was on the 1906 OESA campaign committee; and Mrs. Frederick Eggert, president of the [Portland] Woman's Club from 1907 to 1908, was the 1905 auditor for the OESA.[71] The ties that bound these women together from 1900 to 1906 enabled them to forge new alliances that contributed to suffrage victory in 1912.

After the narrow defeat of a suffrage amendment in 1900, the OESA took the next six years to regroup. During this period Oregon's Initiative and Referendum law passed, making it much easier to put the issue of suffrage before the voters.[72] The coincidence of the Lewis and Clark Exposition, the completion of the Sacajawea Statue, and the annual meeting of the NAWSA in Portland made 1906 seem an auspicious time for launching another effort for Oregon equal suffrage.

After the statue celebrations, with enthusiasm running high, the NAWSA pledged monetary support for a new campaign as well as organizing assistance from national board members Mary Chase and Gail Laughlin. The OESA elected a special campaign committee: Viola Coe, a long-time friend and supporter of Duniway's, was elected to the presidency, and Duniway accepted a position as honorary president. Coe, along with her husband Henry, had donated the copper needed for the statue of Sacagawea, becoming friends along the way with Dye and Evans. The Coes were very well connected to Portland's elite and to the women who held leadership roles in all of the local organizations.

Vice president of the OESA was Dr. Annice Jeffreys Meyers, a well-respected physician and married to the president of the Lewis and Clark Exposition committee. Duniway credited Dr. Jeffreys (who was often called by this name even after her marriage) with "securing the start of our movement through the legislative straits of 1895," and in recognition of her long and dedicated service she was elected auditor to the national convention in 1905.[73] Unfortunately she was taken ill after the 1906 campaign and died shortly thereafter.

Duniway resented the influence of the national leadership on the new OESA executive committee. Despite the fact that three of its seven members were long-time supporters of hers (Coe, Meyers, and Martha Dalton), Duniway commented acidly that "the new administration, chosen in 1905, under direction of our National officers, ignored all the previous work and workers of thirty-four strenuous years."[74] Her disparaging remarks were a harbinger of future conflict.

Unlike Duniway, Evans welcomed the participation of the national suffrage organization in the upcoming 1906 election. As Evans wrote in the *History of Woman Suffrage*, "The national suffrage convention gave to the cause in Oregon a new birth."[75] The efficiency and prestige that the national organization brought to the state impressed Evans, who immediately struck up a friendship with NAWSA President Anna Howard Shaw. Dye also respected and liked Shaw and hosted her at her home on several occasions. Unfortunately Duniway loathed the NAWSA president, which contributed to tensions between leaders in the state and national organizations.[76]

Suffrage was defeated again in 1906, this time by 10,178 votes out of 83,338 cast, in spite of the monetary and organizing support from the

NAWSA.[77] Duniway, in fact, would claim that it was defeated precisely because of the meddling of the national organization and because of the active participation of the Women's Christian Temperance Union (WCTU). The "liquor interest" had come out strongly against suffrage, and many attributed the defeat to intense efforts by anti-prohibition factions in Portland. Others, however, attributed the loss to the lack of cohesion within the OESA itself. Duniway later admitted that she did little if anything to promote the alliance of the national and state organizations, believing that the national leaders did not understand the local political atmosphere and would only stir up the liquor industry by their visible presence.[78]

The debate over who was at fault caused a rift between suffragists that persisted to 1912. The split developed into a chasm during the summer of 1906. Duniway led the attack on August 7, claiming that

> Local White Ribboners, some of them of National reputation
> as prohibitionists, became the field workers of the suffrage
> campaign, and the state president of the WCTU proclaimed
> from the platform of a great suffrage conference that her
> propaganda of prohibition and the aim of the Equal Suffrage
> Association were one.[79]

The president of the state WCTU, Ada Wallace Unruh, was not going to be outdone by Duniway. Wounded but still proud, she shot back on August 19.

> We are indignant at the continual and petty thrusts at our
> organization through Mrs. Duniway, but we are a lot of
> sensible women and, knowing that she does not represent the
> real equal suffrage movement in Oregon and that the WCTU is
> too large for her to inspire, we shall smilingly pursue our way.[80]

In an effort to diffuse the volatile situation and the personal attacks that resulted, Dye contributed her own thoughts on the comments that were exchanged in the *Oregonian*. She opened with an apology for her friend. "It is with regret that I have noted the recent attack on the WCTU. The true leader conserves every force and harmonizes them." She noted that everyone "recognize[s] the splendid pioneer work of Mrs. Duniway, a woman who has stood for a certain principle through days of unpopularity and days of recognition," but that people should not "take too seriously the final flashes of a spirit that has long been accustomed to battle." Dye said instead that people should see Duniway's "tempestuous" temperament as a sign that she was simply impatient to achieve suffrage victory before "answering the summons to a wider hereafter." Dye also astutely noted that "suffrage work in Oregon is now in younger hands, trained in newer and more conservative methods, and averse to the 'hammer and tongs' of yesterday."[81] Dye understood what many historians have failed to recognize–that Oregon's suffrage movement in the twentieth century involved many women and many voices, not just Duniway's. Although she had pioneered the cause in the nineteenth century, Duniway found herself competing with other women for power and authority in the twentieth.

Dye's efforts to mediate the conflict failed. An incensed Duniway wrote Dye in a patronizing tone, commenting that her friend "evidently need[ed] instruction" about the way in which prohibition forces were "scuttling her ship."[82] The opposing camps continued to argue amongst themselves for months until the November election of new state officers. But Dye's even-tempered nature and desire to harmonize these forces did not go unnoticed. Caroline Dunlap, founder of Portland's first kindergarten and a respected civic leader, wrote to Dye in October to request that she stand for election to the OESA's executive board. Dunlap wrote that she believed a new direction in leadership was needed to preserve "our beloved course of Equal Suffrage." Dunlap claimed that a number of women felt Dye's wisdom and "agreeable" nature would be helpful, that Dye could in fact "rescue" Oregon women, "and help us out of the petty contentions that are likely to swamp us."[83]

Also in October, Duniway held out a carrot, or perhaps it was a stick, to those who might be thinking of altering the leadership of the OESA. In a letter to Dye, she slyly mentioned, "[I] am creating an Editorial Advisory Board for the Suffrage Movement; also a Cooperative Board of the *very leading* men and their wives of Oregon, which will aid the next campaign if I am chosen President. Mr. and Mrs. Dye are to be chosen on cooperative Board for Clackamas [County]; also others."[84] What Dye made of this plan is unknown, but in the newspaper coverage of the state convention in November, there was no mention of either Dye or Evans. Out of personal loyalty to Duniway, or perhaps because of other priorities and recent ill health, Dye's response to Dunlap appears to have been in the negative. It is impossible to ascertain from the press coverage of the event whether Dye was even present at the convention. Similarly Evans, who would be such a vocal opponent to Duniway in the 1912 election, was not mentioned in the proceedings of the highly contentious OESA meeting.[85]

Duniway's political skills and determination enabled her to wrest power from her opponents at the convention. She was reelected president and the executive committee that emerged out of the conflict consisted of personal friends and long-time supporters. She in fact refused the participation of anyone on the board who she believed would exhibit contrary views on any subject.

In the next two elections, 1908 and 1910, the NAWSA stayed away and even refused to support the state organization financially because of Duniway's reelection to the presidency. In a letter to Dye, national president Shaw wrote that she "consider[ed] the election of Mrs. Duneway [sic] to the presidency the greatest disaster that has befallen the state for many years." She believed that woman suffrage had not been defeated at the polls in 1906, "but by the women themselves in their State Convention this fall." There is some indication from this letter that Dye had contemplated a more visible presence in the local organization and that, like Evans, she had been offered the support of the national association in this undertaking. Shaw concluded with the realization that "for a person whose health is so precarious as is yours at present time to undertake to deal with such a woman as Mrs. Duneway is a very great task and I don't wonder you shrink from it."[86] Ultimately, however, Dye chose to remain by Duniway's side. Evans, on the other hand, quietly accepted funding from Shaw to further the cause of suffrage from within the Woman's Club.

The 1908 and 1910 suffrage campaigns were extremely peaceful affairs compared with the boisterous one of 1906. Duniway believed it was time again to reassert the "still hunt" approach, whereby newspaper editorials and private correspondence would substitute for mass meetings and public addresses.[87] Feeling burned by the "liquor interests," Duniway's suffragists were eager to keep a low profile. Her executive committee certainly shared this perspective. Duniway wrote to Dye in April 1908, just two months before the election:

> Your feeling that we should keep still, so far as the papers are concerned has been shared by all of us up to the time of circulating the Voters' Pamphlet by the secretary of state, which brought our amendment into the limelight … like you, I think it best to avoid stirring them up when they are armed with ballots and we are not.[88]

Duniway also did not have the national committee's money or personnel to work with, which suited her purposes. Unfortunately, the election results did not support her view that the meddling of the national had been solely to blame for earlier suffrage defeats. Woman suffrage lost by 8,174 votes in 1908, which was a huge margin considering that only 23,950 people voted on the measure.[89] It was certainly not a vindication of Duniway's approach.

In 1910 suffragists chose a different tactic, attempting to pass a limited suffrage amendment that read: "No citizen who is a tax-payer shall be denied the elective franchise on account of sex."[90] Campaign strategy again revolved around the still hunt, without public rallies or addresses. Many citizens were puzzled by the measure, wondering if men who were not taxpayers would be denied the right to vote if the measure passed. The WCTU felt the wording of the measure was confusing and refused to endorse it.[91] Others were preoccupied with the issue of prohibition that was also before the voters and took little time to consider the suffrage measure. The defeat was even more substantial than in previous years, though suffragists, especially Duniway, appeared undaunted.[92]

During this time, Dye's efforts to mediate between the WCTU and Duniway and to remain neutral in the increasingly tense relationship between state and national suffrage leaders drew the respect of many at the NAWSA. Her excellent oratorical skills, even-tempered nature, and grasp of women's history brought an invitation to speak at the NAWSA convention held in conjunction with the 1909 Alaska-Yukon-Pacific Exposition in Seattle. Her speech, entitled "Women in Civic Life," highlighted thirty-eight spheres of influence where women had made a difference in politics, culture, and education. It was one of the keynote addresses at the conference and demonstrated a political awareness born of her literary pursuits. "I sometimes think I should like to write a Bible story with deeds and characters taken from American history, proving that today, as long ago, God lives and moves and has his being in our midst, directing human affairs. And in that story women would have an equal part," she said. Women's rights would bring greater cooperation in society, she argued, and would secure the "gift of human welfare." She ended her address with the idea that women were on a vital quest–equality was "the Holy Grail … [a] mysterious elusive thing" that women sought and that would change human history once it was found.[93]

In Oregon, the search for the Holy Grail continued. Conditions finally changed in 1912, creating a more favorable climate for what would be the final vote on Oregon woman suffrage. Washington (1910) and California (1911) had recently granted suffrage, and nothing dire had happened to either women's sphere or to the political climate, thus taking some of the wind out of the sails of the anti-suffrage argument. Also, Harvey Scott, anti-suffrage brother of Duniway and long-time editor of the *Oregonian*, had died in 1910, thus removing a substantial figure in the opposition press.[94]

Crucial as well were the feelings of women like Sarah Evans, who was not about to let another opportunity for equal suffrage escape her grasp. In her account of the last campaign in the *History of Woman Suffrage* she wrote that after 1910 "women of the State now grew restive and began to agitate for organization for the coming campaign." Apparently during the summer of 1911 many women were urging Duniway to begin a new campaign, but she resisted. In December, Anna Howard Shaw wrote "a very strong letter" to Oregon women "severely criticizing their apathy and lack of preparation for this campaign." Unknown to them, however, Duniway had already planned to launch the campaign in January 1912.[95] By the time she was ready to do so, clubwomen had given up in disgust and vowed to begin their own work on behalf of suffrage. Thus Evans wrote, "Dr. Shaw's letter was submitted to the Woman's Club, an organization which up to this time had taken no active part in work for suffrage. Now a motion prevailed to enter into the campaign."[96] In the midst of these misunderstandings and Duniway's desire to maintain her control of the suffrage movement, the OESA and the Woman's Club both launched campaigns.

The Woman's Club suffrage effort was spearheaded by Sarah Evans, with able assistance provided by several other prominent club members, including Dr. Esther Pohl Lovejoy, head of the Portland City Health Bureau, noted physician, author of the first milk ordinance to pass the city council, and supervisor of market inspector Evans. Also on the committee was Elizabeth Avery Eggert, a physician and long-time member of the Woman's Club who had been a member of the OESA's 1905 campaign committee.[97] According to Evans, this group approached Duniway with a plan to organize all of the clubwomen and suffragists into one body with a central headquarters, the Woman's Club offering to assume the financial responsibility. Duniway turned down the offer, "and the committee and all other groups were compelled to work independently of the State organization."[98]

The rancor with which these two organizations faced each other has been described in Ruth Barnes Moynihan's biography of Duniway, but what has not been presented is the perspective of the Woman's Club and the important role it played in putting suffrage over the top in November 1912. Moynihan attributed success to the "well-organized precinct work" and rallies held by the OESA and the College Women's Club (under the direction of Duniway's friend Dr. Marie Equi). She also mentioned the first "prize-winning Rose Festival Parade float" and the fact that Duniway's recent illness and "long years of dedication" made the public feel sentimental toward the suffrage cause.[99] Missing from her analysis and from Duniway's autobiography is any serious mention of the countless hours of work done by the Woman's Club's suffrage committee and the women they inspired to participate.

Dye's voice was silent in the last contentious battle. She maintained the chairmanship of the OESA in Clackamas County but it is difficult to discern if she played a more active role. She occupied an awkward position between two women she respected and admired and between competing ideologies. As a long-time temperance supporter, Dye believed that the vote would assist women in closing down the liquor interests, an opinion to which Duniway never subscribed. Dye had tried to mediate conflicts between Duniway and the WCTU to no avail, and as Evans became more vociferous in her opposition to Duniway, Dye probably felt pressured to choose sides. Throughout her life Dye had avoided putting her energies where they would not be well used, and fueling the fires of conflict was not her style. She remained neutral and in the background.

Evans was still editor of the *Oregon Journal*'s "Woman's Page," now called simply "Women's Clubs." She provided extensive coverage of the efforts of club members to support suffrage in 1912. She also explained why suffrage was now an issue that the State Federation of Women's Clubs could support.[100] In January 1912, she wrote that the federation had not supported suffrage in prior elections because a significant number of their members were opposed to it, "and the small majority has no right to commit the minority to a policy it does not approve of." But the time seemed auspicious to take a different stance, and she reported that earlier in the month the Woman's Club had taken the first step for the state federation in endorsing suffrage. Explaining its move, she stated, "[The Woman's Club] simply felt the impulse of the times ... and had come to recognize suffrage not as a political issue, not as a fad, nor as a militant movement, but as an advanced step in the progress of civilization."[101] In proposing support for woman suffrage, the Portland group's actions predated the 1914 endorsement of suffrage by the General Federation of Women's Clubs.[102]

Evans continued to use her newspaper column throughout the spring to report on suffrage work and to lobby for its support from clubwomen who may have still resisted affiliation with suffrage. She noted that suffrage would "secure to club women all those things they have been striving for years to do by manual labor, physical energy and nerve-racking influence." She believed that suffrage would give dignity to clubwomen, asking members to reflect on which they would rather have when trying to establish libraries and playgrounds, votes or "influence."[103] Evans's weekly access to the press and her articulate presentation of the benefits of suffrage played an important part in the ultimate victory.

Voters narrowly approved woman suffrage in November 1912, by 4,161 votes out of 118,369.[104] Historians have always attributed that success to the indomitable persistence of Duniway and the favorable winds of change that made 1912 a likely year for passage of the measure. But Duniway's personality and divisive tactics irritated many women who felt more affiliation with their long-time club leader Evans. And while it is difficult to assess the impact of any one group in the successful campaign, the participation of clubwomen may well have provided the margin of victory.

Foreshadowing later developments in the national suffrage fight, the existence of a rival organization helped to politicize women who had previously been uninterested or unconvinced of the worth of the vote.[105] In Oregon, the Woman's Club and the OESA were at odds over power and ideology. As historian Lauren Kessler has argued, Duniway always put forth the "justice" argument when soliciting support for suffrage—that women deserved the vote because it was an inalienable and natural right of both sexes guaranteed by the Declaration of Independence.[106] In contrast, Evans worked with the prevailing ideology of Woman's Club members, presenting the argument that the vote would be an invaluable means to achieving social change in Oregon. Woman's Club members believed the ballot would bring ameliorating legislation to cities and towns, and it was a view that was especially appealing to WCTU members in Oregon. From her earliest writings Dye had embraced both views, but she was clearly more of a mind to support the moral crusaders' perspective than the natural rights argument. She and her husband were very pleased when women helped to enact prohibition in Clackamas County the year following suffrage victory.

Despite the rancorous final campaign, the rivalries among leaders in the Oregon suffrage movement benefited the cause. Tensions forced Duniway, Dye, and Evans to clearly articulate their views, gather their supporters, and develop strategies for success. Although Dye undoubtedly felt uncomfortable caught between friends and rivals, her leadership of the Sacajawea Statue Association and activism in the club movement brought her talents to the attention of the NAWSA and gave her a prominence in women's issues that she would not have otherwise achieved. The organizing skills and leadership lessons that she learned in the women's club movement served her well after Oregon women gained the right to vote.

Romance with Hawaii

1905-1947

The years that followed Dye's success with *The Conquest* and her entry into the suffrage movement unfolded with hope and possibility. Like many Progressives, the Dyes believed in the efficacy of legislation and education to ameliorate the ills of modern society, as Eva's work on behalf of woman suffrage demonstrates. Charles's involvement in Progressive reform is also noteworthy. His legal skills aided him as a state legislator from 1906 to 1908; he served as a Republican representative and chairman of the Committee on Revision of Laws. A long-time supporter of temperance, he formed the "Committee of 100" in 1912 to promote prohibition in Clackamas County.[1] The Dyes celebrated when voters—including newly enfranchised women—banned alcohol from the county in 1913, years before national prohibition was enacted. And when Theodore Roosevelt parted ways with the Republicans in 1912, the Dyes followed the former president into the short-lived Progressive Party.[2]

The coming of age of the Dye children perhaps best illustrates the educational and economic opportunities that arose during the Progressive era and the generational differences that set the youth of the early twentieth century apart from their aging reform-minded parents. Teenagers Emery and Trafton attended Tualatin Academy in Forest Grove. They continued their studies at Pacific University, then left Oregon in 1903 to attend Oberlin College. Graduating in 1905 and 1906 respectively, Emery and Trafton returned to Oregon City, but Trafton's stay was brief. After assisting his father as a law clerk during Charles's first year in the state legislature, he enrolled at Columbia University. In 1910 he obtained his law degree, practiced as an attorney in Portland for seven years, and then settled in Cleveland, Ohio. Emery remained in Oregon City, established himself in the insurance business and later became an attorney.[3] Neither son seemed inclined to either rebel against or resist their conservative upbringing or the educational expectations or career choices that their parents encouraged. Republicans, Congregational Church members, and attorneys, Emery and Trafton embodied the middle-class values of the nineteenth century. The hard-won education of their parents was an unquestioned right of the middle class in the early twentieth century as was a belief in economic opportunity and social progress. Their younger siblings, separated from the older two by ten years, came of age on the brink of World War I. In contrast to their brothers' experience, the possibilities and uncertainties of a modern society marked their choices.

Everett and Eva attended Oregon City High School and Oregon Agricultural College in Corvallis. Their parents suggested a college curriculum for each that reflected more the Dyes' nineteenth-century experience than the transformations wrought by twentieth-century economic and social change. Charles encouraged Everett to choose the agricultural course over the classes in mechanical engineering that his son favored, believing that owning and working a piece of a land would ultimately provide more security and independence. "The mechanical engineers are always compelled to seek employment from other people and to be a wage earner always is not what I would choose for you," Charles wrote.[4] But Everett persevered with his chosen studies and graduated in 1918 with a degree in mechanical engineering.

Eva's aspirations to take chemistry courses and become a laboratory assistant met with disfavor; her parents wanted her to pursue home economics in preparation for teaching and motherhood. Eva chafed at their advice, writing, "in regard to that Chemistry business. I'll drop it for the time but I am more interested in that than in the Home Economics work. It would be a perfect bore to teach sewing and pick everybodies [sic] work to pieces."[5] Eva Emery Dye's views on women's rights and the desirability of women's education were founded on a belief in the primacy of women's roles as mother and teacher; thus it is not surprising that the Dyes never encouraged their daughter to venture far beyond the traditional confines of women's sphere. Eva's letters to her parents during this time reflected her unhappiness at their control. But unlike her brother Everett, Eva ultimately followed the wishes of her parents and graduated in 1919 with a degree in home economics.

In 1917 Eva met Earl Hutchinson, a young man whom the Dyes believed would not be a suitable husband for her. Oregon City employed many unskilled and semi-skilled mill workers, especially during the brief economic revival that accompanied World War I. The small well-educated middle class in Oregon City attributed many social ills, notably the abuse of alcohol, to the growing working class. Marriage into a family that seemed to symbolize the instability and anxiety of the times was not what the

Dyes had in mind for their only daughter. Charles wrote to Trafton and
Everett,

> Earl will work and knows how to run a paper machine and
> their [sic] is nothing particularly objectionable against him
> except I do not like the stock and I think he will be nothing
> more than a mill boss. They are as good as anyone I suppose
> and may be better than anybody else in Russia but I think if
> Eva had kept her head she could have made a far more suitable
> match. I told her that would not give my approval but she
> could choose her own cause.[6]

When Earl left for France in 1918 as part of the Eighteenth Engineers
Regiment, the Dyes probably assumed the relationship had ended. Eva
and Earl had other plans, however, and after his return from Europe, they
were even more determined to be together. After his military service, Earl
used his state military bonus to attend Reed College while Eva taught
school in Raymond, Washington.[7] Little did the Dyes know at the time
that Earl had no intention of becoming a mill boss.

The Dyes unsuccessfully attempted to control their youngest children's
growing independence. When Everett enlisted in May 1918 and departed
for Camp Lee, Virginia, Charles exerted his authority.

> We thought you would write as soon as you got through and
> tell us of your first impressions and perhaps something further
> of your life. We got your night letter but that mainly told of
> your arrival and where we could address you. I suppose you
> thought the night letter was sufficient but there are so many
> things we want to know about everything that I am impatient
> to get word from you. You must write us a long letter at least
> once a week.[8]

Eva in turn barraged her son with questions about his sleeping habits,
his clothing, and his diet. After the war Everett settled near his brother in
Cleveland, perhaps in part to avoid his parents' control. He secured
employment as a mechanical engineer and eventually raised a family in
Ohio.

Letters to their daughter when she was teaching in Raymond reflected
the anxiety the Dyes felt over her growing attachment to Earl. Noting the
recent elopement of a friend's daughter in January 1920, Eva wrote, "I
don't want you to ever do that way. We have only one daughter and we

want her married at home whenever the time comes … That is the nicest way."[9] But to the entire family's amazement and disappointment, Eva eloped with Earl to Vancouver, British Columbia, on May 15, 1920.[10] Charles wrote to Everett and Trafton, "It occurred on May 15th and we knew nothing about it … I was hot about it and have not got over it yet but it's done and they will have to make the best of it."[11] Eventually the furor over the precipitous wedding diminished, and Earl impressed the Dyes by finishing a degree in chemistry, graduating from Reed College in 1923.

The 1910s were years of adaptation in the Dye household as the last of their children reached adulthood and exercised their independence. Ultimately the close-knit family remained intact in spite of the children's momentary rebellions and the departure of Everett for military service. Trafton also left Portland in 1917, and family members' dependence on one another is evidenced by family correspondence that began that year and continued until Dye's death in 1947. The Dyes each wrote to their children weekly, sometimes daily, and, in turn, the boys in Cleveland would respond. Later, when Eva and Earl moved to Los Angeles, they participated in the weekly round of correspondence. Letters followed a route from parents to each child, ending with Everett. In the 1920s Dye began titling her news "The Family Bulletin," or "The Weekly Bulletin," and called herself "Mother Dye," perhaps remembering that precious letters between her parents and grandparents had been signed by Mother Trafton and Mother Smith. The children were expected to stay in contact, and Charles occasionally admonished them when a letter was not forthcoming. In one instance he wrote, "I was just at the P.O. Office [sic] and no letter this week. I think between you you ought to be able to grind out a few lines."[12] Generally, however, letters were enthusiastically written and received, and the voluminous correspondence joined the earlier "Children's Story" as a record of the family's history.

In addition to raising children, Dye continued her literary work with the publication of *McDonald of Oregon* in 1906. She had planted the seeds of this book when she delved into the life of John McLoughlin. While studying the history of Fort Vancouver she was repeatedly told to seek the assistance of Ranald McDonald, son of Archibald McDonald, who was chief factor of Fort Colville during the 1820s and 1830s. When she found McDonald and reported that she was writing a biography of the "King of the Columbia," he informed her that he, not McLoughlin, was the king.[13] Dye and McDonald began a lively correspondence in 1892 that ended with his unexpected death in 1894.

Before his death McDonald told Dye about a diary he had kept during most of his life and provided to Malcolm McLeod of Ottowa, who wanted to write his biography. With diligence she pursued the lead, but she could never get McLeod to respond. After she had interested the private secretary of the premier of British Columbia in her plight, he succeeded in obtaining the diary.[14] As an example of her perseverance, the story of her effort to get the journal copied is worth reprinting in its entirety:

> I received a message from [Mr. R. E. Gosnell] that he had secured the book and I told him I would go to Vancouver B.C., for it. When I got there he refused to let me take the book away, but offered to let me read it. I knew there was no use in causing trouble, so I sat down to try to copy it off. It was a hopeless task. While I was at work a thought struck me. In the next room was a public stenographer. Perhaps I could engage her to make a copy. I rushed in and she accepted the work and got another girl to help her. We flew to the work. I read the pages over and had the girls copy. Their fingers flew over the typewriter keys for days during all their spare time. The man who had the book knew nothing of my operations, being busy in a session of the Parliament.
>
> Finally I got the copy made and paid the girls a large sum for their services. I then rushed back to Portland, got together my facts and set to the task of writing my book.[15]

It had taken ten years to secure McDonald's diary. Together with the information he provided in his letters and extensive research she had already undertaken for *McLoughlin and Old Oregon* the diary supplied rich material for her third historical novel.

McDonald, like her other works, opens with a long prelude and covers the 1820s, when McDonald was a child and other characters occupied center stage at Forts Colville and Vancouver. Although it is similar in style to her first two romances, *McDonald* is a more cohesive effort in which the chapters build on each other and develop a coherent chronology that is missing in her other two books. McDonald himself does not appear as a main character until halfway through the text, the first half of which describes the dangerous and chaotic overland migrations into Oregon during the 1840s, a tale she also had told in *McLoughlin*. McDonald spent much of his adult life sailing the world and taught English in Nagasaki during 1848 and 1849, and Dye used his story to bridge the end of British rule in Oregon country with the development of the state under the Americans.

McDonald was intriguing to Dye because of his connection to overseas expansion. She called him "a hero of the vanguard," arguing that his teaching and the information he brought back paved the way for Commodore Matthew Perry's journey to Japan in 1853 and ushered in trade relations between the United States and Asia. She quoted McDonald at the end of her story:

> Yes, I flatter myself that I was the instigator of Commodore Perry's expedition to Japan. You will find my depositions in executive document number fifty-nine of the Thirty-second Congress. That started Perry. I suggested to Captain Glynn of the ship "Preble" that, in the event of another visit to Japan for the purpose of opening trade, models of Western ingenuity should be taken and exhibited. And Commodore Perry did that … I broke the seal that made Japan a closed empire,–at all events, cracked it; so it was easy for Commodore Perry to do the rest.[16]

This interest in explorers and adventure paralleled her earlier work on Lewis and Clark, and given the time period and subject matter, *McDonald* could have been the sequel to either *The Conquest* or *McLoughlin*. Published in the fall of 1906, the book quickly went into a second edition.

McDonald received positive reviews. Historian Thomas Prosch reviewed the work on behalf of the *Washington Historical Quarterly* and opened with the comment, "This is the latest story of Oregon's famed author. It is one of the best." He gave her high marks for the inclusion of women in the story of westward migration and for the "thrillingly interesting" tale she told of McDonald's life. Recognizing the value of the research she had done, Prosch devoted three out of the four pages of his review to her research enterprise. In addition to searching out McDonald's journal she had also obtained government documents related to McDonald's voyage to Japan in 1848 and an old account of the "Voyage of the Morrison," which she finally located in the Boston Public Library.[17] The anonymous reviewer from the *Oregon Historical Quarterly* generally agreed with Prosch's assessment, stating that Dye's "unique and original contribution" was the recounting of McDonald's role in westward expansion. The book as a whole, the reviewer stated, served as "a grand resume of the results of her explorations in the whole range of early Oregon history."[18]

Not all comments were favorable, however. Her alma mater's alumni magazine did not offer such enthusiastic praise. R. H. Stetson seemed puzzled by both the content and the style and wondered "why it was not published as a set of sketches and short stories … It would not then have the somewhat deceptive appeal of a novel." He reported that the book "seems to have a hero," and "the most tolerant description of its method would be to call it epic." Despite his lackluster commentary, Dye would have accepted Stetson's latter statement as a compliment. She intended it to be epic, as she had her other works.[19]

McDonald sold well initially, and Dye hoped it would be an even greater success than *The Conquest* and *McLoughlin*. However, the Panic of 1907 hit just at the time a third edition was in press, and the bottom fell out of the publishing market. Sales of *McDonald* never recovered, and as of 1919, when she was seeking a new publisher, A. C. McClurg had only sold fifty-three hundred copies compared to over thirty thousand copies of *The Conquest*.[20]

With her usual energy and determination, she did not let the troubles with *McDonald* stand in the way of new research, and she soon undertook her most ambitious literary project to date. This endeavor evolved out of Dye's interest in the history of women and her Progressive values: her belief in the need for cultural, economic, and social intervention overseas, and a fundamental appreciation for American progress and democratic government. The project also arose from her fascination with the Pacific Rim, an interest first sparked in 1878 when her friend Carolyn Eldred became a missionary in Japan. Beginning her research during the height of Progressive confidence and prosperity, Dye believed the timing was auspicious for a work that would far surpass her others in its celebration of the American mission spirit.

In October 1910 Honolulu's *Daily Star* reported that Dye had arrived in Hawaii and was "preparing material for a new volume … which will have for its subject the relations which existed years ago between Oregon and the Hawaiian Islands, and the life history of a woman whose career was spent between both places."[21] The history she planned to write revolved around Charlotte Colcord. Dye had discovered in 1908 that the Emerys were related to the Colcords, a family that had many ties to Hawaii, when she was perusing the Emery Family Record, a genealogical guide sent to her by her father.[22] Her desire to learn more about her relatives in Maine increased after her father's death in November 1909. While settling Cyrus Emery's affairs in Illinois she read again his "Reminiscences of Life" (1903).

In its pages she found references to the Colcord family. As Cyrus's "Reminiscences" explained,

> in the early days of the 19th century, one John Colcord went around Cape Horn to the Sandwich Islands … He was a blacksmith. From the reports of the Hawaiians at that time, they were peaceable, quiet and honest. Stealing was unknown. Whenever they left their house all that was necessary was to stand a broom or stick up against the door. This man John Colcord, made the first locks that were used or needed there to lock out thieves. Christianity, New England rum, and the thieves were introduced at the same time.[23]

In March 1910 Dye wrote to Mrs. Turner, sister-in-law to John Colcord: "I have been repeatedly asked to write something about the Sandwich Islands [Hawaii], and also about our Congregational church, how it began, &c, but never imagined the two subjects w[oul]d ever have any connection."[24] The connection was that John Colcord's half-sister Charlotte had married Peter Hatch, who helped found Oregon City's Congregational church.[25] From her knowledge of Oregon history Dye knew the Hatch family was important to the early church and to the provisional government.

For the first time in her writing career she decided to write a biography about a woman. The pieces of a romance began to fit together as Dye researched Charlotte's history. Charlotte was "about the first white woman here," Dye wrote to Turner and "seems to have made a deep impression on all who ever knew or heard of her. For that reason I wish to preserve her memory among the pioneer mothers of Oregon." She also was intrigued because of Charlotte's connection to the Emery family. She explained to Turner:

> The same day they brought David Hatch back here to his old home to be buried I happened to open my Emery Genealogy and by chance my eye fell on the name[s], David Hatch, Susan Hatch, Peter H. Hatch, Charlotte Colcord, and I began to take notice immediately. Charlotte's mother was my great aunt Elizabeth Emery [Colcord] of Sanford.[26]

Dye soon discovered that Charlotte also had lived in Hawaii. Traveling with her brother John to the islands in 1840, she taught school at Lahainaluna Mission Seminary. While in Honolulu she met Peter Hatch, the first mate on a whaling ship. Coincidentally, Hatch came from

Parsonfield, Maine, the town where Charlotte had attended the Parsonfield Seminary as a young woman. Charlotte and Peter were married in 1841 and left the islands for Oregon City in 1843. Charlotte died of tuberculosis in 1846, leaving two young children behind.[27]

When describing her interest in Hawaiian history to the reporter from the *Daily Star*, Dye also noted that while researching the lives of John McLoughlin and Ranald McDonald she continually encountered stories about the nineteenth-century shipping trade between the Pacific Northwest and the Hawaiian Islands.[28] Thus, in addition to recounting the life of Charlotte Colcord Hatch, the project she undertook in 1910 dealt with trade relations between early Oregon and Hawaii, the influence of the first American missionaries on Hawaiian society, and Hawaii's royal families. Her research and writing on nineteenth-century Hawaii eclipsed her other works in terms of time, energy, and expense. It was to be her masterpiece, and many dreams for the future were tied to its success.

Little is known about Dye's journey to Hawaii in 1910 or her literary endeavors between 1910 and 1917, but she left an impressive research trail. During the course of her investigations into the history of the Hatch and Colcord families she struck up a lively correspondence with Peter Hatch's son and Charlotte Colcord's sister. This enriched her understanding of nineteenth-century Maine and Hawaii. Relatives also provided anecdotes about the romance between Hatch and Colcord and whaling adventures that centered on John Colcord. She unearthed the diary Colcord kept while a resident of Hawaii between 1821 and 1844, which she presented to the Hawaiian Historical Society in November 1910.[29] Similar to her previous research experiences, the contacts she made with Colcord-Hatch relatives netted a treasure trove of letters about nineteenth-century America and Hawaii that is a valuable resource for historians today.

In April 1917 she wrote to historian Edward Dekum that she had finished her manuscript but wished to return to Hawaii for a final revision. She told him that the expense of the trip was prohibitive, especially because Everett and Eva were in college, "and of course I have many other 'irons in the fire.'" Traveling to Hawaii again would allow her to add "divine little touches" in order to paint "a picture of a romantic time." Her hope was that this book would join *McLoughlin and Old Oregon* and *The Conquest* as a "trilogy of the Pacific."[30] Before she could arrange a second journey to the islands, World War I intervened, bringing financial difficulties to the Dyes and travel restrictions that made the journey impossible.

While she waited for an opportunity to resume work on her Hawaii manuscript she kept busy with the other "irons in the fire." The war provoked new interest among women in overseas causes and provided renewed energy for the women's club movement. At the height of American involvement in the war, Dye used the Chautauqua to promote patriotism and women's issues. The women's symposium that had been a successful feature of Chautauqua for years became "a patriotic conference of women" in July 1918. Eva invited "21 leading women of Portland and the state who are at the head of different war activities to tell what they were doing."[31] As an effective speaker and community leader, Dye was appointed county chairperson of the YWCA during the war and nominated as an honorary delegate to the Northwest Congress for a League of Nations in 1919.[32]

In the aftermath of World War I, Dye revived the languishing Oregon City Woman's Club. In 1920 she was elected president, and the membership swelled immediately from 90 to 166. The committees that members subsequently organized reflected the impact of the war and the interests of their president. Among other activities, women could participate in Near East relief, the China fund, and multiple community service projects. The funding of a public library in Clackamas County was one of many endeavors that bore the stamp of president Dye.[33]

After years of waiting, Dye's opportunity to return to Hawaii finally came. She left for the islands in the autumn of 1922 when she was sixty-seven years old. Travelling alone aboard the *S. S. Maui*, Eva disembarked in Honolulu after a six-day journey. She resided at the Blaisdell Hotel, where below her room was a garden "with palms that look like ferns as big as tall trees," she wrote to Charles, and the cost was one dollar fifty per day.[34] Hiring a typist, she immediately started rewriting her manuscript and frequently drove herself to exhaustion in order to keep one step ahead of the "type girl." Her unofficial host, former Hawaiian Historical Society president William D. Westervelt, introduced her to historians and enthusiasts of Hawaiian history, including many family members of the first missionaries. Westervelt, an expert on Hawaiian folklore and languages, had published *Hawaiian Legends of Old Honolulu* in 1915. His assistance meant access to documents at the Bishop Museum and the Hawaiian Historical Society. She gave him a copy of her manuscript, and he promised to read it carefully.[35]

In addition to Westervelt, Dye sought the advice of two prominent individuals whose personal and family histories influenced her work. Sanford B. Dole, whom she had interviewed and consulted in 1910, had been instrumental in the coup to depose Queen Liliuokalani in 1893 and was declared president of the Republic of Hawaii shortly thereafter. Son of missionaries, an attorney, and a successful pineapple plantation owner, Dole had served as territorial governor from 1900 to 1903 and later on Hawaii's Supreme Court. The second key figure she encountered was the Reverend Henry P. Judd, whose grandfather Dr. Gerrit P. Judd and wife Laura Fish Judd were two of the first American missionaries. They had arrived in Honolulu in 1828, and Judd's abilities as a physician, translator, and adviser in foreign affairs resulted in a lengthy career as councilor and minister to King Kamehameha III during the 1840s. Judd in fact was so influential that he was de facto prime minister.[36] The Judd family remained important to Hawaii's civic, cultural, and religious life well into the twentieth century. They and the Doles were also controversial figures of American dominance on the islands.

Because of the prominence and hospitality of the Judds and the Doles, Dye's original manuscript underwent a major transformation. She was no longer featuring Charlotte Colcord at the center; she wrote to Charles that "one supreme hero is developing, one of whom I had but a glimpse before." She was intrigued with the missionaries' accomplishments and influence and wrote that "the descendants of these old missionaries are like a clan, numerous and jealous of their honor." Her hero was now Dr. Gerrit Judd, and she told her husband that "so many writers have, like Jack London, gone absolutely out of their way to cast reflections on the morals and motives of the fathers of civilization here."[37] In her estimation, other writers had a distorted view of nineteenth-century events that did not reflect the achievements of the American missionaries; thus she intended to correct this perspective with a heroic history. She noted more than once that "Dr. Judd was really the man who saved Hawaii to the United States in those old days when he organized the Government."[38]

She also became interested in the Hawaiian royal family, especially those kings and queens who had extensive educational and cultural contacts with Americans as a result of intermarriage and *hanai*, the practice of interfamily adoption. King Kamehameha III (1813-1854) was the focus of her study, along with his royal brothers, sisters, and cousins.[39] The influence of the mission schools on the royal children was of particular interest. Her ambition was to write something "more romantic, more appealing than anything I have done before," and she exuberantly articulated a central theme of her book to Charles:

I am telling of the kings and queens as they grew up from childhood in the Royal School of the missionaries and actually came to the throne with all the royal glamors [sic] borrowed from Europe. But they were every one of them weak, incompetent kings and queens as any we read of in history, sustained only by American cabinets and advisors. By and by they ran out, the bubble burst, the monarchy was an empty shell. I tell the story, gently indicating the weaknesses that led to extinction, and Judge Dole comes in at last in such a wonderfully conservative, conciliatory way, the choice of all. I am trying to make it a piece of *literature*.[40]

She reported that Hawaiians were captivated more by the folklore and legends of old Hawaii, but she brushed their interests aside and admitted she only was enthralled with the period after whites arrived. Believing that Americans on the mainland would share her fascination with stories of America's religious and economic rise to power on the islands, she wrote about "the contact of races with the whites" that had driven all of her work to date.[41]

Dye's interest in the missionaries arose not just from her belief in the benefits of American expansion but also from a long-held fascination with and admiration of the mission spirit. Oberlin College had first instilled in the Dyes the idea that teachers in the mission field and their religious counterparts were to be emulated and admired. She noted years later that "my people, as most of the missionaries of early Hawaii came with the Puritans to Boston. I felt I knew the character and intent to do good."[42] Throughout their lives the Dyes avidly read the American Board of Foreign Mission's newsletters and contributed financially to mission causes throughout the world. Dye had first explored the importance of missionaries when she praised the virtues of the Whitmans and the Spaldings in *McLoughlin and Old Oregon*. Her Hawaiian research reconfirmed her sentiment that contact between missionaries and native peoples was a subject worthy of historical fiction, but as in her other works enthusiasm for the conquerors resulted in a one-sided account that never presented Native Hawaiian perspectives.[43]

When Dye left for Honolulu in October 1922 she anticipated returning to Oregon City by the first of 1923. Instead, the letters her husband received at Thanksgiving indicated she would be in Hawaii much longer as she incorporated new material in her manuscript. He asked her how much longer she thought she would be away. "I am almost afraid to ask," he wrote, "for fear you will think I am hurrying you home. Take your time and get it just as good as you possibly can before leaving it. Even if you have to stay until spring. I will manage this end of it."[44] As it turned out, she was gone until the end of April, and the letters they exchanged during her six-month absence offer a wealth of information about their relationship and their children.

Although Charles and Eva had been separated several times while she researched her other books, this six-month separation was difficult. They missed each other's company, and both worried about the trip's expense. Charles's letters were full of reassurances that Eva could take as much time as she needed to finish her book, and he would supply the financial means for an extended stay. "You say you wish you could take all the time you want," he wrote in February. "I don't see why you can't. It has cost a lot of money and time and it would be a pity to spoil it now by hurrying home." He reminded her that her time would be taken up with speaking engagements and interruptions from visitors when she returned. "My advice is for you to stay away until [you] get the work done. You are too well known here to be able to command your time."[45]

Interlaced with his reassurances, however, were warnings about their financial situation. During the 1910s and 1920s Charles expanded his business interests beyond real estate law to include the acquisition and management of a number of properties in Oregon City and Portland. The maintenance and repair of these sites, which consisted of apartment-style housing, kept Charles busy and frequently in need of ready cash. He wrote in January, "I paid today $2,500 on the mortgage on the Everett St. property. That leaves a balance of $6,000 due in 2 yrs.," and in his next letter he told her he would need to spend one thousand dollars on the property at East 11th and Harrison. "So I am going to be pressed for cash this summer again as I was last."[46] The funds for property improvement competed with the money necessary to send his wife to Hawaii. To help pay for her journey, they cashed in a number of government war bonds and used additional savings. The trip cost nearly one thousand dollars, approximately one-fifth of Charles's annual income.

Their long-distance discussions about money provided some of the few instances of tension in their relationship. She reported that she constantly worried about "running short," and waited anxiously for Charles to send an additional one hundred dollars on two separate occasions. She seemed oblivious to any financial difficulties he might be facing. He reassured her that he had no intention of letting her run out of money and told her to draw on his credit if necessary. He also made it clear, however, that he had to plan carefully for the checks he sent. It was obvious that financial considerations had delayed her return to Hawaii, and she blamed Charles for it. When he commented that he was "in much better fix to stand it [financially] than ever before," she replied, "I am glad you are able to bear it than ever before. Perhaps it is best that I waited so long. The thought of all the wasted years however sometimes makes me sick."[47]

Although finances provided the fuel for occasional discontent and worry, the hope that Eva's book would earn handsome royalties inspired new dreams for the future. Charles often wrote that he was "hoping and praying" that she would "make a hit with it," and assured her it would be "a fine book and ... it will go off like hot cakes."[48] Her success would mean he could take a year off from work or retire altogether. At the least, he hoped to close his law office in the winters so he and Eva could travel and take life a little easier. "If you could make a hit with the book it would put us on easy street," he wrote.[49] After paying some unexpected expenses, he told her, "It seems to me that I am getting a little more than my share just at this time ... I don't think I want to quit business but I would like to get my nose off the grindstone long enough for the scabs to heal up."[50]

Eva's success would not only ease their financial situation; it also would allow them to leave Oregon City. Charles wrote often of his desire to leave behind this "abominable climate in the winter," and more importantly, he made the claim that they were not well suited for life in a blue-collar city.[51] He explained his wish to live elsewhere in one of his March letters.

> if your book succeeds we will not be long in Oregon City
> anyway. I would like a change. Oregon City is a mill town and
> never will be anything else. Mill towns are all right and very
> necessary but as we are not mill people and are not particularly
> congenial to them there is no reason why we should always
> remain here.[52]

Leaving Oregon City was also appealing because of difficulties they were having with their son Emery. Following his graduation from Oberlin

College and a brief attempt at serving in the military in 1907, Emery had returned to Oregon City. He had seemed destined for the kind of social and financial successes enjoyed by his siblings, but from 1907 onward he exhibited symptoms of what probably would be diagnosed today as paranoid schizophrenia. In October 1907 Eva wrote to her father, "If necessary we will sell our place here in town and go out in the country where he can have some out door interests ... by a quiet life and freedom from excitements he may gradually get better." He was twice committed to the state sanitarium, and the Dyes searched in vain for the reason for his illness. Eva queried her father, "Was your brother John like this, or any of your family?" She believed he had been injured at birth during a forceps delivery, but she also wondered if he had harmed his "cranial nerves" when playing football.[53]

The need to monitor Emery's troubling behavior was one reason Eva traveled without Charles to Hawaii, and worries about Emery also added to the pressure the Dyes felt to make the Hawaii endeavor a success. She wrote to Charles, "I do not think he sh[oul]d live in Oregon City,–a change of environment will be a great help to him. I do not seem to want to stay there myself anymore."[54] Charles found Emery's behavior puzzling and frustrating. "I am at a loss to know how to control his mania for clipping and making little notes and religiously keeping them until he has bushels of them," he told Eva. Emery spent the better part of the autumn "nailing up boxes" to store his clippings. "I think he must have a full dray load," commented Charles in exasperation.[55] Eva in turn worried that Emery's chronic unemployment would lead to trouble. She cautioned her husband, "Do not let Emery get so out of money that he will do anything wrong," such as stealing to support himself.[56]

The hope that Eva would produce a best seller undoubtedly weighed on them both, but the most remarkable thing about their Hawaii correspondence is the evidence it provides of their love for each other. On board the *S. S. Maui*, Eva wrote, "I wish every minute you were here, it w[oul]d be so much nicer together," and again in December she commented, "I always wish you were here to walk with me when the day's work is over."[57] She wanted most of all for him to enjoy the sites of Hawaii with her. Near the end of her trip she traveled to Kilauea Volcano. Journeying to Hilo, she commented, "I wish you c[oul]d see how lovely this boat is, all in white with Greek bas-relief panels in white ... Also there are island paintings by a noted Honolulu artist." Once at the volcano she described lava tubes and rivers of fire in vivid detail to Charles. Her enthusiasm was tempered by his absence, and she wrote, "I hate to see all these interesting things without you."[58]

For his part, Charles rarely wrote a letter to his wife without mentioning how much he missed her or offering support for her endeavors. He told her in November, "It has been one of the nicest falls Oregon has experienced for some time. More like an Iowa fall than Oregon. If you were here it would be a day to take a long ride but with you so far away I can only enjoy it in my imagination." The holidays were especially difficult for Charles because the children were only able to join him briefly at Christmas. Alone on New Year's Day, he wrote, "I am reminded that this is the first Holiday season that we have passed apart in the forty years of our married life." Charles understood how important this project was to Eva and offered continual encouragement that she should stay until she felt satisfied with her work. "I miss you very much," he wrote, "but I know if you do not finish the work before you come home you will have no chance to finish it afterwards and you will be so disappointed there will be no living with you." He was clearly lonely without her, however, and in February he commented, "It seems like a long time since you left home and I am beginning to think I would like to hear the train whistling on which you would arrive in Oregon City."[59]

In addition to demonstrating the affectionate support he offered Eva, Charles's letters also bear witness to his sense of humor. On November 28 he told her, "I bought a turkey for Thanksgiving today. Cost $5.00 which seemed terrible steep but the children were coming home and I thought we must celebrate even if you were not with us. I think though I ought to have bought a chicken and sent the difference to the starving of Asia." He also teased her upon receipt of one her letters, responding "yours of 'Nov. 31st' … came duly to hand. We ended up November here with the 30th." Friends asked Charles repeatedly when she would return. To one man he responded, "I told him you had fallen in love with the climate of Hawaii and I did not think your love for me would draw you away until I could give you assurance of better weather than we have been having since 1923 came in." Knowing how busy she was, he sent Christmas cards to her friends, writing on them, "Honolulu Dec. 16th 1922. I wish [you] a Merry Christmas and a Happy New Year Your Friend Eva Emery Dye." In his letter he told her, "They all thought you had prepared them and were much pleased that you remembered them … When you come back you must not be surprised and give me away."[60]

Charles's lengthy letters to Eva offer more than just a rare glimpse into their relationship. They provide a wealth of information about Oregon City in the 1920s, which was not a time of prosperity. High unemployment in the shipping, lumber, and agricultural industries after the war brought disillusionment to laborers and provoked distrust among their middle-class counterparts. Despite the advent of automobile transportation, better roads, and improvements in health and social conditions, the twenties in Oregon "seemed to be bracketed by the general malaise that opened the decade and the even more severe economic trouble that closed it."[61] Charles's letters mirror this sentiment, and while Eva was gone he kept her and their children abreast of local events.

One major social and political development in Oregon was the rebirth of the Ku Klux Klan. In the postwar atmosphere of anxiety in Oregon, the Klan rose to power, targeting Catholics, Jews, and the Japanese. According to historian Eckard Toy the Klan enrolled thirty-five thousand members in Oregon by 1923 from a total population that numbered about eight hundred thousand.[62] The election of 1922 highlighted the Klan's influence and demonstrated the degree of nativist sentiment in the Pacific Northwest. The Klan backed an anti-Catholic measure to make public school compulsory that passed by a wide margin, and Charles noted that "religious fanaticism seems to have controlled the election." Democrat Walter Pierce, who enjoyed widespread KKK support, ousted anti-Klan Governor Ben Olcott. Charles argued that the voters' anger over taxation also contributed to Olcott's downfall. He commented that the people "voted the Governor out because taxes were too high and they are 9/10 of them voted by the people themselves and to show their consistency all the measures on ballot to increase taxes carried."[63] Disgusted by the returns and the influence of the KKK, he wrote,

> the Ku Klux and all other radicals seemed to have full swing. The Catholics fought hard against the Compulsory School Bill but it was of no avail. Fanaticism was in the saddle. Catholics are always fanatics when they are on top but I was in hopes that Protestants were different but the influence of agitation by the K. K. K. has so inflamed people that instead of acting with toleration they have shown the same spirit of intolerance as is shown by the Catholics ... I can't help feeling that it has caused a division in society that will be long in healing up.[64]

Religious fanaticism was not the only rift in Oregon during this period. Anti-labor sentiment ran high in the Pacific Northwest as a result of labor strife in the 1910s. In 1916 and 1919 there were three significant episodes of labor unrest in Washington, and all involved the Industrial Workers of the World, or Wobblies. The first incident, involving a strike by shingle weavers and the Wobblies, occurred in Everett. Known as the Everett Massacre, the violence that resulted in the deaths of seven men and injuries to one hundred others pitted law enforcement officials against radical laborers. In February 1919 a four-day strike by sixty thousand workers in Seattle shut down the city, and later that year Centralia became the site for a gun battle between American Legionnaires and the Wobblies. Despite the fact that the Wobblies were most often the recipients of violent acts rather than the instigators, the events left an indelible impression on an uneasy public that the IWW was violent and unpredictable.[65] Distrust and tension between labor and capital continued into the twenties. In the fall and winter of 1922-23 there were a number of fires in Oregon City and around the state, which many people attributed to the Wobblies. In Oregon City, the Elks Lodge burned in early December, and Charles noted, "The fire was evidently incendiary." A few days later the entire business district of Astoria burned, "about 27 blocks in all. 2500 people are homeless," he wrote. "It appears like an organized effort of the Wobblies or some one of like principles to destroy as much property as possible."[66]

Most devastating to the Dyes personally was the complete destruction of the Congregational Church on February 4, 1923. Charles penned a quick letter to Eva that morning: "Just a line to tell you that Cong. church burned about 5 a.m. today, total loss. Parsonage saved … Fire thought to be incendiary … People indignant but determined not to be wholly disheartened." Three days later Charles mentioned that the members were gathering to plan for the future. "We are going to have our roll call for the church on tomorrow evening at the banquet room of the Masonic Temple. I wish you were here." Luckily the church was insured, and the two hundred members vowed to rebuild as quickly as possible.[67] Appointed to the committee to find a new church site, Charles reported that he probably would be expected to contribute one thousand dollars to the effort to raise the necessary fifteen thousand dollars, because the minister and the other members of the committee were likely to do the same. The letter he wrote the day before the church's burning seemed prophetic: "So it looks like I will need a best seller or something else to meet all the extra expenses for 1923."[68]

Charles's commitment to the church dovetailed with his support of prohibition, which he mentioned numerous times in his letters. In the early twenties Charles, with the support of the Congregational Brotherhood, revived the "Committee of 100" that had successfully put Clackamas County in the "dry" column in 1913. Charles's intent in reviving his committee was "to assist police officers in stemming the tide of liquor traffic" in the wake of passage of the Eighteenth Amendment.[69] He wrote frequently to Eva about temperance addresses he attended, including a banquet and speech by the superintendent of the Anti-Saloon League. The death of a superintendent at Hawley's Paper Mill in Oregon City gave Charles an occasion to speculate on the cause of Henry Henningsen's death, stating that there was a rumor that "it was caused by drinking moonshine." He noted that a day or two after Henningsen died the police raided the paint shop at the mill and found "nine quarts of moonshine and about as many empty containers." The superintendent of the paint shop was fined three hundred dollars and fired by the mill owner.[70] Eva's support for prohibition was as strong as it had been in the 1870s, and she shared his enthusiasm for the cause. One of the highlights of her journey was attending an address by Kathleen Norris, who spoke in San Francisco about her own family's war with alcohol and the need for stricter prohibition laws. "It was one of the finest temperance talks I ever heard, appealing to the women of California to sustain the law of the land," she reported to Charles.[71]

The six-month period of Eva's absence was a time of change and loss in Oregon City, as Charles's letters demonstrate. In addition to the fires that raged that winter, Oregon City experienced the worst flooding since 1890 and unusually harsh winter weather. There were also numerous deaths of friends and neighbors in the city; many of Charles's letters began with sad news of illness or accident. Coupled with the animosity fostered by the election of 1922 and the poor economic outlook, these misfortunes increased the anticipation that Eva's book would transform their lives. While his letters often expressed loss and loneliness, hers attested to the confidence she felt in her work and her purpose.

In December she wrote to Charles, "I understand that a prize of $10,000 has been offered for the best book on Hawaii. I hope I may win it, but say nothing." She believed "there is a feverish interest in Hawaiian literature," but asserted that what the people hungered for was a "standard work," not one that revolved around myth and legend. Myths, she argued, were "very pretty, locally interesting, but this age demands something more practical and that is why I think my book will be of national interest rather than local." She felt pressured to finish her writing and send it off to a publisher because she had met several authors working on histories of Hawaii. She was confident of the quality and unique attributes of her contribution, however, and wrote to Charles, "So far no book equal to it is known."[72]

On March 22, after months of work and upon receipt of favorable criticism from Judge Dole, she told Charles that she was almost finished. She had decided to title the work "The King's Eagles: The Royal Romance of Hawaii." What began as an intensive study of Kamehameha III became a sweeping account of the reign of Hawaiian kings and queens throughout the nineteenth century. The book ended with the downfall of Queen Liliuokalani in 1894, when Dole took center stage. Dye compared Dole to George Washington and described the queen as a "headstrong" woman "determined to be a Queen Elizabeth three hundred years too late." The "king's eagles" were the missionaries and American statesman who had paternalistically steered domestic and foreign policy for eighty years. She lavishly praised their abilities. "From the beginning," she wrote, "the monarchy had existed only by the assistance and toleration of kindly, good-natured and well-disposed Americans who for a hundred years had practically controlled the country."[73] As with her other works, an analysis of the conflicts between native peoples and American colonizers was missing entirely, and the absence of tension around class, ethnic, or religious issues allowed her to create a heroic and patriotic romance. A few days after selecting the title she triumphantly reported, "The book is done, done, done … Judge Dole seems to think the book a great accomplishment. I regard it myself as my *Magnum Opus*."[74]

Once her manuscript was complete her impatience to rejoin Charles increased. On March 27 she wrote, "It is a wonderful day, sun shining, birds singing, flowers blooming, but now my work is done I want to fly right to you." Anxious to be home, she was delayed weeks because of the timing of ships departing for the mainland and was unable to leave until April 21. "I am so homesick to see you all," she wrote, reluctant to make a stop in Long Beach to visit Charles's relatives because it would delay her return to Oregon City until May 1. In her April letters she wrote briefly about the support Charles had given during their long separation, acknowledging, "Your lovely letters are a great encouragement." The months apart had been challenging for them both, and prior to boarding the *S. S. Calawaii* she wrote to Charles, "Keep a stiff upper lip. I will soon be home."[75]

Before leaving Honolulu, she sent her manuscript to Doubleday Page
& Company. In 1919, Dye had purchased the plates and copyrights of her
books from A. C. McClurg and Company, and Doubleday Page had
assumed the responsibility of publishing later editions of her works. She
was confident they would look favorably upon the work she believed had
much greater appeal than *The Conquest* or *McLoughlin*. Knowing that it
would probably be her last major literary undertaking, she and Charles
anxiously awaited its publication.

In June 1923 Dye wrote to Sanford Dole that "New York publishers"
considered her manuscript and they would attend to it as soon as the
spring books were in press. She feared that publishers would view her
work as fiction, not history, which might harm her chances of getting it
published. She requested that Judge Dole write a letter on her behalf. "It
w[oul]d be simply to reassure them that what appears to be a tale is really
fact and not fiction at all. And altogether a tale highly creditable to those
brave Americans who literally made themselves trustees of Kamehameha's
kingdom." Dole responded favorably, writing an open letter "To the
Publishers of a Royal Romance." Stating that he had "gone over this
manuscript with much interest," he reassured possible skeptics that "the
work has had the benefit of a great amount of careful research and the
author may be congratulated for the success with which she has reproduced
the Hawaiian atmosphere and the skill with which she has avoided
unimportant and uninteresting details."[76]

In spite of Dole's support, the editors rejected her manuscript. Doubleday
Page and other publishers told Dye that "there is not sufficient interest in
that subject." She also mentioned that one reviewer thought her work was
"too enthusiastic."[77] Dye's tale, which was similar in style and form to *The
Conquest* and *McLoughlin*, assumed that the average reader would grasp the
intricacies of a complicated history and could sort fact from fiction. Although
she was certain there was national interest in the islands, eastern publishers
remained unconvinced.

For the remaining years of her life Dye periodically revised her manuscript
and sent it to publishers. In 1935 she thought the time was auspicious for
another attempt. "I am offering it to the Atlantic Monthly, encouraged by
the fact their leading article recently was on Hawaii," she wrote to Henry
Judd. "Maybe the time has come." But the time never came. The *Atlantic
Monthly* turned it down, and so did Macmillan in 1936. "Our eastern
publishers seem to need *confirmation* of the historical data of the volume,
need to know that it is approved by Hawaiian authorities," she told Judd

with frustration. She sent the manuscript back to Hawaii for further review, but her efforts were to no avail. The manuscript had been revised several times over a twenty-five year period and had received three different titles. None of the revisions could alter the fact that Dye's exuberant style and heroic themes marked her as a turn-of-the-century writer with a shrinking readership.[78]

Dye's unsuccessful attempts to bring "The Royal Romance" before the public battered her self-confidence, yet she never stopped writing. Four years after her return from Hawaii she wrote to her children that she was revising *McDonald of Oregon* "into practically a new book." She believed the work, entitled "Beyond the Rockies," would be "even more loved out here than McLoughlin and Old Oregon." She persevered for several more years, collecting new tales and revising chapters from her previous works. The result was the publication of *The Soul of America: An Oregon Iliad* (1934). After years of embedding stories about women in her biographies of men, Dye crafted a work that celebrated pioneer women's achievements. Perhaps after all the years of weaving women's history into the history of great men, she finally felt freed–or compelled–to place women at the center of a story. She noted in press releases that she had conceived of the idea twenty-five years earlier in the aftermath of her successful portrayal of Sacagawea. A reviewer in the *Oregonian* enthused that it was "a glowing impressionistic interpretation of Oregon history, with emphasis on what the women did and what was accomplished by a group of pioneers who also have been overlooked by historians."[79]

Writing had been Dye's lifetime obsession, and Charles acknowledged its importance in a letter he wrote to their children in 1928. At the age of seventy-two, his wife never wavered from her single-minded determination, and he was willing to give up his own dream of leaving Oregon City in order to support her efforts. He commented,

> Mama complains about not having more time to write but she tires out easily and is not as spry as she once was … If we could sell and go south for the winter where we would not have to keep fires it might help but mama wants to stay here until she finishes the book she is working on as her material is all here.[80]

She realized that others close to her had paid a price for her commitment to a literary life, and as she aged she often wondered if she should have taken a different path. Her grandchildren's experiences gave her an opportunity to reminisce about the years when her children were young. In March 1927 she wrote to the children:

> I suppose it w[oul]d have been wise for me to have celebrated you children's birthdays more, but with my writing and all it never seemed possible to do so much. I often think my family w[oul]d have been much happier if I had never written anything, but looking back over it I hardly see how I c[oul]d have been happy without it. From earliest childhood, the best escape from loneliness or sorrow or disappointment of any kind has been to forget it in writing. And it does not seem to me that having a family sh[oul]d prohibit one entirely from any thing so comforting. Other women played bridge, or spent most of their time on dress and visiting, &c, &c. But if I c[oul]d write, artistically, it was like painting, or music, or any other creative art.[81]

The comfort she derived from her writing carried her through many crises and provided an outlet for anxiety. Shortly after her return from Hawaii Emery's health took a turn for the worse. His paranoia-turned-obsession about a family friend landed him in jail in May 1924 but not before the scuffle on the streets of Portland to subdue him and remove a loaded pistol made the front page of the *Oregon Journal*.[82] Mortified over the publicity and worried that Emery would refuse to cooperate with efforts to place him in the state sanitarium, Eva wrote to her children: "We are urging him to go quietly and make no trouble and it will be easier for us to get his release later when we may go somewhere else."[83] He was committed to the sanitarium in July 1924 and remained there for several years. Emery's mental illness was a constant worry and jeopardized many of the Dyes' relationships with friends. As Eva once told Everett, "I hate to speak of it, it is our great sorrow. Do not mention it in your letters to us. The least said the better."[84] Writing provided a welcome relief from worry, but even that enjoyment was tempered by Emery's troubles. Although she reported she was often able to "rush along rapidly" with her work, she also acknowledged that "at other times such a deep depression comes over me at [the] thought of you all so far away, and of our dear Emery, that it floors me completely."[85]

The ending of thirty years of Chautauqua festivities in 1928 was another upsetting event, though it was not unexpected. Clackamas County would not abate the taxes on the property owned by the Willamette Valley Chautauqua Assembly, and rising costs for speakers and entertainment had outpaced ticket sales during much of the twenties. Charles Dye and several other board members had regularly dipped into their own pockets to keep the annual event afloat, but it became clear in the spring of 1928 that the cost of salvaging the operation was financially prohibitive. Although historians argue that Chautauqua activities declined nationwide in the twenties because of movies, the automobile, and radio, one newspaper article claimed that greater mobility and communication had been an asset to the Oregon Chautauqua rather than a detriment.[86] The WVCA continued to enjoy large and enthusiastic crowds even in its last years. The board was committed to keeping the event affordable for as many families as possible, and ticket prices remained static from 1913 until the end. The Dyes and their friends had provided quality education and entertainment at a low cost, which was the reason for Chautauqua's great success and its failure.

As 1928 came to a close the Dyes found themselves embattled by illness and other misfortunes. While visiting her daughter in California, Eva had been injured in an automobile accident. With a broken arm she was reduced to typing with one hand, a frustrating experience that left her weary and annoyed that her writing was interrupted. Both she and Charles were slow to recover from a bout with influenza in December, and Charles struck an uncharacteristically pessimistic tone in a letter he wrote to Everett shortly after Christmas. "I hope there will be another Christmas coming and that the coming year will not be so unfortunate for us as the last year has been."[87]

Economic uncertainties added to the air of malaise in the Dye household during the late twenties. Hard times had prevented the sale of all of Charles's properties in Portland, which in turn meant that they were unable to relocate nearer to their children. Charles seemed dispirited in May 1929 when he wrote to Everett, "I wish you were all not so far away. Life is so short and we have to spend it here by ourselves … I would like to sell everything and retire and spend the rest of my days free from responsibility but it does not seem that I can."[88] Charles's weekly, informative letters that he had sent to his children for many years ended shortly thereafter. He suffered a stroke while attending church services on a summer Sunday, the day after his and Eva's forty-seventh wedding anniversary. He died a week later on July 22, 1929, at the age of seventy-three.

Charles had been Eva's champion for years, supporting her in all her endeavors, believing in her abilities and giving her freedom to explore her ideas. His loss must have been crushing, but true to form, Eva persevered in the aftermath of his death, with memories of her husband and her own independence to sustain her. She soon resumed her work, rarely admitting to the deep loneliness that accompanied his death. "The saddest time for me," she wrote to the children, "is to go to church and papa not there. I cannot bear to stop to speak to people, fearing I shall break down crying, as I did today." By the following spring she noted, "I have been very busy with my literary work, am trying to finish several things. I have always been interrupted so that now I am trying to make the best of the quiet time. All my life literary work has made me forget my troubles."[89]

A few months after Charles's death Eva decided that she would remain in Oregon City. This decision was made partly out of necessity. The advent of the Great Depression continued to make it impossible for her to sell any of the properties Charles had accumulated over the years; in fact, during the thirties she often let families live in the apartments rent-free just to keep them occupied. To her credit she managed to keep all of the real estate intact, although it took many years to bring the property taxes current after the economic upheaval of the Depression. She also stayed in Oregon City because it was her home. She did not wish to leave the house she and Charles built in 1894, the church they attended, or her many friends. She told the children,

> At church this morning the new organ sounded just as sweetly as it did that day at papa's funeral. And when the hymns were sung I seemed to hear his voice at my side just as full and as sweet as in all the 40 years when we went to church together here. He was one of the best singers in the church, if not the best among the men. Sitting there I realized as never before that this is home and Mr. Dye will always seem to be here with me. I shall fix up the home place as best I can and always live here where you can come and visit me.[90]

Dye remained in the yellow house at the corner of Ninth and Jefferson streets for all but the last year of her life, when a broken hip necessitated a move to a convalescent center. She was still actively writing and speaking about Oregon history in 1940 to students from kindergarten through college, though she wrote to her long-time friend Henry Judd, "the depressions, death of my husband, and other discouraging things have battered my courage."[91]

Dye's confidence was never battered enough to prevent her from promoting her own work or the history of the region. In 1937 she was actively seeking a producer to make movies out of three of her books, and the previous year she boasted that "new boxed editions" of *The Conquest* and *McLoughlin* were selling briskly from publishers Wilson-Erickson, Incorporated.[92] She was proud of the fact that her books were still considered "standard works" in the Pacific Northwest, a label she accepted with satisfaction. Enjoying the publicity and praise that came with her accomplishments and age, she received an honorary doctorate in literature from Oregon State College in 1930 and similar honors in law from the University of Portland in 1939.[93] The former called her "a pioneer of literary culture," and the honors bestowed on her attested to the energy and enthusiasm with which she advocated the history of the Pacific Northwest.

Eva Emery Dye died on February 25, 1947, at the age of ninety-one. She gave one of her last interviews when she was eighty-nine, still exhibiting the vigor and enthusiasm for which she was known. Inspired by the past and hopeful for the future, she told the reporter she wished she could rewrite her books.

> I could do every one of them better now. I may surprise the literary world yet. Perhaps I may leave something which will be published years after I am gone. I still have a number of unpublished manuscripts which I think are better than any which have been on the library shelves for so many years.[94]

She continued writing to the end of her life, confident that her heroic histories made a lasting contribution to the history of the region and the nation.

Epilogue

Eva Emery Dye was a woman both ahead of and behind her time. Her historical chronicles appealed to an eager audience because they evoked an earlier era when white Americans felt assured of their destiny and confident of their claims to the nation and the world. By the 1920s the reading public was enjoying the works of Ernest Hemingway, F. Scott Fitzgerald, and Sinclair Lewis, writers who criticized "feel good" nostalgia and questioned middle-class values in the aftermath of World War I. The heroic and romantic style and imperialistic themes that had served Dye well in 1900 were outdated by the time she was ready to publish her last work on Hawaii.

But she was ahead of her times in other ways. Her books read like screenplays, and with the advent of moving pictures she became interested in bringing her work to the cinema. She negotiated a contract with "a scenario writer" in 1919 but because A. C. McClurg and Company still maintained the copyrights to her books and they were unwilling to settle for the compensation offered, negotiations faltered. In 1927 her *McLoughlin and Old Oregon* and *The Conquest* were used as the basis for Raymond Wells's film *The Pilgrimage of Faith*. She wanted her books to become feature-length films, however, and in 1937 she was still trying to find film producers. Her dramatic style and appreciation of pageantry were well suited for the screen; perhaps if she had come of age in the twentieth century she would have chosen to write screenplays instead of romantic history.[1]

In her quest to restore women to history she was also ahead of her time. Although her books are laden with traditional adventures featuring "great" men, she endeavored in all of her works to explore women's experiences. There is a sense one gets from her writing that if someone, perhaps a fellow writer or a noted historian, had given more encouragement she would have undertaken the history of women in the West as her primary subject. Instead she felt that her work was discredited because she included women. In a speech given at the National American Woman Suffrage Association convention in 1909, she commented, "Have you noticed that schoolboys sometimes call American history dull? But let some one name all the deeds of women—at once the average dry as dust historian lifts deprecating hands, 'Romance, fiction, not real history.'"[2] Her last published work, *The Soul of America* (1934), was her most comprehensive effort to recognize the achievements of pioneer women. Published during the midst of the Depression, it was her least financially successful book.

The balancing act between history and fiction that is so apparent in her work had a significant impact on Dye's career as an author. Writing at a time when the historical profession in America was attempting to set professional standards and become more "scientific," her desire to enliven the past put her at odds with people she respected and admired, such as historian Frances Fuller Victor. She expressed her frustration with traditional history and professional historians in an unpublished review of Reuben Thwaites's 1904 edition of the Lewis and Clark journals.

> Is it a crime to tell history as it was enacted in real life? Must history be stupid to be true? … Of course, though, the conscientious historian that tells history as a story, is very likely to be confounded with certain romancers who simply take the names of history, and without any more than a smattering of the facts, proceed to weave any sort of a fanciful tale. But afterall, the one that tells the true story and tells it well, will live and be remembered.[3]

Dye was conscientious in her research, so she was all the more perturbed when critics did not take her writing seriously. She was so persistent in pursuit of details, in fact, that she gained a reputation for badgering her respondents. She clearly did not want to be "confounded with certain romancers," yet romance, mythology, and legend were important influences in her choice of subject matter, style, and interpretation. As librarian Melva Garrow Ellingsen put it, "Rather than be classified as dull and right, she chose to be romantic and probable."[4] In the end, her desire to maintain editorial control over her characters and the manner in which her pen brought them to life meant that her work was considered fiction. Her work has not stood the test of time as she had hoped, but it is more the style and not the substance that prevented her from being the Homer of the Pacific Northwest. In 1911 noted historian Joseph Gaston wrote that Dye had "done more than any other writer since Irving to popularize the dramatic story of the new northwest,"[5] and for that reason her literary work and her lifelong commitment to writing about the history of the region deserves mention.

Dye did not ever claim to be a historian, but it is clear that she wanted the same opportunities to write and lecture about history that her contemporaries in the historical profession enjoyed. For the most part they welcomed her literary efforts, offered supportive reviews and encouragement, and appreciated her enthusiasm. She maintained close ties with historians Frederic Young, Edmond Meany, James B. Horner, and Joseph Gaston as well as with her friends at the Hawaiian Historical Society. She was a tireless promoter of Oregon history, and her abilities and enthusiasm as a speaker drew crowds to her lectures in a way that many traditional historians could not. She once wrote to Meany, "As you know many 'scientific historians' are loath to admit that anything can be history written in other than depressing detail."[6] She proved throughout her life that her brand of history was much more appealing to the public than the tomes produced by academic historians.

Dye was a consummate historical researcher and had, as her husband put it, "a nose for finding out things."[7] Her home was cluttered with the ephemera collected from her many research trips, and she regularly boxed up materials and sent them to the Oregon Historical Society. Dye understood the value of the details that allow one to recreate history, and she passed that appreciation down to her children and grandchildren. She once told her son Everett to save all of the family letters because "one day [they may] be all we have left to refer to for facts."[8]

Finally, it is worth noting that Dye was an accomplished organizer of people. Her grandchild Dolly Hutchinson once mentioned that Grandma Dye liked to form committees and initiate projects and then turn them over to others. She would then move on to the next interesting task that came her way. A list of committees she chaired and organizations she led over her lifetime would encompass several pages. One of her primary enjoyments in life was her women's club work, and from the Chautauqua women's symposium to the Woman's Club of the Lewis and Clark Exposition to the Oregon City Woman's Club, she devoted years of her life to organizing women. She once commented that "like the public school the Woman's Club is a school in citizenship for all women," and she recognized the importance of connecting women's domestic world with the public sphere.[9] At the age of seventy she was elected president of the Clackamas County Federation of Women's Clubs, an organization she had helped to build, and she remained an active member until her death.

In customary self-confident fashion she wrote her own tribute in 1924. It summarized her many accomplishments, her unswerving devotion to the history of Oregon, and her indomitable spirit. "If you remember me," she offered, "let it be as one who loved Oregon and who wanted its people to have the best the world has to offer in history, literature, art, music, and social service."[10]   Her desire to connect history to every facet of American society and culture enabled her not simply to educate but also to enliven the past for several generations of readers. Perhaps, after all, she was a historian, in the best sense of the word.

Notes

List of Abbreviations

EED   Eva Emery Dye
CHD   Charles Henry Dye
EWD   Everett Willoughby Dye
CED   Charlotte Evangeline Dye
EDH   Eva Dye Hutchinson (the married name of Charlotte Evangeline Dye)
OHS   Oregon Historical Society

Introduction

1 "Phrenological Examination of Eva Emery Dye, Oberlin, 188[]," Hutchinson collection. A description of phrenology can be found in Paul Boyer, Clifford E. Clark, Jr., Joseph Kett, et al., *The Enduring Vision: A History of the American People* (Lexington: D. C. Heath, 1993), 361-62.

2 Melva Garrow Elingsen, "Eva and Clio; Or, The Muse Meets Its Mistress," *Call Number* (Fall 1957):20; "News and Comment," *Oregon Historical Quarterly* vol. 48 (March 1947):52.

3 Jean M. Ward and Elaine A. Maveety, eds., *Pacific Northwest Women, 1815-1925: Lives, Memories, and Writings* (Corvallis: Oregon State University Press, 1995); Gordon B. Dodds, ed., *Varieties of Hope: An Anthology of Oregon Prose* (Corvallis, OR: Oregon State University Press, 1993).

4 EED to Children, July 17, 1937.

Chapter 1

1 The fire, groundbreaking, and building of the church on a new site is described in Horace Lyman Bachelder, *The Liberal Church at the End of the Oregon Trail* (Portland: Watson Printing Co., 1969), 48 and 55-59.

2 Untitled newspaper account from the *Oregonian*, April 26, 1959 (Dye biographical file at OHS).

3 For changes from a frontier economy to industrialization see Thomas Dublin, *Women at Work: The Transformation of Work and Community in Lowell, Massachusetts, 1826-1860* (New York: Columbia University Press, 1979);

Suzanne Lebsock, *The Free Women of Petersburg: Status and Culture in a Southern Town, 1784-1860* (New York: W. W. Norton, 1984); Mary P. Ryan, *Cradle of the Middle Class: The Family in Oneida County, New York, 1790-1865* (New York: Cambridge University Press, 1981); Christine Stansell, *City of Women: Sex and Class in New York, 1789-1860* (New York: Alfred A. Knopf, 1986).

4 Cyrus Emery, "Reminiscences of Life" (unpublished ms., Prophetstown, IL, 1903, Hutchinson collection), 11 see also 4, 75.

5 Ibid., 4.

6 Ibid., 5.

7 Ibid., 4, 19.

8 Lebsock, 57-60; Norma Basch, *In the Eyes of the Law: Women, Marriage, and Property in Nineteenth-Century New York* (Ithaca: Cornell University Press, 1982), chapter three.

9 Emery, 11.

10 On the revival movement in general and New York in particular see Paul E. Johnson, *A Shopkeeper's Millenium: Society and Revivals in Rochester, New York, 1815-1837* (New York: Hill and Wang, 1978); Ryan, chapter two.

11 Emery, 46.

12 Ibid., 16-17.

13 Ibid., 60, 39, 59.

14 Ibid., 40, 49.

15 Flyer from "Maine Wesleyan Seminary and Female College, Kent's Hill," with handwritten note from Eva: "This is where my mother went to school; at Kent's Hill, Maine about 1850. Specialized in music" (n.d., Hutchinson collection).

16 Emery, 71.

17 Ibid., and Lucinda Smith to Children, December 9, 1855. Unless otherwise noted, letters from and to Lucinda Smitth and Caroline Emery are part of the Hutchinson Collection.

18 Lucinda Smith to Caroline Trafton Emery, October [ ], 1855 and April 12, 1855.

19 Caroline Trafton Emery to John and Malina Trafton, August 19, 1854.

20 Emery, 124.

21 Ibid., 91, 94-95.

22 Lucinda Smith to Caroline Trafton Emery, June 25, 1854; Emery, 93.

23 Lucinda Smith to Children, July 25, 1854 and September 9, 1854.

24 Ibid., July 25, 1854.

25 Caroline Trafton Emery to John and Malina Trafton, August 19, 1854.

26 Lucinda Smith to Children, July 25, 1854 and September 9, 1854.

27 Lucinda Smith to Cyrus Emery, August 16, 1855.

28 Salter Emery to Cyrus Emery, August 13, 1855.

29 Lucinda Smith to Cyrus and Caroline Emery, February 6, 1857.

30 Lucinda Smith to Caroline Trafton Emery, March 8, 1857.

31 Lucinda Smith to Caroline and Cyrus Emery, April 11, 1857.

32 Lucinda Smith to Cyrus Emery, May 2, 1857.

33 Ibid.

34 EED to EDH, December 14, 1939.

35 Eva Emery Dye, autobiographical fragment (n.d., Hutchinson collection).

36 [Oregon City] *Morning Enterprise,* "Extensive War Work is Being Outlined by Local Chapter of D.A.R." May 5, 1918; Fred Lockley, *The History of the Columbia River Valley* (Chicago: S. J. Clarke Publishing Co., 1928) vol. 2, 290.

37 Quoted in Verne Bright, "Historian of the Pioneers," *Northwest Literary Review* 1 (Nov.-Dec. 1935), 4.

38 Emery, 36-37, 23, 104-5.

39 EED to EWD, February 23, 1920.

40 Fred Lockley, "Impressions and Observations of the Journal Man," [Oregon] *Daily Journal,* (March 18, 1936).

41 Emery, 94.

42 Eva Emery Dye, autobiographical fragment.

43 Eva Emery Dye, "Sketch of Eva Emery Dye," autobiographical fragment (n.d., Hutchinson collection).

44 Lockley, *The History of the Columbia River Valley,* 293.

45 Lockley, "Impressions and Observations of the Journal Man."

46 Dye, "Yesterday at Oberlin," *Oberlin Alumni Magazine* (May 1909), 321.

Chapter 2

1 Untitled clipping from "Jennie Juniper" (pseudonym for Eva Emery) March 28, 1875, Oberlin, Ohio, in scrapbook (OHS Dye collection, box 2).

2 Eva Emery Dye, "Yesterday at Oberlin," *Oberlin Alumni Magazine* (May 1909):321.

3 Lockley, "Impressions and Observations of the Journal Man"; Charles R. Hutchinson, "The Story of Eva Emery and Charles H. Dye" (unpublished ms., 1989, Hutchinson collection), 1.

4 Barbara Miller Solomon, *In the Company of Educated Women: A History of Women and Higher Education in America* (New Haven: Yale University Press, 1985), 62.

5 Eleanor Flexner, *Century of Struggle: The Woman's Rights Movement in the United States* (Cambridge: Harvard University Press, 1979), p. 69.

6 For another helpful comparison, consider the early life and struggles of Jane Addams. From her mother's early death to her father's domineering presence, and Addams's later efforts to educate herself and find a meaningful career, her life has many parallels with that of Eva Emery Dye. See the essays in Anne Firor Scott, *Making the Invisible Woman Visible* (Chicago: University of Illinois Press, 1984); and Alice S. Rossi, ed., *The Feminist Papers from Adams to de Beauvoir* (Boston: Northeastern University Press, 1973).

7 Nancy F. Cott, *The Bonds of Womanhood: "Woman's Sphere" in New England, 1780-1835* (New Haven: Yale University Press, 1977); Sara M. Evans, *Born for Liberty: A History of Women in America* (New York: Free Press, 1997), chapter five; Kathryn Kish Sklar, *Catharine Beecher: A Study in American Domesticity* (New Haven: Yale University Press, 1973).

8 Solomon, 21-24, 63.

9 Lockley, *The History of the Columbia River Valley,* 293.

10 *Oberlin Review* 2 (5) April 21, 1875.

11 Ibid., 2 (10) July 7, 1875.

12 Ibid., 5 (3) October 17, 1877, 30 and 35.

13 Ibid., 5 (18) May 15, 1878, 207.
14 Ibid., 5 (6) November 28, 1877, 66.
15 Ibid., 6 (18) May 14, 1879, 211.
16 Ibid., 5 (14) March 20, 1878, 164.
On Romanticism, see Richard H.
Fogle,ed., *The Romantic Movement in
American Writing* (New York: Odyssey
Press, 1966), 1-24. "The badge A.B."
refers to the bachelor's degree; the Latin
is *artium baccalaureus*. Elizabeth Jewell
and Frank Abate, eds. *The New Oxford
American Dictionary* (New York: Oxford
University Press, 2001), 1.
17 *Oberlin Review*, 5 (14) March 20,
1878, 164.
18 Ibid.
19 Ibid., 6 (9) January 8, 1879, 103.
20 Ibid., 5 (5) November 14, 1877, 55.
21 Ibid.
22 Ibid., 5 (7) December 7, 1877, 78.
23 Ibid., 6 (16) April 16, 1879, 187.
24 Ibid., 7 (17) April 30, 1879, 198.
25 Ibid., 9 (2) February 4, 1882.
26 Homer, *The Odyssey* (London:
Penguin Books, 1991 edition, trans.
D.C.H. Rieu), xxxv.
27 *Oberlin Review*, 8 (4) November 6,
1880.
28 Ibid., 4 (12) August 1, 1877.
29 Ibid.
30 Dye, autobiographical fragment.
31 Verne Bright, "Historian of the
Pioneers," *Northwest Literary Review*, 1
(Nov.-Dec. 1935), 4.
32 *Oberlin Review* 8 (17) May 14, 1881.
33 Ibid., 8 (16) April 30, 1881, 189.
34 Nancy F. Cott, *The Grounding of
Modern Feminism* (New Haven: Yale
University Press, 1987), chapter one.
35 Evans, 125-26.
36 *Oberlin Review* 6 (15) April 2, 1879,
170.
37 Evans, 127.
38 Eva L. Emery, "Women of Genius,"
n.d. [c. 1880], Hutchinson collection.
39 Margaret Fuller, "The Great Lawsuit.
Man Versus Men. Woman Versus
Women," in Alice S. Rossi, *The Feminist
Papers* (Boston: Northeastern University
Press, 1988), 168. For Fuller's
discussions of self-dependence, see her
Woman in the Nineteenth Century (New
York: W. W. Norton & Co., 1971), 40,
118, 121, 128, 175.

40 *Oberlin Review* 8 (10) February 5,
1881, 111.
41 Lockley, *History of the Columbia River
Valley*, 294.
42 *Oberlin Review* 9 (10) January 21,
1882, 117.
43 Ibid., 6 (6) November 20, 1878, 71;
and 6 (18) May 14, 1879.
44 Lockley, "Impressions and
Observations of the Journal Man."
45 *Oberlin Review*, 9 (20) June 17, 1882,
"Graduating Classes," 239.

Chapter 3

1 Souvenir postcards from Sidney, Iowa,
with Eva Emery Dye's notes on the
obverse (n.d., Hutchinson collection); no
history of Sidney, Iowa exists, but many
pertinent facts were provided by
Librarian Bev Finnigan at the Sidney
Public Library.
2 Howard R. Lamar, ed., *The New
Encyclopedia of the American West* (New
Haven: Yale University Press, 1998),
552; Dorothy Schweider, *Iowa: The
Middle Land* (Ames: Iowa State
University Press, 1996), 62-63; Bev
Finnigan states that the railroad reached
Sidney in 1878.
3 Bev Finnigan; Dye Family Record
(Hutchinson collection), 166; souvenir
postcards from Sidney, Iowa (see note
1).
4 Fred Lockley, *History of the Columbia
River Valley From the Dalles to the Sea*
(Chicago: S. J. Clarke Publishing
Company, 1928) vol. II, 294; draft
biographical sketch of C. H. Dye for the
"Alumni Necrology, 1925-30," and
alumni questionnaire (December 1894),
Oberlin College Archives.
5 "Sidney School Column" (n.d.,
newspaper clipping, Hutchinson
collection).
6 Eva Emery Dye, poetry journal, n.p.
(1880-c. 1900, Hutchinson collection).
7 Ibid.
8 Confirmation for Charles Dye's degree
from Tammy Martin at the Oberlin
College Archives; for Eva Emery Dye's
degree, the *Oberlin Weekly News* June 27,
1889; Oberlin graduates could receive
an honorary A.M., an A.M. in "Course
and Prescribed Work," or an A.M. for
postgraduate study. Charles and Eva

Emery Dye both received degrees for "Course and Prescribed Work." For information on the granting of A.M. degrees prior to 1898 see the Oberlin College Alumni Register (1960), Oberlin College Archives.

9 Ibid, May 1884.

10 Ibid, c. 1886, 166.

11 Charles H. and Eva Emery Dye, alumni questionnaires (1888 and December 1894), Oberlin College Archives.

12 Ibid.

13 Eva Emery Dye, "The Amana Commune," *Chicago Daily News* (September 13, 1888). For this essay Eva was paid six dollars (notes made on a page in her journal, n.d.). See also her notes for the essay, recorded on p. 67 of her journal. Eva was meticulous about noting the date and day, "Thursday evening," that this essay was published and the payment; however, the essay could not be located on extant microfilm copies of the *Chicago Daily News*.

14 Press review from *Iowa City Republican* (n.d. [c. 1889] news clipping, Hutchinson collection).

15 Eva Emery Dye, "The Historic Capital of Iowa," *Magazine of American History* (vol. XXI, no. 6, June, 1889), 443-55.

16 Ibid., 446.

17 Other favorable reviews came from the *St. Paul Pioneer Press* and *Chicago Herald* (press review clipping, n.d., Hutchinson collection).

18 CHD to EED, July 3, 1889.

19 Ibid.

20 Charles R. Hutchinson, "Story of Eva Emery and Charles H. Dye" (1989), 2.

21 [Portland] *Oregonian* (March 20, 1936), 10.

22 Ibid. For Reverend Lucas's tenure at the Congregational Church, see Horace Lyman Bachelder, *The Liberal Church at the End of the Oregon Trail* (Portland, Watson Printing Co., 1969), 30-38.

23 Eva Emery Dye poetry journal (December 1888, Hutchinson collection), 52.

24 Ibid., "The Children's Story," (January 1889), 53-54.

25 Ibid., 59, 63.

26 Ibid., 55.

27 Ibid., 58.

28 Ibid., poetry journal, 220-21.

29 Ibid., 52.

30 Ibid., "The Children's Story" (c. 1898), 45.

31 Ibid., 58.

32 Ibid., 68

33 Ibid., 90.

34 Ibid., 85.

35 Ibid., poetry journal, 165.

36 The two classic studies of women's revolutionary experience are Linda K. Kerber, *Women of the Republic: Intellect and Ideology in Revolutionary America* (Chapel Hill: University of North Carolina Press, 1980) and Mary Beth Norton, *Liberty's Daughters: The Revolutionary Experience of American Women, 1750-1800* (Boston: Little, Brown and Company, 1980); see also Sara M. Evans, *Born for Liberty: A History of Women in America* (New York: Free Press, 1997), chapters three and four; Ruth H. Bloch, "The Gendered Meanings of Virtue in Revolutionary America," *Signs* 13 (1987): 37-58; Jan Lewis, "Virtue and Seduction in the Early Republic," *William and Mary Quarterly* 44 (October 1987): 689-721.

37 Mary Earhart Dillon, "Frances Willard," in Edward James, et al., eds. *Notable American Women, 1607-1950: A Biographical Dictionary* (Cambridge, MA: Harvard University Press, 1971), vol. III, 617; Evans, 126-30.

38 Edward Bellamy, *Looking Backward* (New York, 1960 ed.). For a discussion of Bellamy's views and their appeal to socialist women, see Mari Jo Buhle, *Women and American Socialism, 1870-1920* (Urbana: University of Illinois Press, 1981) 75-77; see also Buhle's discussion of Willard and Nationalism, 80-81.

39 Bellamy, *Looking Backward*, 176, 180, as quoted in Buhle, 76.

40 For Bellamy's influence in Oregon, particularly in Nationalist clubs that sprang up in many rural communities, see James J. Kopp, "Looking Backward at Edward Bellamy's Influence in Oregon, 1888-1936," *Oregon Historical Quarterly* 104 (1): 63-95.

41 Eva Emery Dye, "Blue Monday Must Go," *The Housekeeper* (December 1, 1889).

42 Ibid.

43 See the essay on Gilman and the selections from *Women and Economics* in Alice S. Rossi, *The Feminist Papers from Adams to de Beauvoir* (Boston: Northeastern University Press, 1988).

44 Dye, "Blue Monday Must Go."

45 Kathryn Kish Sklar, *Catharine Beecher: A Study in American Domesticity* (New Haven: Yale University Press, 1973), 163. Catharine Beecher, *Treatise on Domestic Economy for the Use of Young Ladies at Home and at School* (1841), as quoted in Sklar, 160.

46 Dillon, 615-16.

47 For the intellectual roots of the nineteenth-century woman's rights movement see Nancy Cott, *The Grounding of Modern Feminism* (New Haven: Yale University Press, 1987), chapter one.

48 For a discussion of the "justice" versus "expediency" argument during the Progressive Era see Aileen S. Kraditor, *The Ideas of the Woman Suffrage Movement, 1890-1920* (New York: W. W. Norton & Co., 1981), chapter three. Evans provides a useful summary of these ideas, 152-56. See also Estelle Freedman, "Separatism As Strategy: Female Institution Building and American Feminism, 1870-1930," *Feminist Studies* 5, no. 3 (Fall 1979); Nancy Cott states that the dual argument of justice and expediency had a "see-saw quality: at one end, the intention to eliminate sex-specific limitations; at the other the desire to recognize rather than quash the qualities and habits called female, to protect the interests women had already defined as theirs and give those much greater public scope" (19-20).

49 Eva Emery Dye, "Only A Woman," *Union Signal* (May 8, 1890).

50 Ibid.

51 Ibid. On the racist and nativist tone of the late nineteenth-century suffrage movement, see Louise Newman, *White Women's Rights: The Racial Origins of Feminism in the United States* (New York: Oxford University Press, 1999); Kraditor, chapter six; Evans, 155-56. After 1890 black voters were increasingly the targets of intimidation

and violence throughout the nation. Poll taxes, fraudulent election tactics, and terrorism made their enfranchisement tenuous at best.

52 Eva Emery Dye, poetry journal (February 1890), n.p. Eva Emery Dye, "A Woman Led the Deed," *Union Signal* (February 27, 1890).

53 Ibid.

54 Ibid. "For God and Home and Native Land" was the slogan of the WCTU. An alternate version in her poetry journal states, "For God and Home and Woman's Hand"/Shall slay him by and by," 228-29.

Chapter 4

1 Eva Emery Dye to children, July 13, 1924 (Hutchinson collection).

2 Eva Emery Dye, untitled speech to the Daughters of the American Revolution, 1906 (OHS Dye collection, box 4).

3 Ibid.

4 Eva Emery Dye, "Introduction to History," (n.d. [c. 1889], in poetry journal, Hutchinson collection), 188.

5 Gordon B. Dodds, *The American Northwest: A History of Oregon and Washington* (Wheeling, IL: Forum Press, Inc., 1986), 70 and 102-6; for patterns of settlement in the region and information on the ethnicity of the first migrants, see Carlos A. Schwantes, *The Pacific Northwest: An Interpretive History* (Lincoln: University of Nebraska Press, 1996), 225-32.

6 Schwantes, 226.

7 Charles R. Hutchinson, "The Story of Eva Emery and Charles H. Dye," (unpublished ms., 1989), 2.

8 Quoted in Alfred Powers, *History of Oregon Literature* (Portland: Metropolitan Press, 1935), 404.

9 Schwantes, 111-12.

10 Works Projects Administration, *End of the Trail* (Portland: Binfords and Mort, 1940), 191.

11 Ibid.

12 Quoted in Powers, 405.

13 *History of the Bench and Bar* (Portland, 1910); Eva Emery Dye to Lena, June 5, 1906 (OHS Dye collection, box 1).

14 Amanda Laugesen, "George Himes, F. G. Young, and the Early Years of the Oregon Historical Society," *Oregon*

Historical Quarterly vol. 101, no. 1 (Spring 2000): 18.

15 Quoted in Verne Bright, "Historian of the Pioneers," *Northwest Literary Review* 1 (Nov.-Dec. 1935): 4.

16 Eva Emery Dye, "autobiographical fragment," (n.d., c. 1905, Hutchinson collection). A condensed version of this autobiographical account appeared in *The National Cyclopaedia of American Biography* (New York: James T. White & Co., 1906), vol. 13, 346.

17 Eva Emery Dye, "Longfellow," (Oberlin, 1881-82, in poetry journal, Hutchinson collection), 173.

18 Henry Wadsworth Longfellow, *Evangeline and Selected Tales and Poems* (New York: New American Library, 1964), 74.

19 Ibid., xvi.

20 Dye, "Longfellow," 174.

21 Ibid., 175.

22 Washington Irving, *Astoria, Or Anecdotes of an Enterprize Beyond the Rocky Mountains* (Boston: Twayne Publishers, 1976), 58-59, 101, 239-44, 310-11.

23 In his discussion of the Rocky Mountain Fur Company Bernard DeVoto recorded an important note on Irving: "This is a good place to remark on Irving's usual trustworthiness and on the curious decline in reputation which *Astoria* and *Bonneville* have suffered. They are little used by modern writers and yet both are original sources, in some contexts the only sources, and both have remarkable accuracy. Their literary quality is superb." Bernard DeVoto, *Across the Wide Missouri* (Boston: Houghton Mifflin Company, 1998 reprint of 1947 edition), chapter V, note 11, pages 401-2.

24 Eva Emery Dye, *McLoughlin and Old Oregon* (Chicago: A.C. McClurg & Co., 1910 ed.), 9-10.

25 Ibid., 66.

26 Profiles of McLoughlin and the Hudson's Bay Company can be found in Dodds, 39-47; Schwantes, 70-79; Keith Murray, "The Role of the Hudson's Bay Company in Pacific Northwest History," in G. Thomas Edwards and Carlos A. Schwantes, eds., *Experiences in a Promised Land: Essays in Pacific Northwest History* (Seattle: University of Washington Press, 1986), 28-39.

27 Richard G. Montgomery, *The White-Headed Eagle: John McLoughlin, Builder of an Empire* (Freeport, NY: Books for Libraries Press, 1971), 84.

28 Murray, 36; Dodds, 98.

29 Dye, *McLoughlin*, 67-68.

30 Ibid., 19.

31 For a balanced analysis of Narcissa Whitman's personal relationships and role as a missionary spouse see Julie Roy Jeffrey, *Converting the West: A Biography of Narcissa Whitman* (Norman: University of Oklahoma Press, 1991).

32 Numerous examples of Narcissa's discontent can be found in Narcissa Whitman, *The Letters of Narcissa Whitman* (Fairfield, WA: Ye Galleon Press, 1986).

33 Longfellow, xvi.

34 Dye, *McLoughlin*, 223-25, 336, 205.

35 Whitman, 142-45, 225-26, 94. The last example is also reprinted in Nancy F. Cott, ed., *Root of Bitterness: Documents of the Social History of American Women* (Boston: Northeastern University Press, 1986), 232.

36 Dye, *McLoughlin*, 236.

37 Ibid., 282.

38 For a discussion of history and literature in the region, see Dodds, 158-62.

39 See especially Dye's chapters "Elijah" and "Dr. Whitman and His Cayuses."

40 Dye, *McLoughlin*, 55, 147, 148, 204, 205.

41 An anonymous reviewer of *McLoughlin* noted that Dye "correctly conceives of the motive that is primary in this culminative course of events. A lower race is to be dispossessed by a higher." Review of *McLoughlin and Old Oregon*, *Oregon Historical Quarterly* vol. 1, no. 4 (1900): 208.

42 It was not until after the turn of the century that histories of the region began to break free from a purely heroic stance on the first pioneers. See Dodds, 158-62. Schwantes also notes, "The tragic story of the Whitmans eventually generated an enormous body of writing that has nearly overshadowed the rest of Pacific Northwest history, transformed Marcus and Narcissa Whitman from well-meaning missionaries into long-suffering and sacrificing saints, and for

years sustained the legend that Marcus Whitman saved Oregon" (90). Clifford Drury provides an excellent summary of the Whitman literature in *Marcus and Narcissa Whitman and the Opening of Old Oregon* (Glendale: Arthur H. Clark Company, 1973), vol. 2, Appendices three and four.

43 Dye, *McLoughlin*, 346.

44 "Stirring Epic of Old Oregon Becomes Opera 'Narcissa,'" *Oregonian*, September 5, 1926.

45 Dye, *McLoughlin*, 380.

46 Eva Emery Dye, "Woman's Part in the Drama of the Northwest," *Oregon Pioneer Transactions* (Portland, 1895), 39, 42.

47 Drury, vol. 2, 345-46.

48 Eva Emery Dye, alumni questionnaire (December 1894). Oberlin College Archives.

49 Quoted in Alfred Powers, *History of Oregon Literature* (Portland: Metropolitan Press, 1935), 409.

50 Ibid. See also Bright, 4.

51 Dodds, 159.

52 Frances Fuller Victor, "Review of *McLoughlin and Old Oregon: A Chronicle*," *American Historical Review* vol. 6, no 1 (1900), 148.

53 Ibid., 150.

54 Whitman, 40.

55 Melva Garrow Ellingsen, "Eva and Clio; Or, the Muse Meets Its Mistress," *Call Number* (Fall 1957): 17.

56 William A. Mowry to Dye, October 12, 1900 (OHS Dye collection, box 1). Mowry wrote *Marcus Whitman* (1901), which also painted a heroic picture of Whitman. Drury, vol. 2, 386.

57 Review of *McLoughlin* in the *Oregon Historical Quarterly*, 207 and 210.

58 Quoted in Bright, 14.

59 George Sparks (A. C. McClurg & Co.) to Dye, November 10, 1919 (Hutchinson collection).

60 Patricia Nelson Limerick, *The Legacy of Conquest: The Unbroken Past of the American West* (New York: W.W. Norton & Company, Inc., 1987), 26.

61 Review of *McLoughlin* in the *Oregon Historical Quarterly*, 207.

62 EED to Mr. Levison, July 2, 1901 (OHS Dye collection, box 4).

63 The national Chautauqua movement is described in Victoria and Robert Ormand Case, *We Called It Culture, The Story of Chautauqua* (Garden City, NY: Doubleday & Co., Inc., 1948). The best local histories of Chautauqua in Oregon are Herbert K. Beals, *Gladstone, Oregon, A History: Part Two: Civil War to the Eve of the Great Depression* (Gladstone, OR: Gladstone Historical Society, 1998), chapter ten; and Donald Epstein, "Gladstone Chautauqua: Education and Entertainment, 1893-1928," *Oregon Historical Quarterly* vol. 80, no. 4 (Winter 1979): 391-403.

64 Eva Emery Dye, "Portland-Oregon City Chautauqua at Gladstone Park," [Oregon City] *Morning Enterprise* (n.d. c. 1911), Hutchinson collection.

65 Ibid. Eva Emery Dye, "Answers to Yesterday's Questions," (n.d., OHS Dye Collection, box 4); "Big Chautauqua at Gladstone Opens July 12," *Gladstone Reporter*, June 30, 1921; Beals, 80-81.

66 "Big Chautauqua at Gladstone Opens July 12," and Beals, 82.

67 Dye, "Portland-Oregon City Chautauqua at Gladstone Park."

68 EED to Children, April 13, 1924.

69 Beals, 84.

70 Abigail Scott Duniway, *Path Breaking: An Autobiographical History of the Equal Suffrage Movement in Pacific Coast States* (New York: Source Book Press, 1970, reprint of 1914 edition), 110; Susan B. Anthony and Ida Husted Harper, eds., *History of Woman Suffrage*, vol. 4 (1902), 892-93.

71 Epstein, 394; Beals states that by the 1920s "the Gladstone Chautauqua [grew] to be the largest Chautauqua on the West Coast," 92.

72 Eva Emery Dye to Mrs. Franklin, May 4, 1922 (OHS Dye collection, box 4). Beals does not note the evolution of the Symposium into a forum for women, 91-92.

73 Eva Emery Dye, "Answers to Yesterday's Questions."

74 Eva Emery Dye, "Chautauqua Congressman," (n.d, OHS Dye collection box 4).

75 Ibid.

76 Epstein, 391.

77 EED to Levison.

78 Ibid.

79 Epstein, 402-3.

80 EED to Levison.

Chapter 5

1 Eva L. Emery, "The Poet of the Future," (n.d., Hutchinson collection).

2 Ella E. Clark and Margot Edmonds, *Sacagawea of the Lewis and Clark Expedition* (Berkeley: University of California Press, 1979), 90-92, 102; Jan C. Dawson, "Sacagawea: Pilot or Pioneer Mother?" *Pacific Northwest Quarterly* 83, no. 1 (January 1992):22; Harold P. Howard, *Sacajawea* (Norman: University of Oklahoma Press, 1971), 182; Donna Kessler, *The Making of Sacagawea: A Euro-American Legend* (Tuscaloosa: University of Alabama Press, 1996), 67; Gail Landsman, "The 'Other' as Political Symbol: Images of Indians in the Woman Suffrage Movement," *Ethnohistory* vol. 39, no. 3 (1992): 271; David Remley, "Sacajawea of Myth and History," in Helen Winter Stauffer and Susan J. Rosowski, eds., *Women and Western American Literature* (Troy, NY: Whitston Publishing Company, 1982), 72; James Ronda, *Lewis and Clark Among the Indians* (Lincoln: University of Nebraska Press, 1984), 256; Ronald W. Taber, "Sacagawea and the Suffragettes: An Interpretation of a Myth," *Pacific Northwest Quarterly* (January 1967): 7-8.

3 One noteworthy exception is Kimberly Swanson's, "Eva Emery Dye and the Romance of Oregon History," *The Pacific Historian*, vol. 29, no. 4. (1987): 59-68.

4 Eva Emery Dye journal, January 31, 1898. (Hutchinson collection), 94.

5 Ibid., January 11, 1898, 90.

6 Quoted in Alfred Powers, *History of Oregon Literature* (Portland: Metropolitan Press, 1935), 405. See also "On the Explorers' Trail: How the Author Searched the Land for Historical Material," [Portland] *Oregonian*, November 2, 1902.

7 Dye journal, October 13, 1896, 81. Throughout her married life, Mrs. Dye had the benefit of domestic help, first with a series of unnamed and unacknowledged "girls," and later from Gertie Humphreys, a woman of some renown among the grandchildren. Gertie was as old as, if not older than, Mrs. Dye, and her inability and unwillingness to do heavy work was a point of contention between them. Mrs. Dye's letters to the children are full of exasperated complaints about the lack of competent help, especially in late summer when the fruit from numerous trees and vegetables from an abundant garden needed to be picked and canned. Like most middle-class women of the late nineteenth century, Mrs. Dye never commented on the irony of her domestic situation: her writing, civic participation, and activism for women's rights was made possible by the labor of frequently exploited, working-class women.

8 Ibid., June 19, 1902, 26.

9 *Oregonian*, July 29, 1934 (Dye biographical file, OHS); Dye to Mr. Gill, September 1, 1906 (OHS Dye collection, box 1).

10 Eva Emery Dye, "The Hudson's Bay Company Regime in the Oregon Country," in F. G. Young, *Semi-Centennial History of Oregon* (Eugene, OR: University Press, 1898), 52.

11 F. G. Young, "The Oregon Trail," *Quarterly of the Oregon Historical Society* 1 (December 1900): 339, 341, as quoted in Amanda Laugesen, "George Himes, F.G. Young, and the Early Years of the Oregon Historical Society," *Oregon Historical Quarterly*, vol. 101, no. 1 (Spring 2000): 21 and 32. See also Thomas Vaughan, "A Century of the Oregon Historical Quarterly," in the same issue of the *Quarterly*, 6-17.

12 Oregon Historical Society, *Proceedings of the Oregon Historical Society* (1898-99), 1-23.

13 EED to EDH, March 9, 1941 (Hutchinson collection).

14 Rita Bell, "Eva Emery Dye, Writer Whose Work Has Awakened New Interest in Oregon History," November 17, 1901 (OHS scrapbook, 41:204).

15 Dye, "The Hudson's Bay Company Regime in the Oregon Country," 51.

16 F. G. Young, "The Lewis and Clark Expedition in American History," *Oregon Historical Quarterly* vol. 2, no. 4 (December 1901): 416. See also Young, "The Lewis and Clark Centennial, The Occasion and Its Observance," *Oregon*

Historical *Quarterly* vol. 4, no. 1 (March 1903): 1-20; and Young, "The Higher Significance in the Lewis and Clark Exploration," *Oregon Historical Quarterly* vol. 6, no. 1 (March, 1905): 1-25.

17 Carl Abbott, *The Great Extravaganza: Portland and the Lewis and Clark Exposition* (Portland: Oregon Historical Society Press, 1981), 14.

18 On the Louisiana Purchase and Jefferson's "empire of liberty," see Merrill D. Peterson, *Thomas Jefferson and the New Nation, A Biography* (New York: Oxford University Press, 1970), 771-76.

19 Eva Emery Dye, *The Conquest: The True Story of Lewis and Clark* (Chicago: A. C. McClurg & Co., 1902), 126.

20 Ibid., 143.

21 Ibid., 395. Dye always believed that America's manifest destiny would lead to expansion across the Pacific to Asia, and she was an early promoter of the importance of the Pacific Rim. She believed Jefferson had the same idea, but there is certainly no proof that he did.

22 John Palmer Spencer, "'We Are Not Dealing Entirely with the Past': Americans Remember Lewis and Clark," in Mark Spence and Kris Fresonke, eds., *Lewis and Clark: Legacies, Memories, and New Interpretations* (Berkeley: University of California Press, 2004), 169.

23 Eva Emery Dye, autobiographical sketch (n.d., Hutchinson collection).

24 Eva Emery Dye to children, December 25, 1919 (Hutchinson collection).

25 David Healy, *U.S. Expansionism: The Imperialist Urge in the 1890s* (Madison: University of Wisconsin Press, 1970); Walter LaFeber, *The New Empire: An Interpretation of American Expansion, 1860-1898* (Ithaca, NY: Cornell University Press, 1963); Emily Rosenberg, *Spreading the American Dream: American Economic and Cultural Expansion, 1890-1945* (New York: Hill and Wang, 1982). The Oregon Volunteer Infantry served in the Philippines, and their experience reflected and shaped concepts of race and imperialism in Oregon. See Sean McEnroe, "Painting the Philippines with an American Brush: Visions of Race and National Mission among the Oregon Volunteers in the Philippine Wars of 1898 and 1899," *Oregon Historical Quarterly* 104:1 (Spring 2003): 24-61.

26 Dye, *The Conquest*, 300.

27 Merrill D. Peterson, *The Jefferson Image in the American Mind* (Charlottesville: University Press of Virginia, 1998), 231-39.

28 Dye, *The Conquest*, 124, 127, 125.

29 Dye, autobiographical sketch.

30 Eva Emery Dye to Mr. [J. Neilson] Barry, June 14, 1933 (OHS Dye collection, box 1).

31 Paul Allen [and Nicholas Biddle], ed., *History of the Expedition Under the Command of Captains Lewis and Clark* (Philadelphia: Bradford and Inskeep, 1814, reprinted by University Microfilms, Inc., Ann Arbor); Elliott Coues, ed., *The History of the Lewis and Clark Expedition* (New York: Francis Harper, 1893, reprinted by Dover Publications, Inc., New York); by far the best history of the various editions of the expedition journals with biographies of the editors is Paul Cutright, *A History of the Lewis and Clark Journals* (Norman: University of Oklahoma Press, 1976).

32 Melva Garrow Ellingsen, "Eva and Clio: Or, The Muse Meets Its Mistress," *Call Number* (Fall 1957): 18.

33 Dye to C. Harper Anderson, September 1901 and October 5, 1901; Dye to H.W. Goode [president of the Lewis and Clark Exposition], April 19, 1905 (OHS Dye collection, box 1).

34 Dye to Reuben Gold Thwaites, February 16, 1902 (OHS Dye collection, box 1).

35 Dye to Mr. Barry, June 14, 1933 (OHS Dye collection, box 1).

36 Eva Emery Dye, "How Mrs. Dye Wrote 'The Conquest,'" speech to Portland Woman's Club (n.d., Dye biographical file at OHS).

37 Frederick Jackson Turner, *The Frontier in American History.* (New York: Dover Publications, 1996), 3.

38 Eva Emery Dye, untitled speech (n.d., OHS Dye collection, box 4).

39 Eva Emery Dye to H.W. Goode [president of the Lewis and Clark Exposition], April 19, 1905 (OHS Dye collection, box 1).

40 Eva Emery Dye to C. Harper Anderson, October 5, 1901 (OHS Dye collection, box 1).

41 Eva Emery Dye undated news clipping (c. 1935), Hutchinson collection.

42 Dye to C. Harper Anderson, October 5, 1901.

43 Mr. Sadtler to General Louis Wagner, May 22, 1901 (Mss 1089 microfilm, Dye, Eva - Correspondence, 1 reel).

44 Dye to OHS Board of Directors, November 26, 1901 (OHS Dye collection, box 1).

45 Dye to Reuben Gold Thwaites, February 16, 1902 (OHS Dye collection, box 1).

46 Dye to Mr. Barry, June 14, 1933.

47 Dye to C. Harper Anderson, October 5, 1901.

48 Eva Emery Dye, "Celebrated Historian of Oregon City Discoverer of Lewis and Clark Diary," *Oregonian*, November 11, 1923.

49 Thwaites, 48; Cutright, 118.

50 Dye, "Celebrated Historian."

51 Ibid.

52 Dye to Thwaites, November 6, 1902; Thwaites to Dye, November 10, 1902 and December 16, 1902; William Hancock Clark to Dye, December 12, 1902 (OHS Dye collection, box 1 and Mss. 1089 microfilm). Thwaites wrote later that he had found in one of Coues's reports on the Lewis and Clark codices that "one of Clark's journals is now in the possession of his son, Mr. Jefferson K. Clark, of St. Louis." He also noted, "upon assuming charge of the proposed publication, the writer at once approached the widow of Mr. Clark – the latter had died in New York soon after the appearance of the Coues edition – and requested an opportunity of examining this notebook, under the supposition that it was the Ordway journal" (Thwaites, 47). However, it is clear from their correspondence that Dye brought to Thwaites's attention the information about Ordway's journal. His note on December 16 is further evidence of this: "I thank you very much for your suggestions relative to Mrs. Clark. I will make an effort as soon as possible to see her."

53 Thwaites, 51.

54 Thwaites to Hays as quoted in Cutright, 119.

55 Thwaites, 48; Cutright, 118.

56 Thwaites to Hays, as quoted in Cutright, 119; Thwaites, 48-49.

57 Cutright, 117.

58 Ibid., 117-18.

59 Dye to Mr. Barry, June 14, 1933.

60 In a February 12, 1904 letter to Dye, Thwaites summarized the timeframe and the discovery (Mss 1089, micofilm).

61 Reuben Gold Thwaites, ed., *Original Journals of the Lewis and Clark Expedition, 1804-1806* (reprint of the 1905 edition, Arno Press, 1969) vol. 1, lix. Two years later Dye wrote to historian James Hosmer, "Now, as to Ordway's journal, I thought I had located it and sent the information to Reuben Gold Thwaites of Wis. He investigated and lo! not the Ordway journal but more of Clark's original letter books came to light" (Dye to Dr. Hosmer, April 4, 1904, OHS Dye collection, box 1).

62 Dye, *The Conquest*, 69, 54, 20, 21.

63 Ibid., 58.

64 For Clark's military career and his role in the settlement of Illinois and Ohio territory, see Lois Carrier, *Illinois: Crossroads of a Continent* (Urbana: University of Illinois Press, 1993), 25-31; see also the sketch of Clark in Howard R. Lamar, ed., *The New Encyclopedia of the American West* (New Haven: Yale University Press, 1998), 220; for Clark and his relationship with Jefferson during this period, see Peterson, *Thomas Jefferson*, 177-83.

65 Dye, *The Conquest*, 114.

66 Ibid., 401.

67 Ronald Takaki, *A Different Mirror: A History of Multicultural America* (Boston: Little, Brown & Co., 1993), 228-38; Patricia Nelson Limerick, *The Legacy of Conquest: The Unbroken Past of the American West* (New York: W.W. Norton & Co., 1987), 196-200; Frederick E. Hoxie, *A Final Promise: The Campaign to Assimilate the Indians, 1880-1920* (Franklin: University of Nebraska Press, 1984).

68 Dye, *The Conquest*, 280, 283.

69 For a discussion of popular writers who did challenge prevailing views of Native peoples, including Northwest author and poet C. E. S. Wood, see Sherry L. Smith, *Reimagining Indians: Native Americans through Anglo Eyes, 1880-1940* (New York: Oxford University Press, 2000).

70 "On the Explorers' Trail," *Oregonian*, November 2, 1902.

71 Quoted in Powers, 410.

72 Ibid.

73 The spelling of Sacajawea's name came from Dye's reading of Biddle and Coues and from anecdotal evidence provided by Clark descendants and the son of expedition member George Shannon. Biddle's text of May 20, 1805 notes, "They also reported that the country is broken and irregular like that near our camp; that about five miles up a handsome river about fifty yards wide, which we named after Chaboneau's wife, Sahcahjahweah, or Birdwoman's river ..." vol. 1, 222. Coues' footnote to this event reads, "Her name is usually spelled Sacajawea." He then adds from Lewis's diary, "About five miles abe [above] the mouth of [the Mussel-] Shell river a handsome river of about fifty yards in width discharged itself into the Shell river on the Stard. or upper side; this stream we called Sah-ca-gee-me-ah or bird woman's River, after our interpreter the Snake woman." vol. 1, 317, n38. Dye also claimed the spelling and pronunciation came from Shannon's son whom she met in California. She said she "argued the matter with him [the pronunciation], but he stuck to it that his father said the Indian woman's name was SakaJAWa." Dye to Grace Hebard, December 18, 1906 (OHS Dye collection, box 4). Today the accepted spelling among ethnographers and historians is Sacagawea, which is believed to mean Bird Woman and is of Hidatsa origin. See Donald Jackson, *Letters of the Lewis and Clark Expedition* (Urbana: University of Illinois Press, 1978), 316n; and Ronda, *Lewis and Clark Among the Indians*, 256-57.

74 Eva Emery Dye, "The College Girl," *Oregon Teachers' Monthly* (n.d., c. 1890, Hutchinson collection).

75 Dawson, 24.

76 Dye, *The Conquest*, 232.

77 Ibid., 237.

78 Biddle, vol. 2, 22 (October 19, 1805).

79 Ibid.

80 Ibid., 227. Of Charbonneau and Sacagawea Dye wrote, "but he had been kind to the captive Indian girl, and her heart clung to the easy-going Frenchman as her best friend. The worst white man was better than an Indian husband," 196-97.

81 Biddle, vol. 1, 381. Coues, vol. 2, 509 (August 17, 1805).

82 Ibid.

83 Dawson, 25.

84 Dye, *The Conquest*, 251.

85 Ibid., 290.

86 Rayna Green, "The Pocahontas Perplex: The Image of Indian Women in American Culture," in Ellen Carol DuBois and Vicki L. Ruiz, eds., *Unequal Sisters: A Multicultural Reader in U.S. Women's History* (New York: Routledge, 1990), 16, 17.

87 Dawson, 26.

88 Dye, *The Conquest*, 290.

89 Gail Bederman, *Manliness & Civilization: A Cultural History of Gender and Race in the United States, 1880-1917* (Chicago: University of Chicago Press, 1995), 144.

90 Ibid., chapters four and five.

91 Taber, 7-8.

92 Remley, 72. Gail Landsman also noted, "The last major use of Indian imagery in the woman suffrage movement was the turning of Sacajawea, the supposed guide to Lewis and Clark, into a heroine. This was largely the work of Eva Marie Dye [sic], chairman of the Oregon Equal Suffrage Association." 271.

93 Clark and Edmonds, 93.

94 Kessler, 67.

95 For criticism of the "guide" motif, see Clark and Edmonds, Kessler, Remley, and Ronda's appendix to *Lewis and Clark Among the Indians*, 256-60.

96 Dye, *The Conquest*, 224.

97 Ibid., 283.

98 Ibid., 285.

99 Biddle, vol. 2, 369-70.

100 Thwaites, *Original Journals*, vol. 5, 260.

101 Eva Emery Dye to J. Neilson Barry, June 10, 1933 (OHS Dye collection, box 1).

102 Advertising pamphlet for *The Conquest* from A. C. McClurg and Company (c. 1902, OHS Dye collection, box 4).

103 "On the Explorers' Trail," *Oregonian*, November 2, 1902.

104 Dye, untitled speech (n.d., OHS Dye collection, box 4).

105 "Saturday Review of Books," *New York Times*, November 29, 1902: 842. A favorable advance review also appeared in the *New York Times*, November 1, 1902: 750, and it was advertised in the fiction category of the "Saturday Review of Books," November 15, 1902: 792.

106 Anonymous review of "The Conquest," *Oregon Historical Quarterly* vol. 3 (1902): 9.

107 Dye quoted from these letters in two speeches, one untitled and undated in box 4 of her collection at OHS and in her speech to the Portland Woman's Club, "How Mrs. Dye Wrote 'The Conquest.'"

108 Dye, "How Mrs. Dye Wrote 'The Conquest.' "

109 Eva Emery Dye to Mr. Brown at A. C. McClurg and Co., January 15, 1903 (OHS Dye collection, box 1).

110 Dye to Mr. Barry, June 14, 1933.

111 Eva Emery Dye, untitled news clipping, March 17, 1901 (OHS scrapbook 39:50).

112 Turner, 9.

Chapter 6

1 Carl Abbott, *The Great Extravaganza, Portland and the Lewis and Clark Exposition* (Portland: Oregon Historical Society, 1981), 50.

2 The historiography on women's culture and its connection to women's politics is substantial. See in particular "Politics and Culture in Women's History: A Symposium," *Feminist Studies* 6, no. 1 (Spring 1980): 26-64; Estelle Freedman, "Separatism as Strategy: Female Institution Building and American Feminism, 1870-1930," *Feminist Studies* 5, no. 3 (Fall 1979): 512-29; Paula Baker, "The Domestication of

Politics: Women and American Political Society, 1780-1920," *American Historical Review*, vol. 89, no. 3 (June 1984): 620-47; Kathryn Kish Sklar, "Two Political Cultures in the Progressive Era: The National Consumers' League and the American Association for Labor Legislation," in Linda K. Kerber et. al., eds., *U. S. History as Women's History, New Feminist Essays* (Chapel Hill: University of North Carolina Press, 1995), 36-62; Mari Jo Buhle, *Women and American Socialism, 1870-1920* (Urbana: University of Illinois Press, 1983); Nancy F. Cott, *The Grounding of Modern Feminism* (New Haven: Yale University Press, 1987).

3 In this chapter, I use "Sacagawea" when referring to the historical Native American woman but retain Dye's "j" spelling for the statue association's title and for the name of the statue itself. For other histories that link clubwomen with suffrage activities see Steven Buechler, *The Transformation of the Woman Suffrage Movement: The Case of Illinois, 1850-1920* (New Brunswick: Rutgers University Press, 1986); Anne Firor Scott, *Natural Allies, Women's Associations in American History* (Chicago: University of Illinois Press, 1991); and June Underwood, "Civilizing Kansas: Women's Organizations, 1880-1920," *Kansas History* (winter-spring 1985): 291-306. Regarding national woman suffrage, see Cott, *The Grounding of Modern Feminism*; Eleanor Flexner, *Century of Struggle: The Woman's Rights Movement in the United States* (New York: Atheneum, 1973); Aileen Kraditor, *The Ideas of the Woman Suffrage Movement* (New York: Columbia University Press, 1965); William O'Neill, *Everyone Was Brave: A History of Feminism in America* (New York: Quadrangle, 1969); Alice S. Rossi, ed., *The Feminist Papers from Adams to de Beauvoir* (Boston: Northeastern University Press, 1988); and the six volumes of the *History of Woman Suffrage*.

4 Oregon Federation of Woman's Clubs, *Fifty Years of Progress, 1899-1950* (1950), 14. On the General Federation in this period see Mary I. Wood, *The History of the General Federation of Women's Clubs for*

the First Twenty-Two Years of Its Organization (Norwood, Mass.: Norwood Press, 1912).

5 Karen Blair, *The Clubwoman as Feminist* (New York: Holmes and Meier Publishers, 1980).

6 Abigail Scott Duniway, *Path Breaking: An Autobiographical History of the Equal Suffrage Movement in Pacific Coast States* (New York: Source Book Press, 1970 [1914 reprint]), 111.

7 On municipal housekeeping see Sara Evans, *Born for Liberty, A History of Women in America* (New York: The Free Press, 1989), chapter seven; Blair, *The Clubwoman as Feminist.*

8 Works Projects Administration, *History of the Portland Woman's Club* (n.d., no page numbers, pamphlet at OHS).

9 Ibid. *Fifty Years of Progress*, 13.

10 *Fifty Years of Progress*, 7.

11 Karen Blair's study suggests that although leaders in the club movement were late to support woman suffrage, many of their rank and file members were staunch supporters of equal voting. She never makes any direct links between these two causes, however. In Oregon the case was a bit different. Rank and file members seemed to have been quite resistant to the idea of endorsing suffrage, while the leadership generally viewed it favorably.

12 Sandra Haarsager's *Organized Womanhood: Cultural Politics in the Pacific Northwest, 1840-1920* (Norman: University of Oklahoma Press, 1997) is one of the only studies to examine the connections between women in clubs and suffrage in the Pacific Northwest. It contains valuable biographies of clubwomen, including Sarah Evans. However, Haarsager does not clearly articulate the impact that clubwomen had on the campaign for suffrage in Oregon, nor does she examine the rivalries that existed among women as they neared suffrage victory in 1912.

13 Joseph Gaston, *Portland, Oregon, Its History and Its Builders* (Chicago: S. J. Clarke Co., 1911), vol. II, 718; Haarsager, 291-95.

14 *Encyclopedia of Northwest Biography*, 221.

15 Portland, *New Northwest*, 26 May 1871, as quoted in G. Thomas Edwards,

Sowing Good Seeds: The Northwest Suffrage Campaigns of Susan B. Anthony (Portland: Oregon Historical Society Press, 1990), 12.

16 The best full-length biography of Duniway is Ruth Barnes Moynihan, *Rebel for Rights, Abigail Scott Duniway* (New Haven: Yale University Press, 1983), though Moynihan accepts uncritically Duniway's viewpoint on everything related to suffrage. Regarding the *New Northwest*, see Jean M. Ward and Elaine A. Maveety, eds., *Yours for Liberty: Selections from Abigail Scott Duniway's Suffrage Newspaper* (Corvallis, OR: Oregon State University Press, 2000). For Duniway's relationship with Susan B. Anthony, see Edwards, *Sowing Good Seeds.*

17 *Oregon Journal*, July 26, 1907, 48.

18 Evans to Dye, October 30, 1903. All letters between Evans and Dye can be found in the OHS Dye Collection, box 2.

19 *Oregon Journal*, July 6, 1906.

20 Gaston, vol. 2, 508-11.

21 Ibid. Undated letter from Sarah A. Evans to donors (OHS Dye collection, box 2); Fred Lockley, *History of the Columbia River Valley* (Chicago: S J. Clarke Co., 1928), vol. 2, 660-65.

22 *Fifty Years of Progress*, 55; "Active Woman's Club to Celebrate 6[5]th Anniversary," [Oregon City] *Enterprise-Courier*, April 30, 1968.

23 June Smelser, "A History of the McLoughlin House," in *Clackamas County Historical 1960* (Oregon City: Clackamas County Historical Society, 1960), 27-55; Thomas W. Prosch, "Effort to Save the Historic McLoughlin House," *Washington Historical Quarterly* vol. 1, no. 2 (January 1907): 36-42; Vara Caufield, "Two Historic Houses: How McLoughlin House Was Saved," *Oregon Historical Quarterly*, vol. 76, no. 3 (1975): 299-301; "Active Woman's Club to Celebrate 6[5]th Anniversary," *Enterprise-Courier.*

24 "Active Woman's Club to Celebrate 6[5]th Anniversary."

25 Caufield, 301; Smelser, 48-49.

26 Undated letter from Sarah A. Evans to donors (OHS Dye collection, box 2).

27 *Oregonian*, July 7, 1905.

28 Ethnohistorian Gail Landsman argues that white portrayals of Native American women depict conflicts between nature and civilization; according to the Anglo-American perspective, those Native American women who did not resist white expansion and adapted to white society had successfully negotiated the boundaries between nature (the "uncivilized") and culture (white civilization). "The 'Other' as Political Symbol: Images of Indians in the Woman Suffrage Movement," *Ethnohistory* vol. 39, no. 3 (Summer 1992): 273-74.

29 Baker, "The Domestication of Politics," 633.

30 *Oregonian*, May 17, 1931.

31 Ibid., July 17, 1931.

32 Evans to Dye, September 3, 1904.

33 For examples of women's auxiliaries that existed simultaneously with men's fraternal organizations and both preserved and augmented traditional values, see Buhle, *Women and American Socialism*, 14-20.

34 Portland Commercial Club of Portland, Oregon, *Constitution and By-Laws, Roster of Members, House Rules, Etc.* (1909), pamphlet at OHS, 5.

35 Ibid., 61; Evans to Dye, June 20, 1904.

36 Evans to Dye, August 1, 1904.

37 Ibid., September 7, 1904.

38 Ibid.

39 Ibid. See also Evans to Dye, September 14, 1904.

40 On voluntary associations and public and private spheres see Evans, *Born for Liberty*, 3-6; Sara M. Evans and Harry C. Boyte, *Free Spaces: The Sources of Democratic Change in America* (New York: Harper and Row, 1987), chapter three; Sara M. Evans, "Women's History and Political Theory: Toward a Feminist Approach to Public Life," and William Chafe, "Women's History and Political History: Some Thoughts on Progressivism and the New Deal," both in Nancy A. Hewitt and Suzanne Lebsock, eds., *Visible Women, New Essays on American Activism* (Urbana: University of Illinois Press, 1993).

41 Baker, 631.

42 Evans, "Women's History and Political Theory," 130.

43 Sarah Evans to Dye, October 25, 1903.

44 Ibid. *Oregon Journal*, July 6, 1906.

45 Sarah Evans to Dye, September 7, 1904.

46 Frank L. Merrick, "Woman's Part at the Centennial," *Lewis and Clark Journal*, vol. 3, no. 5 (February 1905).

47 Ibid. On the exhibits see "The Art Exhibit at the Fair," *Pacific Monthly*, vol. xiv, no. 3 (September 1905).

48 For a comparison of women's activities at the 1876 Centennial Exposition in Philadelphia with the 1893 Columbian Exposition, see Freedman, "Separatism as Strategy," 519-20. Interestingly the rhetoric surrounding women's activities at the New York World's Fair of 1937 was remarkably similar to that of 1905. The Fair Bulletin claimed that women "will not sit upon a pedestal, not be segregated, isolated; she will fit into the life of the Exposition as she does into life itself – never apart, always a part." As Freedman pointed out, "the part in this World's Fair, however, consisted primarily of fashion, food and vanity fair" (522).

49 Sarah Evans to Dye, January 27, 1904.

50 Ibid. Also August 28, 1903.

51 Sarah Evans to Dye, January 27, 1904, October 25 and October 5, 1903.

52 Ibid., February 12, 1904.

53 Ibid.

54 Ida Husted Harper, ed., *History of Woman Suffrage* (New York, 1969), vol. 5, 117; vol. 6, 540.

55 *Oregon Journal*, July 2, 1905.

56 *Oregonian* and *Oregon Journal*, July 6, 1905.

57 *Oregon Journal*, July 6, 1905, front page. On a related note, cultural historian Martha Banta sees a relationship between public statuary and an emphasis on public virtue in the period from 1880 to 1910. "Allegories of perfect beginnings" hearkened back to eras that citizens found more comprehensible and less threatening. Public parks were adorned with statues of Christopher Columbus, Pocahontas,

and Betsy Ross, for example; thus traditional feminine values as well as traditional masculine images underwent a renaissance in the Progressive era. *Imaging American Women: Idea and Ideals in Cultural History* (New York: Columbia University Press, 1987), 411-14.

58 *Oregonian*, July 7, 1905.

59 Ibid.

60 Julie Roy Jeffrey makes this argument explicit in reference to pioneer women in *Frontier Women: The Trans-Mississippi West, 1840-1880* (New York: Hill and Wang, 1979), chapter four.

61 Tom Edwards has noted that the image of Sacagawea did not seem to live on in the minds of campaign organizers. In fact, the symbol of Sacagawea was not used at all in Oregon's 1906 suffrage fight. *Sowing Good Seeds*, 240.

62 For a discussion of changes in ideas put forward by the national suffrage movement in the early twentieth century see Nancy Woloch, *Women and the American Experience* (New York: Knopf, 1984), 325-43; see also Aileen S. Kraditor, *The Ideas of the Woman Suffrage Movement, 1890-1920* (New York: W. W. Norton, 1981).

63 Quoted in Edwards, 239.

64 Dye, 1906 speech to the Daughters of the American Revolution (OHS Dye collection, box 4).

65 Sources on Oregon suffrage include Duniway, *Path Breaking*; Edwards, *Sowing Good Seeds*; Lauren Kessler's articles, "A Siege of the Citadels," *Oregon Historical Quarterly*, vol. 84, no. 2 (1983): 117-49, and "The Ideas of Woman Suffrage and the Mainstream Press," *Oregon Historical Quarterly*, vol. 84, no. 3 (1983): 257-75; Martha Frances Montague, "The Woman Suffrage Movement in Oregon" (M.A. thesis, University of Oregon, 1930); Ward and Maveety, *Yours for Liberty*; the Abigail Scott Duniway papers at the University of Oregon Library; Eva Emery Dye and Bethenia Owens-Adair papers, Oregon Historical Society Library. For a comparison with the Washington woman suffrage movement, see T. A. Larson, "The Woman Suffrage Movement in Washington," *Pacific Northwest Quarterly* (April 1976): 49-62.

66 On the Oregon Congress of Women see Edwards, 160-68, 186-201.

67 Anna Howard Shaw's addresses are mentioned in Susan B. Anthony and Ida Husted Harper, eds., *History of Woman Suffrage* (1902), vol. 4, 892-93, and in Duniway, 110. For Dye's leadership of Clackamas County see Anthony and Harper, vol. 4, 896.

68 Duniway to Dye, May 10, 1905.

69 Ibid., May 15, 1905.

70 Ibid.

71 Author's analysis based on a number of sources, including newspaper clippings in scrapbooks at OHS; letterhead from the OESA in the Dye collection; *Fifty Years of Progress* and the *History of the Portland Woman's Club*; and Harper, *History of Woman Suffrage*, vol. 6. Sarah A. Evans wrote the chapter on Oregon in the *History of Woman Suffrage*.

72 Kessler, "The Ideas of Woman Suffrage," 258-59.

73 Duniway, 107.

74 Ibid., 84.

75 Harper, vol. 6, 541.

76 For Duniway's relationships with national suffrage leaders, see Edwards, *Sowing Good Seeds*.

77 *Oregonian*, June 17, 1906 (OHS scrapbook 89:46).

78 Moynihan, chapter twelve; Duniway, chapter twenty-three.

79 Members of the WCTU adopted the white ribbon to symbolize the purity of the home and their fight against alcohol. *Oregonian*, August 7, 1906.

80 Ibid., August 19, 1906.

81 Ibid.

82 Duniway to Dye, August 26, 1906.

83 Dunlap to Dye, October 1, 1906. For information on Dunlap herself, see her biographical file, OHS and Mary Osborn Douthit, *The Souvenir of Western Women*, 195.

84 Duniway to Dye, October 2, 1906.

85 *Oregonian* and *Oregon Journal*, November 4, 1906.

86 Anna Howard Shaw to Dye, November 19, 1906.

87 Montague, 96.

88 Duniway to Dye, April 27, 1908.

89 *Oregonian*, June 3, 1908.

90 Quoted in Montague, 88-89.

91 Montague, 99.

92 Harper, vol. 6, 544.

93 Eva Emery Dye, "Women in Civic Life," speech given at the National American Woman Suffrage Association," July 2, 1909, Seattle, Washington (OHS Dye collection, box 4).

94 Ibid.; Moynihan, 214.

95 Harper, vol. 6, 545.

96 Ibid.

97 Lockley, vol. II, 65-66.

98 Ibid.

99 Moynihan, 215.

100 Kessler's "The Ideas of Woman Suffrage and the Mainstream Press," never addressed the "Woman's Page" and the ideas put forth by Sarah Evans. Instead she argued that "the Oregon press denied access to the ideas of woman suffrage during the 1912 campaign" (263-64).

101 "Women's Clubs," *Oregon Journal*, January 12, 1912.

102 Evans, *Born for Liberty*, 168.

103 *Oregon Journal*, March 3, 1912.

104 Harper, vol. 6, 548; Duniway, 265; Montague cites 3,800 (107).

105 Historians Anne F. Scott and Andrew M. Scott have described the rivalries between the NAWSA and the Congressional Union, arguing that the radicalism of the latter made the more moderate claims of the NAWSA look appealing to male voters. Instead of being an obstacle to the suffrage movement, as the NAWSA claimed, the radical stance of the Congressional Union was a benefit to the cause and assisted in the passage of the Nineteenth Amendment. Anne F. Scott and Andrew M. Scott, *One Half the People: The Fight for Woman Suffrage* (Philadelphia: J. B. Lippincott, 1975), chapters three and four.

106 Kessler, "A Siege of the Citadels," 132-33.

Chapter 7

1 See Charles H. Dye's biographical file at OHS and undated newspaper clippings in the Hutchinson collection. Charles ran for re-election in 1908 but was defeated (George Himes to EED, May 11, 1908, OHS Dye collection, box 1); for lists of state legislators and their educational and economic backgrounds, see Cecil L. Edwards, *Alphabetical List of Oregon's Legislators* (Salem, OR: Legislative Administrative Committee, 1993).

2 For Progressivism in Oregon see Gordon Dodds, *The American Northwest: A History of Oregon and Washington* (Wheeling, IL: Forum Press, 1986), 182-86, 190-94; Carlos Schwantes, *The Pacific Northwest: An Interpretive History* (Lincoln: University of Nebraska Press, 2nd ed., 1996), 345-62; Thomas J. Rykowski, "Preserving the Garden: Progressivism in Oregon" (Ph.D. dissertation, University of Oklahoma, 1981).

3 Information on Trafton's and Emery's education and employment comes from alumni questionnaires submitted to Oberlin College over the years, which are included in their alumni files (Oberlin College Archives).

4 CHD to EWD, September 22, 1914 (all letters between the Dyes and their children can be found in box 5 of Dye's collection at OHS, with the exception of the correspondence between Eva and Charles during her trip to Hawaii, 1922-23. Those letters remain in the possession of the Hutchinson family).

5 CED to EED, May 9, 1916.

6 CHD to Children, January 31, 1920.

7 CED to EWD, July 24, 1919 and August 23, 1919; Earl Hutchinson to CED, June 22, and July 2, 1917.

8 CHD to EWD, May 14, 1918.

9 EED to CED, January 4, 1920.

10 Even Everett, who was closest to Eva and one of her confidantes, was upset about the marriage. "I cannot understand why you chose such a course which so utterly disregarded your own future, which will be a great handicap to you and Earl, which left out the hopes, happiness, and comfort of the folks at home, and disregarded the attitude and consideration of your friends," he wrote (EWD to EDH, June 17, 1920).

11 CHD to Children, June 18, 1920.

12 Ibid., May 15, 1920.

13 Ranald McDonald to Mrs. C. H. Dye, July 24, 1892 (OHS Dye collection, box 1).

14 Thomas W. Prosch, "Review of *McDonald of Oregon*," *Washington Historical Quarterly* vol. 1 (1906): 67-69.

15 As quoted in Alfred Powers, *History of Oregon Literature* (Portland: Metropolitan Press, Publishers, 1935), 411.

16 Eva Emery Dye, *McDonald of Oregon: A Tale of Two Shores* (Chicago: A. C. McClurg & Company, 1907, 2nd ed.), 394.

17 Prosch, 66-70.

18 "Review of *McDonald of Oregon*," *Oregon Historical Quarterly* 7, no. 4 (December 1906): 436.

19 R. H. Stetson, "Review of *McDonald of Oregon*," *Oberlin Alumni Magazine* (December 1906): 107.

20 George Sparks to EED, November 10, 1919 (Hutchinson collection).

21 "Oregon Writer at Honolulu: Mrs. Eva Emery Dye Arrives on Hawaiian Islands," [Honolulu] *Daily Star*, as reprinted in the *Oregon City Courier*, November 11, 1910.

22 Dye wrote to Mrs. Taylor, a distant cousin, December 27, 1908 and expressed her interest in the Colcord family's connection to the Emerys (OHS Dye collection, box 2).

23 Cyrus Emery, "Reminiscences of Life," (unpublished ms., 1903, Hutchinson collection), 31-32.

24 Dye to Mrs. Turner, March 24, 1910 (OHS Dye collection, box 2).

25 Founded in 1844, the church was originally called The Presbyterian Church of the Willamette Falls. Its name was changed to the First Congregational Society of Oregon City in 1849. For Peter Hatch's contribution to founding the church see Horace Lyman Bachelder, *The Liberal Church at the End of the Oregon Trail* (Portland: Watson Printing Company, 1969), 1-14.

26 Dye to Mrs. Turner.

27 A brief sketch of Peter Holt Hatch can be found in Howard McKinley Corning, *Dictionary of Oregon History* (Portland: Binfords & Mort Publishers, 1956), 108. Corning states Hatch was from Parsonville, Maine; however, letters to Dye from the Hatch family clearly state it was "Parsonfield." See also

the letters from Colcord and Hatch family members to Dye in her manuscript collection at the Oregon Historical Society.

28 "Oregon Writer at Honolulu."

29 The receipt from the Archives of Hawaii reads: "RECEIVED from Mrs. E. E. Dey, [sic] a Journal (sixteen pages cut out) kept by John N. Colcord, a resident of Honolulu from 1821 to November 20, 1844. This Journal is received with the understanding between Mrs. Dey and the undersigned, that it will be returned to her, or any descendent of the said John N. Colcord, on demand." Colcord himself removed the missing pages, according to family history. (November 21, 1910, OHS Dye collection, box 2).

30 Dye to Edward Dekum, April 14, 1917 (OHS Dye collection, box 1).

31 EED to EWD, July 18, 1918.

32 Biographical sketch of Eva Emery Dye in OHS Dye Collection box 4; EED to EWD, September 7, 1918.

33 Undated clippings pertaining to the Oregon City Woman's Club, c. 1921, in the Hutchinson collection; EED to Children, May 17, 1920; [Oregon City] *Morning Enterprise*, September 24, 1920; "Active Woman's Club to Celebrate 65th Anniversary," [Oregon City] *Enterprise-Courier*, April 30, 1968.

34 EED to CHD, October 23 and 24, 1922.

35 Ibid., October 24, 1922. William D. Westervelt, *Hawaiian Legends of Old Honolulu* (Tokyo: Charles E. Tuttle Company, 1963, reprint of 1915 edition). Westervelt served as president of the Hawaiian Historical Society in 1910 and 1911 (Barbara Dunn, Hawaiian Historical Society).

36 Lela Goodell, "Judd, Gerrit Parmele," *American National Biography Online* (London: Oxford University Press, 2000). For Laura Fish Judd, see Patricia Grimshaw, *Paths of Duty: American Missionary Wives in Nineteenth-Century Hawaii* (Honolulu: University of Hawaii Press, 1989).

37 EED to CHD, December 10, 1922.

38 Ibid., January 15, 1923 and December 3, 1922.

39 A useful account of Hawaiian royal succession and the relationship between King Kamehameha III and his siblings can be found in George S. Kanahele, *Emma: Hawaii's Remarkable Queen* (Honolulu: The Queen Emma Foundation, 1999), 4-7. See also Kanahele's description of *hanai* and other religious and cultural practices, 3-4, 13-20.

40 EED to CHD, February 22, 1923.

41 Ibid., and January 6, 1923. See also February 20 and 23, 1923.

42 Dye to Mrs. Walter Frear, February 27, 1939 (OHS Dye collection, box 2).

43 Missionary influence, the history of the first groups of missionaries to Hawaii, and the importance of mission schools are described in Grimshaw, Kanahele and Hiram Bingham, *A Residence of Twenty-One Years in the Sandwich Islands* (Tokyo: Charles E. Tuttle Company, 1981, reprint of 1847 edition).

44 CHD to EED, December 1, 1922.

45 Ibid., February 9, 1923.

46 Ibid., January 31, 1923 and February 3, 1923.

47 EED to CHD, December 12, 1922 and December 26, 1922.

48 CHD to EED, January 4, 1923 and January 18, 1923.

49 Ibid., January 4, 1923.

50 Ibid., February 7, 1923.

51 Ibid., January 18, 1923.

52 Ibid., March 8, 1923.

53 Dye to father, October 3 and October 6, 1907 (OHS Dye collection, box 4). The theory that he was injured at birth comes from an unpublished poem Eva wrote and from a letter from EED to their children, June 22, 1930: "No doubt that injury to his temple when he was born broke something" (OHS Dye collection, box 5).

54 EED to CHD, January 27, 1923.

55 CHD to EED, November 28, 1922 and October 14, 1922.

56 EED to CHD, January 27, 1923.

57 Ibid., October 19, 1922 and December 28, 1922.

58 Ibid., April 3 and 4, 1923.

59 CHD to EED, November 23, 1922; January 1, 1923; March 9, 1923; February 7, 1923.

60 Ibid., November 28; December 12, 1922; January 30, 1923; December 26, 1922.

61 Schwantes, 363.

62 Eckard V. Toy, "The Ku Klux Klan in Oregon," in G. Thomas Edwards and Carlos A. Schwantes, eds., *Experiences in a Promised Land: Essays in Pacific Northwest History* (Seattle: University of Washington Press, 1986), 272.

63 CHD to Children (and then sent on to EED), November 9, 1922. Charles was incorrect that all the tax measures passed, and the most controversial one, a graduated income tax, did not. For Oregon politics in the twenties, see Dodds, 216-21.

64 CHD to EED, November 10, 1922.

65 Schwantes, 339-44 and 357-61; Dodds, 339-41.

66 CHD to EED, December 4 and 9, 1922.

67 The fire and the rebuilding efforts are also described in Bachelder, 48-59.

68 CHD to EED, February 4, 1923; February 7, 1923; March 29, 1923; February 3, 1923.

69 undated newspaper clippings, c. 1920, Hutchinson collection.

70 CHD to EED, January 24 and January 30, 1923.

71 EED to CHD, October 17, 1922.

72 Ibid., December 20, 1922 and January 19, 1923.

73 Eva Emery Dye, "The King's Eagles: A Royal Romance," (unpublished ms., 1923, OHS Dye collection box 2), 386, 384.

74 EED to CHD, March 22, 1923 and March 24, 1923.

75 Ibid., March 27, 1923; April 5, 1923; April 7, 1923 and undated [April 18], 1923.

76 Dye to Sanford B. Dole, June 2, 1923; Sanford B. Dole to Publishers of a Royal Romance, June 24, 1923 (OHS Dye collection, box 2).

77 Dye to Henry P. Judd, March 11, 1935; Dye to Mrs. Walter Frear, February 27, 1939 (OHS Dye collection, box 2).

78 Dye to Henry P. Judd, March 11, 1935, July 12, 1937, and November 26, 1937 (OHS Dye collection, box 2); EED to EWD, February 6, 1936.

79 [Portland] *Oregonian*, July 15, 1934.

80 CHD to Children, January 22, 1928.

81 EED to Children, March 24, 1927.

82 "Maniac is Captured in Street Fight," *Oregon Journal*, May 13, 1924, 1; *Oregonian*, May 14, 1924, 8.

83 EED to Children, May 30, 1924.

84 EED to EWD, February 23, 1920.

85 EED to Children, March 24, 1927.

86 Undated newspaper clipping [c. 1938], Hutchinson collection; "Chautauqua Never Before Missed Assembly," unidentified newspaper clipping, dated May 21, 1928 (Hutchinson collection); Herb Beals, *Gladstone, Oregon: A History* (Gladstone, OR: Gladstone Historical Society, 1998), 93-94.

87 CHD to EWD, December 29, 1928.

88 Ibid., May 21, 1929.

89 EED to Children, September 8, 1929 and May 25, 1930.

90 Ibid., April 6, 1930.

91 Dye to Mr. Judd, February 18, 1940 (OHS Dye collection, box 2).

92 EED to Children, January 4, April 7, May 5, 1937; August, 23, 1936.

93 *Oregon Journal*, undated clipping in Dye's biographical file at OHS; Ibid., June 4, 1939.

94 "'First Lady' of Literature Surprises," *Banner-Courier* [Oregon City], January 26, 1945.

Epilogue

1 Dye to Miss Marvin, September 9, 1919 (OHS Dye collection, box 1); Dye to W. H. McMonies, Lifeograph Co., April 9, 1920 (OHS Dye collection, box 1); EED to Children, March 6, 1927, January 4, 1937, April 7, 1937, and May 5, 1937 (OHS Dye collection, box 5).

2 Eva Emery Dye, "Women in Civic Life," presented at the National American Women Suffrage Association convention, July 2, 1909, Seattle, Washington (OHS Dye collection, box 4).

3 Eva Emery Dye, "Review of Reuben Gold Thwaites, ed.., 'The Journals of Lewis and Clark,' " (unpublished, OHS Dye collection, box 4).

4 Melva Garrow Ellingsen, "Eva and Clio: Or, The Muse Meets Its Mistress," *Call Number* 19 (Fall, 1957), 21.

5 Joseph Gaston, *Portland, Oregon, Its History and Builders* (Chicago: S. J. Clarke Co., 1911), vol. 3, 185.

6 Dye to Prof. Meany, October 28, 1931 (OHS Dye collection, box 1).

7 CHD to EED, March 13, 1923 (Hutchinson collection).

8 EED to EWD, October 16, 1919 (OHS Dye collection, box 5).

9 Eva Emery Dye, untitled speech for the Oregon City Woman's Club, (n.d., c. 1920, Hutchinson collection).

10 Louise F. Shields, "Originator of Gladstone Chautauqua Noted Author," *Sunday Oregonian*, June 1, 1924, as quoted in Kimberly Swanson, "Eva Emery Dye and the Romance of Oregon History," *The Pacific Historian* vol. 29, no. 4 (1987):68.

Bibliography

Unpublished Works

Dye, Eva Emery. "The King's Eagles: A Royal Romance." Unpublished ms., 1923. Eva Emery Dye Papers. MSS 1089. Oregon Historical Society.

Emery, Cyrus. "Reminiscences of Life." Unpublished ms., 1903. Charles Hutchinson collection.

Hutchinson, Charles. "The Story of Eva Emery Dye and Charles H. Dye." Unpublished essay, 1989. Charles Hutchinson collection.

Oberlin College. Alumni Register. Oberlin College Archives, 1960.

Portland Commercial Club of Portland, Oregon. Constitution and By-Laws, Roster of Members, House Rules, Etc. Pamphlet, Portland, OR; 1909. Oregon Historical Society.

U.S. Works Projects Administration. History of the Portland Woman's Club. Pamphlet, n.d. Oregon Historical Society.

There are numerous unpublished essays and speeches in Dye's manuscript collection at the Oregon Historical Society.

Oral History Interviews

Caldwell, Roberta Schubel. August 24, 1994.

Hutchinson, Charles R. March 23, 1995.

Archival Collections

Alumni Records. 1833–1991. Series 3. Oberlin College Archives.

Charles Hutchinson collection. Privately held.

Duniway, Abigail Scott. Duniway Family Papers, Collection 232, Series B. University of Oregon Library.

Dye, Charles H. Biographical file. Oregon Historical Society.

Dye, Eva Emery. Biographical file. Oregon Historical Society.

Dye, Eva Emery. Eva Emery Dye Papers. MSS 1089. Oregon Historical Society.

Owens-Adair, Bethenia. Bethenia Owens-Adair Papers. Oregon Historical Society.

Scrapbooks. Oregon Historical Society.

Selected Published Writings of Eva Emery Dye

Essays:

"The Amana Commune." Chicago Daily News. September 13, 1888.

"Blue Monday Must Go." The Housekeeper. December 1, 1889.

"Celebrated Historian of Oregon City Discoverer of Lewis and Clark Diary." Oregonian [Portland]. November 11, 1923.

"The Evolution of Laws, Constitutions and Politics …" The Centennial History of Oregon, 1811-1912. Joseph Gaston. Chicago: S. J. Clarke, 1912. 639-73.

"The Historic Capital of Iowa." Magazine of American History 22 (1889): 443-55.

"The Hudson's Bay Company Regime in the Oregon Country." Semi-Centennial History of Oregon. Ed. F. G. Young. Eugene, OR: University Press, 1898.

"Longfellow," The Dakota Educator. n.d., c. 1884.

Oberlin Review. 1875-1882.

"Woman's Part in the Drama of the Northwest." Oregon Pioneer Transactions. Portland, OR: George Himes & Company, 1895: 36-43.

"Yesterday at Oberlin." Oberlin Alumni Magazine. May 1909: 321.

Poetry Cited

"A Woman Led the Deed." Union Signal. February 27, 1890.

"The College Girl." Oregon Teachers' Monthly. n.d., c. 1890.

Oberlin Review. 1872-1882.

"Only A Woman," Union Signal. May 8, 1890.

Historical Fiction

The Conquest: The True Story of Lewis and Clark. Chicago: A. C. McClurg & Co., 1902.

McDonald of Oregon: A Tale of Two Shores. Chicago: A. C. McClurg & Co., 1906.

McLoughlin and Old Oregon. Chicago: A. C. McClurg & Co., 1900.

Stories of Oregon. San Francisco: Whitaker and Ray Company, 1900.

The Soul of America: An Oregon Iliad. New York: The Press of the Pioneers, 1934.

Reviews

McLoughlin and Old Oregon 1900

"Review of McLoughlin and Old Oregon." *The Freeman* [New York] December 6, 1922.

"Review of McLoughlin and Old Oregon." *Oregon Historical Quarterly* 1 (1900): 207-10.

"Stirring Epic of Old Oregon Becomes Opera 'Narcissa.'" *Oregonian* [Portland] September 5, 1926.

Victor, Frances Fuller. "Review of McLoughlin and Old Oregon: A Chronicle." *American Historical Review* 6 (1900): 148-50.

The Conquest 1902

New York Times. November 1, 1902: 750.

"Review of The Conquest." *Oregon Historical Quarterly* 3 (1902): 427-28.

"Saturday Review of Books." *New York Times* November 29, 1902: 842.

McDonald of Oregon 1906

Prosch, Thomas W. "Review of McDonald of Oregon," *Washington Historical Quarterly* 1 (1906): 66-70.

"Review of McDonald of Oregon," *Oregon Historical Quarterly* 7 (December 1906): 435-37.

Stetson, R. H. "Review of McDonald of Oregon," *Oberlin Alumni Magazine* (December 1906): 107.

Soul of America 1934

Johnson, Robert C. "Review of Soul of America," *Oregon Historical Quarterly* 35 (1934): 279-80.

"Review of Soul of America," *Oregonian* [Portland] July 15, 1934.

Newspapers

Banner-Courier [Oregon City]
Enterprise-Courier [Oregon City].
Morning Enterprise [Oregon City].
Oregon Journal [Portland].
Oregonian [Portland].

Contemporary Works

Allen, Paul [and Nicholas Biddle], ed. *History of the Expedition Under the Command of Captains Lewis and Clark.* Philadelphia: Bradford and Inskeep, 1814. Reprinted by University Microfilms, Inc., Ann Arbor. 2 volumes.

"The Art Exhibit at the Fair," *Pacific Monthly* 14 (September 1905): 279-83.

Coues, Elliott, ed. *The History of the Lewis and Clark Expedition.* New York: Francis Harper, 1893. Reprinted by Dover Publications, New York. 3 volumes.

Douthit, Mary Osborn. *The Souvenir of Western Women.* Portland, OR: Presses of Anderson & Duniway, 1905.

Duniway, Abigail Scott. *Path Breaking: An Autobiographical History of the Equal Suffrage Movement in Pacific Coast States.* 1914. New York: Source Book Press, 1970.

Fuller, Margaret. "The Great Lawsuit. Man Versus Men. Woman Versus Women." *The Feminist Papers from Adams to de Beauvoir.* Alice S. Rossi, ed. Boston: Northeastern University Press, 1988. 158-82.

———. *Woman in the Nineteenth Century.* 1855. New York: W. W. Norton & Co., 1971.

Gaston, Joseph. *Portland, Oregon, Its History and Its Builders.* Chicago: S. J. Clarke Co., 1911.

History of the Bench and Bar. Portland, Oregon, 1910.

Lockley, Fred. *The History of the Columbia River Valley From the Dalles to the Sea.* Chicago: S.J. Clarke, 1928. 2 volumes.

———. "Impressions and Observations of the Journal Man." *Daily Journal* [Portland]. March 18, 1936.

Merrick, Frank L. "Woman's Part at the Centennial," *Lewis and Clark Journal.* 3 (February 1905): 13.

"On the Explorers' Trail: How the Author Searched the Land for Historical Material." *Oregonian* [Portland]. November 2, 1902.

Oregon Historical Society. *Proceedings of the Oregon Historical Society, 1898-99.* Portland, OR: Oregon Historical Society, 1899.

Portland Chamber of Commerce. *Men of Oregon.* Portland, Oregon, 1911.

Thwaites, Reuben Gold, ed. *Original Journals of the Lewis and Clark Expedition, 1804-1806.* 1904-05. New York: Arno Press, 1969. 7 volumes.

———. "The Story of Lewis and Clark's Journals," *Oregon Historical Quarterly* 6 (1905): 26-53.

Young, F. G. "The Higher Significance in the Lewis and Clark Exploration," *Oregon Historical Quarterly* 6 (1905): 1-25.

——. "The Lewis and Clark Centennial, The Occasion and Its Observance," *Oregon Historical Quarterly* 4 (1903): 1-20.

——. "The Lewis and Clark Expedition in American History." *Oregon Historical Quarterly* 2(1901): 410-22.

Secondary Sources

Abbott, Carl. *The Great Extravaganza: Portland and the Lewis and Clark Exposition*. Portland, OR: Oregon Historical Society Press, 1981.

Anthony, Susan B. Anthony et al., eds. *History of Woman Suffrage*. Rochester, N.Y.: C. Mann, 1887-1922. 6 volumes.

Bachelder, Horace Lyman. *The Liberal Church at the End of the Oregon Trail*. Portland, OR: Watson Printing Company, 1969.

Baker, Paula. "The Domestication of Politics: Women and American Political Society, 1780-1920." *American Historical Review* 89 (1984): 620-47.

Banta, Martha. *Imaging American Women: Idea and Ideals in Cultural History*. New York: Columbia University Press, 1987.

Basch, Norma. *In the Eyes of the Law: Women, Marriage, and Property in Nineteenth-Century New York*. Ithaca: Cornell University Press, 1982.

Beals, Herbert K. *Gladstone, Oregon, A History: Part Two: Civil War to the Eve of the Great Depression*. Gladstone, OR: Gladstone Historical Society, 1998.

Bederman, Gail. *Manliness & Civilization: A Cultural History of Gender and Race in the United States, 1880-1917*. Chicago: The University of Chicago Press, 1995.

Bellamy, Edward. *Looking Backward, 2000-1887*. New York: New American Library, 1960.

Bingham, Hiram. *A Residence of Twenty-One Years in the Sandwich Islands*. 1847. Tokyo: Charles E. Tuttle Company, 1981.

Blair, Karen. *The Clubwoman as Feminist*. New York: Holmes and Meier, 1980.

Bloch, Ruth H. "The Gendered Meanings of Virtue in Revolutionary America." *Signs* 13 (1987): 37-58.

Bright,Verne. "Historian of the Pioneers." *Northwest Literary Review* 1 (Nov.-Dec. 1935): 4.

Boyer, Paul et.al. *The Enduring Vision: A History of the American People*. Lexington: D. C. Heath, 1993.

Buechler, Steven. *The Transformation of the Woman Suffrage Movement: The Case of Illinois, 1850-1920*. New Brunswick: Rutgers University Press, 1986.

Buhle, Mari Jo. *Women and American Socialism, 1870-1920*. Urbana: University of Illinois Press, 1983.

Carrier Lois. *Illinois: Crossroads of a Continent*. Urbana: University of Illinois Press, 1993.

Case, Victoria and Robert Ormand Case. *We Called It Culture, The Story of Chautauqua*. Garden City, NY: Doubleday, 1948.

Caufield,Vara. "Two Historic Houses: How McLoughlin House Was Saved," *Oregon Historical Quarterly* 76 (1975): 299-301.

Chafe, William. "Women's History and Political History: Some Thoughts on Progressivism and the New Deal. " *Visible Women, New Essays on American Activism*. Nancy A. Hewitt and Suzanne Lebsock, eds. Urbana: University of Illinois Press, 1993.

Clark, Ella E., and Margot Edmonds. *Sacagawea of the Lewis and Clark Expedition*. Berkeley: University of California Press, 1979.

Corning, Howard McKinley. *Dictionary of Oregon History*. Portland, OR: Binfords & Mort, 1956.

Cott, Nancy F. *The Bonds of Womanhood: "Woman's Sphere" in New England, 1780-1835*. New Haven: Yale University Press, 1977.

——. *The Grounding of Modern Feminism*. New Haven: Yale University Press, 1987.

——, ed. *Root of Bitterness: Documents of the Social History of American Women*. Boston: Northeastern University Press, 1986.

Cutright, Paul. *A History of the Lewis and Clark Journals*. Norman: University of Oklahoma Press, 1976.

Dawson, Jan C. "Sacagawea: Pilot or Pioneer Mother?" *Pacific Northwest Quarterly* 83 (1992): 22-28.

DeVoto, Bernard. *Across the Wide Missouri*. 1947. Boston: Houghton Mifflin Company, 1998.

Dodds, Gordon B. *The American Northwest: A History of Oregon and Washington.* Wheeling, IL: Forum Press, 1986.

——, ed. *Varieties of Hope: An Anthology of Oregon Prose.* Corvallis, OR: Oregon State University Press, 1993.

Drury, Clifford M. *Marcus and Narcissa Whitman and the Opening of Old Oregon.* Glendale, CA: The Arthur H. Clark Company, 1973. 2 volumes.

Dublin, Thomas. *Women at Work: The Transformation of Work and Community in Lowell, Massachusetts, 1826-1860.* New York: Columbia University Press, 1979.

Edwards, Cecil L. *Alphabetical List of Oregon's Legislators.* Salem, OR: Legislative Administrative Committee, 1993.

Edwards, G. Thomas. *Sowing Good Seeds: The Northwest Suffrage Campaigns of Susan B. Anthony .* Portland, OR: Oregon Historical Society Press, 1990.

Ellingsen, Melva Garrow. "Eva and Clio; Or, the Muse Meets Its Mistress." *Call Number* (Fall 1957): 17.

Epstein, Donald. "Gladstone Chautauqua: Education and Entertainment, 1893-1928." *Oregon Historical Quarterly* 80 (1979): 391-403.

Evans, Sara M. *Born for Liberty: A History of Women in America.* New York: Free Press, 1997.

——. "Women's History and Political Theory: Toward a Feminist Approach to Public Life." *Visible Women, New Essays on American Activism.* Nancy A. Hewitt and Suzanne Lebsock, eds. Urbana: University of Illinois Press, 1993.

—— and Harry C. Boyte. *Free Spaces: The Sources of Democratic Change in America.* New York: Harper and Row, 1987.

Flexner, Eleanor. *Century of Struggle: The Woman's Rights Movement in the United States.* Cambridge: Harvard University Press, 1975.

Fogle, Richard H., ed. *The Romantic Movement in American Writing.* New York: Odyssey Press, 1966.

Freedman, Estelle. "Separatism As Strategy: Female Institution Building and American Feminism, 1870-1930." *Feminist Studies* 5 (1979): 512-29.

Green, Rayna. "The Pocahontas Perplex: The Image of Indian Women in American Culture," *Unequal Sisters: A Multicultural Reader in U.S. Women's History.* Ellen Carol DuBois and Vicki L. Ruiz, eds., New York: Routledge, 1990.

Grimshaw, Patricia. *Paths of Duty: American Missionary Wives in Nineteenth-Century Hawaii.* Honolulu: University of Hawaii Press, 1989.

Haarsager, Sandra. *Organized Womanhood: Cultural Politics in the Pacific Northwest, 1840-1920.* Norman: University of Oklahoma Press, 1997.

Healy, David. *U.S. Expansionism: The Imperialist Urge in the 1890s.* Madison: University of Wisconsin Press, 1970.

Homer. *The Odyssey.* London: Penguin Books, 1991.

Horner, John B. *Oregon Literature.* Portland, OR: J.K. Gill Company, 1902.

Howard, Harold P. *Sacajawea.* Norman: University of Oklahoma Press, 1971.

Hoxie, Frederick E. *A Final Promise: The Campaign to Assimilate the Indians, 1880-1920.* Franklin: University of Nebraska Press, 1984.

Irving, Washington. *Astoria, Or Anecdotes of an Enterprize Beyond the Rocky Mountains.* Boston: Twayne Publishers, 1976.

Jackson, Donald. *Letters of the Lewis and Clark Expedition.* Urbana: University of Illinois Press, 1978. 2 volumes.

Jeffrey, Julie Roy. *Converting the West: A Biography of Narcissa Whitman.* Norman: University of Oklahoma Press, 1991.

——. *Frontier Women: The Trans-Mississippi West, 1840-1880.* New York: Hill and Wang, 1979.

Johnson, Paul E. *A Shopkeeper's Millenium: Society and Revivals in Rochester, New York, 1815-1837.* New York: Hill and Wang, 1978.

Kanahele, George S. *Emma: Hawaii's Remarkable Queen.* Honolulu: The Queen Emma Foundation, 1999.

Kerber, Linda K. *Women of the Republic: Intellect and Ideology in Revolutionary America.* Chapel Hill: University of North Carolina Press, 1980.

Kessler, Donna. *The Making of Sacagawea: A Euro-American Legend.* Tuscaloosa: University of Alabama Press, 1996.

Kessler , Lauren. "A Siege of the Citadels." *Oregon Historical Quarterly* 84 (1983): 117-49.

———. "The Ideas of Woman Suffrage and the Mainstream Press." *Oregon Historical Quarterly* 84 (1983): 257-75.

Kopp, James J. "Looking Backward at Edward Bellamy's Influence in Oregon, 1888-1936," *Oregon Historical Quarterly* 104 (1): 63-95.

Kraditor, Aileen S. *The Ideas of the Woman Suffrage Movement, 1890-1920.* New York: W. W. Norton & Co., 1981.

LaFeber, Walter. *The New Empire: An Interpretation of American Expansion, 1860-1898.* Ithaca, NY: Cornell University Press, 1963.

Lamar, Howard R., ed. *The New Encyclopedia of the American West.* New Haven: Yale University Press, 1998.

Landsman, Gail. "The 'Other' as Political Symbol: Images of Indians in the Woman Suffrage Movement." *Ethnohistory* 39 (1992): 247-84.

Larson, T. A. "The Woman Suffrage Movement in Washington." *Pacific Northwest Quarterly* 40 (1976): 49-62.

Laugesen, Amanda. "George Himes, F.G. Young, and the Early Years of the Oregon Historical Society." *Oregon Historical Quarterly* 101 (2000): 18-39.

Lebsock, Suzanne. *The Free Women of Petersburg: Status and Culture in a Southern Town, 1784-1860.* New York: W. W. Norton & Co., 1984.

Lewis, Jan. "Virtue and Seduction in the Early Republic." *William and Mary Quarterly* 44 (October 1987): 689-721.

Limerick, Patricia Nelson. *The Legacy of Conquest: The Unbroken Past of the American West.* New York: W. W. Norton., 1987.

Longfellow, Henry Wadsworth. *Evangeline and Selected Tales and Poems.* New York: New American Library, 1964.

McEnroe, Sean. "Painting the Philippines with an American Brush: Visions of Race and National Mission among the Oregon Volunteers in the Philippine Wars of 1898 and 1899." *Oregon Historical Quarterly* 104: 1 (Spring 2003): 24-61.

Montague, Martha Frances. "The Woman Suffrage Movement in Oregon." M.A. thesis, University of Oregon. 1930.

Montgomery, Richard G. *The White-Headed Eagle: John McLoughlin, Builder of an Empire.* Freeport, NY: Books for Libraries, 1971.

Moynihan, Ruth Barnes. *Rebel for Rights, Abigail Scott Duniway.* New Haven: Yale University Press, 1983.

Murray, Keith. "The Role of the Hudson's Bay Company in Pacific Northwest History." *Experiences in a Promised Land: Essays in Pacific Northwest History.* G. Thomas Edwards and Carlos A. Schwantes, eds., Seattle: University of Washington Press, 1986. 28-39.

Newman, Louise M. *White Women's Rights: The Racial Origins of Feminism in the United States.* New York: Oxford University Press, 1999.

Norton, Mary Beth. *Liberty's Daughters: The Revolutionary Experience of American Women, 1750-1800.* Boston: Little, Brown and Company, 1980.

O'Neill, William. *Everyone Was Brave: A History of Feminism in America.* New York: Quadrangle, 1969.

Oregon Federation of Woman's Clubs,. *Fifty Years of Progress, 1899-1950 .* Portland, OR: n. p., 1950.

Peterson, Merrill D. *Thomas Jefferson and the New Nation, A Biography.* New York: Oxford University Press, 1970.

———. *The Jefferson Image in the American Mind.* Charlottesville: University Press of Virginia, 1998.

"Politics and Culture in Women's History: A Symposium." *Feminist Studies* 6 (1980): 26-64.

Powers, Alfred. *History of Oregon Literature.* Portland: Metropolitan Press, 1935.

Prosch, Thomas W. "Effort to Save the Historic McLoughlin House," *Washington Historical Quarterly* 1 (January 1907): 36-42.

Remley, David. "Sacajawea of Myth and History," *Women and Western American Literature.* Helen Winter Stauffer and Susan J. Rosowski, eds., Troy, NY: Whitston, 1982. 70-89.

Rosenberg, Emily. *Spreading the American Dream: American Economic and Cultural Expansion, 1890-1945.* New York: Hill and Wang, 1982.

Ronda, James. *Lewis and Clark Among the Indians.* Lincoln: University of Nebraska Press, 1984.

Ryan, Mary P. *Cradle of the Middle Class: The Family in Oneida County, New York, 1790-1865.* New York: Cambridge University Press, 1981.

Rykowski, Thomas J. "Preserving the Garden: Progressivism in Oregon." Ph.D. thesis, University of Oklahoma. 1981.

Schwantes, Carlos A. *The Pacific Northwest: An Interpretive History.* Lincoln: University of Nebraska Press, 1996.

Schweider, Dorothy. *Iowa: The Middle Land.* Ames: Iowa State University Press, 1996.

Scott, Anne Firor. *Making the Invisible Woman Visible.* Chicago: University of Illinois Press, 1984.

——. *Natural Allies: Women's Associations in American History.* Chicago: University of Illinois Press, 1991.

——, and Andrew M. Scott. *One Half the People: The Fight for Woman Suffrage.* Philadelphia: J.B. Lippincott, 1975.

Sklar, Kathryn Kish. *Catharine Beecher: A Study in American Domesticity.* New Haven: Yale University Press, 1973.

——. "Two Political Cultures in the Progressive Era: The National Consumers' League and the American Association for Labor Legislation," *U. S. History as Women's History, New Feminist Essays.* Linda K. Kerber, et. al., eds. Chapel Hill: University of North Carolina Press, 1995. 36-62.

Smelser, June. "A History of the McLoughlin House," *Clackamas County Historical 1960.* Oregon City, OR: Clackamas County Historical Society, 1960. 27-55.

Smith, Sherry L. *Reimagining Indians: Native Americans through Anglo Eyes, 1880-1940.* New York: Oxford University Press, 2000.

Solomon, Barbara Miller. *In the Company of Educated Women: A History of Women and Higher Education in America.* New Haven: Yale University Press, 1985.

Spencer, John Palmer. "'We Are Not Dealing Entirely with the Past': Americans Remember Lewis and Clark," *Lewis and Clark: Legacies, Memories and New Interpretations.* Mark Spence and Kris Fresonke, eds. Berkeley: University of California Press, 2004.

Stansell, Christine. *City of Women: Sex and Class in New York, 1789-1860.* New York: Alfred A. Knopf, 1986.

Swanson, Kimberly. "Eva Emery Dye and the Romance of Oregon History." *The Pacific Historian* 29 (1987): 59-68.

Taber, Ronald W. "Sacagawea and the Suffragettes: An Interpretation of a Myth." *Pacific Northwest Quarterly* 31 (1967): 7-13.

Takaki, Ronald. *A Different Mirror: A History of Multicultural America.* Boston: Little, Brown & Co., 1993.

Toy, Eckard V. "The Ku Klux Klan in Oregon," *Experiences in a Promised Land: Essays in Pacific Northwest History.* G. Thomas Edwards and Carlos A. Schwantes, eds., Seattle: University of Washington Press, 1986. 269-86.

Turner, Frederick Jackson. *The Frontier in American History.* New York: Dover Publications, 1996.

Underwood, June. "Civilizing Kansas: Women's Organizations, 1880-1920." *Kansas History* 7 (1985): 291-306.

U.S. Works Projects Administration. *End of the Trail.* Portland, OR: Binfords and Mort, 1940.

Vaughan, Thomas. "A Century of the Oregon Historical Quarterly." *Oregon Historical Quarterly* 101 (Spring 2000): 6-17.

Ward, Jean M. and Maveety, Elaine A. *Pacific Northwest Women, 1815-1925: Lives, Memories, and Writings.* Corvallis, OR: Oregon State University Press, 1995.

——, eds. *Yours for Liberty: Selections from Abigail Scott Duniway's Suffrage Newspaper.* Corvallis, OR: Oregon State University Press, 2000.

Westervelt, William D. *Hawaiian Legends of Old Honolulu.* 1915. Tokyo: Charles E. Tuttle Company, 1963.

Whitman, Narcissa. *The Letters of Narcissa Whitman.* Fairfield, WA: Ye Galleon Press, 1986.

Woloch, Nancy. *Women and the American Experience.* New York, McGraw-Hill, 1984.

Wood, Mary I. *The History of the General Federation of Women's Clubs for the First Twenty-Two Years of Its Organization.* Norwood, Mass.: Norwood Press, 1912.

Index

Abbott, Carl, 77
A. C. McClurg and Company, 65-66, 72, 76, 87, 146, 152, 167
Addams, Jane, 157 (n. 6)
Amana Colonies, 41-42, 47, 159 (n. 13)
American Board of Foreign Missions, 62, 137
American Renaissance, 2, 59
Anderson, C. Harper, 81-82
Andrews, William, 10
Andrews & Emery, 10
Anthony, Susan B., 49, 103, 113, 115, 168
Anti-Saloon League, 144
Astor, John Jacob, 58, 61
Astoria, 58, 63, 143, 161 (n. 23)
Atlantic Monthly, 33, 146

Baker, Paula, 107, 109
Bancroft, Hubert Howe, 63, 66
Bederman, Gail, 93
Beecher, Catharine, 49
Bellamy, Edward, 47-48
Biddeford (Maine), 10-11
Biddle, Nicholas, 79-82, 88, 90-91, 95-96, 166 (n. 73)
Bishop Museum, 135
Blackfeet, 58, 87
Blackwell, Antoinette Brown, 23
Blair, Karen, 101, 168 (n. 11)
"Bleeding Kansas," 30
"Blue Monday Must Go," 48
Boone, Daniel, 79-80
Boone, Rebecca, 88
Bozeman Pass, 92, 95
Bride of Lammermoor, The, 30
British Columbia, 103, 129-30
British Romantics, 2. *See also* Romanticism
Bryan, William Jennings, 69, 73

Carlyle, Thomas, 25, 32-33
Cartwright, Charlotte M., 104-5
Caufield, E. G. and Charles, 106
Cayuse War, 63-64
Charbonneau, Toussaint, 90-91, 166 (n. 80)
Chautauqua, 1, 5, 55, 67-71, 73, 115, 135, 149, 154: Literary and Scientific Circles, 67; New York Chautauqua, 70; Women's Symposium, 69, 154. *See also* Willamette Valley Chautauqua Assembly

Civil War, 17, 68
Clackamas County (Oregon), 73, 115, 119, 123-24, 126, 135, 144, 149, 154
Clark, Ann Rogers, 88
Clark, Ella, 94
Clark, George Rogers, 3, 79-80, 85-86, 97-98
Clark, Mrs. Jefferson Kearney, 82
Clark, John O'Fallon, 81-83, 87
Clark, Julia Hancock, 87-88
Clark, William, 3, 79-82, 85-86, 98, 105. *See also* Lewis and Clark Expedition
Clark, William Hancock, 81-82, 105
Coe, Henry Waldo, 107, 117
Coe, Viola, 107, 117
Colcord, Charlotte, 132-33. *See also* Hatch
Colcord, Elizabeth Emery, 133
Colcord, John, 3, 133-34
"College Girl," 88-89
Columbia River, 61, 65, 77, 89, 129
Columbia University, 126
"Committee of 100," 126, 144
Compulsory School Bill, 142
Congregational Brotherhood, 144
Congregational Church (Oberlin), 21, 35. *See also* First Congregational Church
conquest, as Dye theme, 28-30, 54, 61-62, 64, 66-67, 71-72, 75, 78
Conquest, The: The True Story of Lewis and Clark, 3-4, 58, 96-97, 104, 107, 115-16, 126, 131-32, 146, 151-52; and Clark brothers, 84-86; and Clark descendants, 80-83; frontispiece to first edition, 88; and guide motif, 95-96; heroic themes in, 67, 98; and Thomas Jefferson, 78-79; Lewis and Clark as icons in, 99; and Lewis and Clark journals, 82; and Native Americans, 58, 86-87; and research for, 98; structure of, 84; timing of publication, 72; and Theodore Roosevelt, 78; and Sacajawea Statue Association, 100; and "trilogy of the Pacific," 134; and woman suffrage, 94-95; portrayal of women in, 54, 87-94
Cooper, Alice, 107, 111
Corbett, Henry, 77
Cortes, Hernando, 29
Coues, Elliott, 80, 84, 91, 95
"Courtship of Miles Standish, The," 33
Cross, Harvey, 68
Crown, Lyman, 12, 14, 17-18
"cult of true womanhood," 23
Cutright, Paul, 84

Dalton, Martha, 105, 117
Daughters of the American Revolution, 102, 105, 114
Dawes General Allotment Act, 86
Dekum, Edward, 134
Des Moines (Iowa), 42
Detroit, 80-81, 85
Dole, Sanford B., 135-37, 145-46
Doubleday Page & Company, 146
Douglas, James, 58, 62
"Dreamland," 17
Drury, Clifford, 65, 161-62 (n. 42)
Duniway, Abigail Scott, 3, 68-69, 100-104, 113, 115-24
Dunlap, Caroline, 119
Dye, Andrew, 35
Dye, Charles Henry, 4, 22, 80, 154: career in teaching, administration, and public service, 38, 41, 73; and the Chautauqua, 69, 149; and children, 43-44, 46, 126-29; and Congregational Church, 6, 45; correspondence with Eva, 138-45, 147; death of, 150; described by Eva, 44-46; education of, 35-36, 39, 43; and Emery Dye, 139-40; and Eva's Hawaii project, 136-40, 144-45; family background of, 35; financial situation of, 74, 138-39, 149-50; health concerns of, 149; as lawyer, 41, 43, 55-56; on Oregon City, 142-45; and political office, 56, 73, 126; and Progressive reform, Prohibition, and temperance, 43, 45, 126, 149; relationship with Eva, 2, 35-36, 43-45, 53, 141-45; and relocation, 37-38, 41, 43, 54-55
Dye, Charlotte Evangeline, 46, 73-74, 127-29, 134, 172 (n. 10)
Dye, Emery Charles, 39-40, 44, 73-74, 126, 140, 148
Dye, Eva Emery, 1, 6-7, 14, 16, 18, 36, 43, 53, 57, 59, 65, 71, 75-76, 135, 141, 152, 157 (n. 6): and Chautauqua, 67-70; death of, 151; desire to go to college, 19; discovery of Lewis and Clark documents, 3, 84; and domestic help, 163 (n. 7); early married life of, 37-43; and epic poetry, 28-30; and factual documentation of her work, 62-63; and historical essays, 41-42; influence of historical fiction on, 57; Jeffersonian ideals and, 1, 78-79; literary contribution of, 2, 73, 75, 153; and mental illness of Emery Dye, 140, 148;

as mother, 44-47, 73-74, 127-29; motivations for writing, 4, 17, 72; portrayal of Native Americans, 58, 63, 86-87; at Oberlin College, 21-24, 26; and Oregon City, 54-56, 68, 142, 144; and Oregon Historical Society, 76; and Progressive era, 78-79, 126; relationship with Abigail Scott Duniway, 115-16, 118-20; relationship with Charles Dye, 35-36, 44, 45, 138-39, 140-41, 149-50; relationship with father, 9, 16-17; relationship with grandmother, 7, 18; relationships with historians, 66, 75-77, 154; relationship with stepmother, 19; Romanticism and, 2, 26-28, 32-33, 57-59; and self-education, 38-39, 40; and sense of humor, 24; and "story of the children," 43-44; and temperance, 32, 47, 123-24, 144; women characters in her works, 54, 59-62, 64-65, 87-94; women's rights and, 4, 31-34, 50-52, 127
Dye, Everett Willoughby, 17, 46, 73-74, 127-29, 134, 148-49, 154, 172 (n. 10)
Dye, Jane Mickelwait, 35
Dye, Sarah Minor, 35
Dye, Trafton Mickelwait, 39-41, 44-45, 73-74, 126, 128-29

Edmonds, Margot, 94
Eldred, Carolyn, 35, 132
Ellingsen, Melva Garrow, 153
Emerson, Ralph Waldo, 25, 45
Emery, Caleb, 10, 16
Emery, Caroline Ernestine, 14
Emery, Caroline Trafton, 7, 11, 18
Emery, Cyrus, 7-19, 22, 133
Emery, Hannah Willard, 7-8, 11
Emery, Iroline May, 17
Emery, Laura, 19
Emery, Leonard, 19
Emery, Martha Ann Rose, 16
Emery, Salter, 8, 13
Emery, Thomas Salter (Captain), 7
Emery, William, 8, 10
Epstein, Donald, 71
Equi, Marie (Doctor), 123
"Evangeline," 33, 46, 57-58, 62
Evans, Sarah A., 100-104, 106-8, 110-12, 114, 117, 119-20, 122-24
Evans, Sara M., 32, 109
Evans, William, 103

Fairchild, James H., 36, 41
Fall of Anahuac, The, 28-29
"Family Bulletin, The" 129
"Family Record," 40, 132
First Congregational Church (Oregon City), 6, 43, 45, 126, 133, 143
First Congregational Church (Portland), 112
Fort Colville (Oregon Territory), 3, 129
Fort Madison (Iowa), 35
Fort Vancouver (Washington), 3, 58, 60, 66, 129
Franklin (Nebraska), 41: Franklin Academy, 41
Fremont County (Iowa), 37
Fremont County Herald, 37-38
French and Indian War, 16, 57
From the West to the West, 116
Fuller, Margaret, 25-26, 32-34, 38

Gaston, Joseph, 153-54
Gilman, Charlotte Perkins, 48, 93-94
Gladstone (Oregon), 5
Gladstone Park, 68, 73
Garden Plain (Illinois), 12
Great Depression, 150
Greek culture/literature, 2, 22-23, 26, 28, 30, 41, 57, 69-70, 72, 140
Green, Rayna, 92

Hatch, Charlotte Colcord, 133-34
Hatch, David, 133
Hatch, Peter, 133-34
Hawaii, 3, 6, 132-41, 144-48, 152, 154
Hawaiian Historical Society, 134-35, 154
Hawley, Willis, 70
Hays, Isaac (Secretary), 81
"Hiawatha," 58
Higginson, Ella, 3
"Historic Capital of Iowa," 42
History of Woman Suffrage, 117, 122
Homer, 26, 28, 55, 57-58, 63, 153
Honolulu Daily Star, 132, 134
Horner, John B., 66, 154
Hudson's Bay Company, 3, 57-60, 63, 75, 77
Hutchinson, Dolly, 154
Hutchinson, Earl, 127-29
Hutchinson, Eva Dye. *See* Dye, Charlotte Evangeline

Iliad, The, 28-30
"Iliad of the West," 77
Improved Order of Red Men (IORM), 108, 110, 112-13

Industrial Workers of the World (IWW), 143
Iowa City (Iowa), 41-43, 47
Irving, Washington, 2, 38, 57-58, 153, 161 (n. 23)

Jacksonian politics/reform, 9
Jefferson, Thomas, 1, 72, 78-79, 84-85, 92, 98
Judd, Gerrit P., 136
Judd, Henry P. (Rev.), 136, 146, 151
Judd, Laura Fish, 136
Juniper, Jennie, 18

Kamehameha III, King, 136
Kent's Hill (Maine), 10
Kentucky and Ohio Valley, 86
Kentucky County, 85
Kessler, Donna, 94
Kessler, Lauren, 124
"King of the Columbia," 65, 130
"King's Eagles, The: The Royal Romance of Hawaii," 145-47
Ku Klux Klan, 142

Laugesen, Amanda, 75
Lee, Jason (Rev.), 59-60
Lewis, Lucy Meriwether, 88
Lewis, Meriwether, 3, 79, 84-86, 98. *See also* Lewis and Clark Expedition
Lewis and Clark Centennial Exposition, 77-78, 100, 104-6, 111-17, 154
Lewis and Clark Expedition, 2-4, 30, 77, 92-93, 98-99, 105, 106, 113; Biddle-Allen text and, 88; and discovery of original documents, 83-84; Dye's motivation for researching, 77-79; first popularized, 3, 72-73; Lewis and Clark as icons, 97; original journals of, 81-82, 84, 96, 153; portrayal in *The Conquest*, 85; research endeavor and, 82
Lewis and Clark Fair Commission, 110-12
Leyba, Donna de, 85, 88
Liliuokalani, Queen, 136, 145
Limerick, Patricia Nelson, 66
liquor interests, 118, 120, 123, 144
Longfellow, Henry Wadsworth, 2, 33, 47, 57-59, 62
Lord Dunmore's War, 84-85
Louisiana Purchase, 78, 85
Louisiana Purchase Centennial Exposition, 77, 81
Lucas, Oramel (Rev.), 43
"Lyra Hellenica," 28

McDonald, Ranald, 3, 129-32, 134

McDonald of Oregon, 3, 116, 129-32, 147

McKay, Alexander, 61

McKay, Margaret, 60-61

McKinley, William, 78

McLeod, Malcolm, 130

McLoughlin, Eloise, 61, 66

McLoughlin, John, 3-5, 57-66, 73-77, 81, 105, 129, 134

McLoughlin and Old Oregon,   3, 54, 57-59, 62, 65-67, 71-72, 77, 87, 97, 106, 130, 134, 137, 147, 152

McLoughlin House, 5, 106

McLoughlin Memorial Association, 106

Macedonia (Ohio), 35

Madison (South Dakota), 43, 55

Madison (Wisconsin), 82-83

Magazine of American History, 42

Maine Wesleyan Seminary and Female College, 10

Mexican-American War, 29

Meyers, Annice Jeffreys (Doctor), 112, 117

Meyers, Jefferson, 112

missionaries, 3, 6, 30, 39, 57, 59-60, 63, 78, 134-37, 145, 161-62 (n. 42), 173 (n. 43)

Missouri Historical Society, 84

Monroe, Anne Shannon, 3

Montgomery, Mrs. J. B., 105

mothers as force in history, 88-89, 107, 113-14: Republican motherhood, 46, 114

"Mothers of Great Men, The," 46

Mowry, William, 66

Moynihan, Ruth Barnes, 122-23

Narcissa, 64-65

National American Woman Suffrage Association (NAWSA), 49, 112, 114, 117-18, 120-21,125, 152, 171, (n. 105)

Native Americans, 2, 29-30, 58, 60, 67, 74, 80; Dye's portrayal of, 61-63, 86-87, 137

native peoples. *See* Native Americans

New Northwest, The, 103

New York Times, 97

Nez Perce, 58, 90

North West Company, 60, 75, 77

Northwest Congress for a League of Nations, 135

Oberlin Alumni Magazine, 19

Oberlin College, 1-2, 19-27, 30-32, 34-39, 41, 43, 46, 53-54, 57-58, 126, 137, 139

Oberlin Review, 23-28, 31, 34-35, 38

"Octoginta Duo," 28

Odyssey, The, 28-29, 58

Olcott, Ben, 142

"Only a Woman," 50-51

Ordway, John (Sergeant), 82-83, 165 (n. 52, 61)

Oregon, 2, 59, 66, 76-77, 83, 100, 102-3, 106-8, 112-13, 130-31, 147, 150, 155, 159 (n. 40); and authors of fiction and history, 2-3; Dyes' relocation to, 43, 55; Dye's success in, 76-77, 151, 154; Hawaii manuscript and, 132-34; historians of, 66, 75-76; histories of, 63, 73, 75-76; in the 1880s, 55; in 1890, 56; in the 1920s, 141-43, 173 (n. 63); John McLoughlin and, 59-62, 66, 73, 106; Oregon Pioneer Association, 57, 62; significance of Lewis and Clark to, 77; Lewis and Clark Centennial Exposition and, 77; *Stories of Oregon*, 74, 76; Whitman myth and, 63-64, 161-62 (n. 42); and woman suffrage, 73, 100, 102-3, 114-15, 117-19, 121-22, 124-25, 168 (n. 11 and n. 12), 170 (n. 61 and n. 71), 171 (n. 100); women's clubs in, 100-104, 114, 124-25, 168 (n. 11 and n. 12). *See also* Chautauqua, *McDonald of Oregon*, *McLoughlin and Old Oregon*, Oregon City, Oregon Equal Suffrage Association

Oregon Agricultural College, 127

Oregon City (Oregon), 2, 57, 73, 84, 88, 105, 115, 134, 138, 141, 145, 147; and Chautauqua, 67-70; description of, 56; Dye children and, 126-27, 139-40; Dyes' relocation to, 54-55; First Congregational Church in, 6, 43, 133; in the 1920s, 142-44; and John McLoughlin, 4-5, 57, 60, 64, 105; Oregon City Woman's Club, 105, 133-35, 138-45, 147, 150, 154

Oregon Equal Suffrage Association (OESA), 34, 94, 102, 113, 115-19, 122-24

Oregon Historical Quarterly, 66, 75-77, 97, 131

Oregon Historical Society, 3, 5, 76-77, 81, 98, 104, 154

Oregonian, The, 76, 118, 122, 147

Oregon Journal, 106, 110, 112-13, 148

Oregon Pioneer Association, 57, 62

Oregon Trail, 2, 76

Pacific Northwest, 55-59, 64, 103, 108, 113, 134, 142-43: Chautauqua and, 55, 71; and Abigail Scott Duniway, 103; Dye and historical fiction about, 2-3, 151, 153; Dye's historical interest in, 42, 61; Dye's portrayal of Native Americans in, 63; early histories of, 57-58; historians of, 63; history of women in, 5
Page, Laura Trafton, 11-12
Page, Samuel, 12
panic of 1837, 8, 10
panic of 1893, 65
panic of 1907, 132
Parsonfield (Maine), 134
"Pen Possessed, The," 24-25
Perry, Matthew (Commander), 131
Peterson, Merrill, 79
phrenology, 1, 19
Pierce, Walter, 142
Pilgrimage of Faith, The, 152
Pocahontas, 92, 97, 108, 170 (n. 57)
Pohl, Dr. Esther, 103-4, 122
Portland (Oregon), 56, 68, 77, 101-2, 105-8, 111-12, 117-18, 126
Portland Commercial Club, 108, 112
Portland Flouring Mills, 108
Portland Woman's Club, 97, 101-2, 104-5, 116, 120, 122-24, 135, 154
Progressive Era, 79, 94, 102-3, 126, 132, 160 (n. 48), 170 (n. 57)
Progressive Party, 126
Prophetstown (Illinois), 7, 12, 16-19, 23
Prosch, Thomas, 131
public statuary, 170 (n. 57)

Reed College, 128-29
"Reminiscences of Life," 9, 17, 132-33
Remley, David, 94
Republican Party, 17, 103-4, 126
Revolutionary War, 16, 35, 45
Richardson, Tom, 108
River of the West, 65
Rob Roy, 30
Rock Island (Illinois), 12
Romantic Period (Romanticism), 2, 25, 26-28, 32-33, 57-59
Roosevelt, Theodore, 78, 93, 126
"Royal Romance," 145-47. See also "King's Eagles, The"

Sacagawea (Sacajawea) 52, 72, 90, 93, 98-99, 108, 115, 117, 147; in The Conquest, 72, 91, 97; as "guide" to Lewis and Clark Expedition, 95-96, 166 (n.

92); as heroine, 87; historians' interpretations of, 94; as icon, 4, 96; as pioneer mother, 88-89, 90, 94, 107, 114; in relation to Pocahontas, 92; reunion with Shoshone, 91; Sacajawea Statue Association, 4, 100, 102, 104-16, 125; spelling of name, 166 (n. 73), 167 (n. 3); statue concept at Lewis and Clark Centennial Exposition, 110-111; as princess, 92-93; as wife to Charbonneau, 90, 166 (n.80); and woman suffrage 4, 106-7, 111-14, 170 (n. 61)
Sacajawea Statue Association, 4, 100, 102, 104-16, 125
Salter, Titus, 16
Sanford (Maine), 7, 9-11, 16, 133
S. B. Emery and Company, 10
Schliemann, Heinrich, 28
Scott, Harvey, 76-78, 122
Scott, Sir Walter, 2, 30, 57-59
Second Great Awakening, 9
Shaw, Anna Howard, 69, 114-15, 117, 120, 122
Shoshone, 4, 87, 90-93, 95-96
Sidney (Iowa), 37-38, 41
"Sidney School Column," 38
Simpson, Sir George, 60, 66
"Sixty Thousand, The," 31, 47
Sklar, Kathryn Kish, 49
Smith, Henry (Doctor), 12
Smith, Lucinda Clark Trafton, 7, 10-15, 18
Solomon, Barbara, 22
Sons of Temperance, 17
Soul of America, The: An Oregon Iliad, 147, 153
Spanish-American War, 78
Spalding, Eliza, 42, 60-61, 64-65, 88-89, 137
Spalding, Henry, 42, 60-61, 137
Spencer, John Palmer, 78
Spike (Prophetstown, Illinois), 17, 21
S.S. Calawaii, 145
S.S. Maui, 135, 140
Stanton, Elizabeth Cady, 49
State Historical Society of Wisconsin 81-82
Stone, Lucy, 22
Stories of Oregon, 74, 76
Stowe, Harriet Beecher, 52
suffrage. See woman suffrage
Sumner, Charles, 30

Taber, Ronald, 94
Taft, Laredo, 107, 111
temperance movement, 31-32, 47, 49, 56, 102, 107, 118; Abigail Scott Duniway and, 103, 123; Charles Dye's advocacy of, 43, 45, 126, 144; Eva Emery Dye's advocacy of, 1, 31-32, 47, 104, 123, 144; Cyrus Emery's advocacy of, 17; founding of WCTU and connection to women's rights, 36, 44, 47, 49, 51, 64, 116
Thwaites, Reuben Gold, 3, 81-84, 96, 153
Toy, Eckard, 142
Trafton, John, 10-11
Trafton, Jordan, 11
Trafton, Lucinda Clark, 7, 10-12
Troy (Ohio), 35
Troy, ancient city of, 28, 30
"True Lady, The," 32-33
Turner, Fredrick Jackson, 80-81, 84, 98

Union Signal (WCTU), 47, 49-50
University of Wisconsin, 80-81
Unruh, Ada Wallace, 118

"Vernal Lyric, A," 23
Victor, Frances Fuller, 3, 65-66, 153
Voorhis, Eleanor Glasgow, 82, 84
Voorhis, Julie Clark, 82, 84, 88

Waiilatpu Mission, 62
Washington Equal Suffrage Movement, 101
Washington Historical Quarterly, 131
Weatherred, Edyth, 111
Wells, Raymond, 152
Westervelt, William D., 135, 173 (n. 35)
Wheeler, Olin, 80
Whitaker and Ray (Publishers), 74, 76
White Ribboners, 118
Whitman, Marcus, 61-64
Whitman, Narcissa, 61-66, 88-89, 161-62 (n. 42)
Whitman and Spalding missions, 42, 60-61, 137
Whitman massacre, 62-64
Whitman myth, 63-64, 161-62 (n. 42)
Whittier, John Greenleaf, 32-33
Wilcox, Theodore, 108-110
Willamette Valley Chautauqua Assembly (WVCA), 5, 68-69, 149. *See also* Chautauqua
Willard, Frances, 47-48

Willard, Samuel Jr., 8
Willard, Stephen, 8
Wobblies. *See* IWW
"Woman Led the Deed, A," 51-52, 111, 115
"Woman's Page," 106, 112, 123, 171 (n. 100)
woman suffrage, 4, 47, 112, 120-24, 126, 166 (n. 92),: California suffrage, 121; Oregon suffrage, 4, 73, 100, 102-3, 114-15, 117-19, 121, 122, 124-25, 168 (n. 11 and n. 12), 170 (n. 61 and n. 71), 171 (n. 100); Washington suffrage, 101, 121. *See also* NAWSA, OESA
Women and Economics, 48, 93
"Women in Civic Life," 121
"Women of Genius," 33
Women's Christian Temperance Union (WCTU), 32, 102, 116, 118. *See also* temperance movement
women's club movement, 4, 100-103, 114, 125, 135, 168 (n. 11): Clackamas County Federation of Women's Clubs, 154; College Women's Club, 123; General Federation of Women's Clubs, 101, 124; Oregon City Woman's Club, 105, 135, 154; Oregon Federation of Women's Clubs, 101, 104. *See also* Portland Woman's Club
Women's Congress, 69, 73, 115
women's rights. *See* Dye, Eva Emery; woman suffrage; women's club movement; temperance movement
Wood, C. E. S., 111, 166 (n. 69)
World Columbian Exposition, 110
World War I, 127, 134-35, 152
Wyeth, Nathaniel, 59, 61

Young, Frederic G., 75-77, 154